Versions of these devotions originally appeared in various volumes of the magazine, *My Devotions.* This book is dedicated to the authors of these devotions, who have contributed their God-given time and talents to nurturing the faith of God's children.

Preface

For a number of years, the title *Little Visits* has been associated with devotions that share the saving Gospel of Jesus Christ with children. From the very first edition of *Little Visits with God* to this current volume, these devotions reinforce scriptural truths and faith concepts centered on God's love for us through Christ.

Setting aside time for devotions is an excellent way to lead children to the Savior and to bring them face-to-face with God's Word. In Romans 10:7, we read that "faith comes from hearing the message, and the message is heard through the word of Christ."

Find a time that best suits your family and be consistent. Set a format that is most harmonious with the ages and stages of your children. Using the order of worship provided on the facing page will build a sense of tradition and ritual into your family devotions. Developing such rituals or traditions helps to lay important building blocks for faith formation and creates a link between worship in the family of faith and worship within your own family.

These devotions have been written by pastors and educators who have drawn upon their experiences to provide illustrations from daily life and link them to God's Word. May you and your children be blessed as the Holy Spirit works through these words to teach your minds and to touch your hearts.

The Editors

Daily Devotion for Family Use

Parents may feel free to adapt according to the children's ages and ability to participate.

____ The Invocation

The parent may open the devotion with a call to worship.
Leader: In the name of the Father and of the Son and of the Holy Spirit.
Family: Amen.

____ The Hymn

The family may sing together a related hymn or song of praise.

____ The Scripture Reading

The designated Scripture may be read by parent or child.

____ The Devotional Reading

The designated devotion may be read by parent or child.
The parent may lead the family in discussion using the questions provided.

____ The Closing Prayer

The parent may lead the family in the closing prayer.

january

Contributors for this month:

Diana Lesire Brandmeyer

Kristine Moulds

Jeanette A. Dall

Interference

Dakota pushed the buttons on the TV remote. Every channel had disappeared and was replaced by a blue screen. Outside, thunder clapped loudly.

What had happened to Dakota's television? Interference. The storm outside was interfering with the television signals. Without a clear signal the television screen turned blank.

Sometimes we don't pick up God's signals. The activities in our lives may cause interference. We know God is with us all the time, but we forget that He desires to speak to us.

Psalm 46:10 reminds us to stop and listen for God's voice. But how can we hear Him?

God's voice is found in His Word, the Bible. You can hear His voice through your pastor's sermons, your parents, and even your Christian friends.

This week listen for how many times you hear God's voice. Ask God to guide you through your day. Thank God for His gift of Jesus, our Savior from sin.

Read from God's Word

God is our refuge and strength, an ever-present help in trouble. Therefore we will not fear, though the earth give way and the mountains fall into the heart of the sea, though its waters roar and foam and the mountains quake with their surging. ... The LORD Almighty is with us; the God of Jacob is our fortress. Come and see the works of the LORD, the desolations He has brought on the earth. He makes wars cease to the ends of the earth; He breaks the bow and shatters the spear, He burns the shields with fire. "Be still, and know that I am God; I will be exalted among the nations, I will be exalted in the earth." The LORD Almighty is with us; the God of Jacob is our fortress. Psalm 46

_____Let's do: Take some time to sit quietly and read your Bible. Ask God to help you hear His voice and to understand what He wants you to do.

_____Let's pray: Heavenly Father, I'm thankful that You want to talk to me and guide me. Help me to recognize and remove any interference that keeps me from hearing Your voice. Amen.

D. L. B.

Read from God's Word

My son, if you accept my words and store up my commands within you, turning your ear to wisdom and applying your heart to understanding, and if you call out for insight and cry aloud for understanding, and if you look for it as for silver and search for it as for hidden treasure, then you will understand the fear of the LORD and find the knowledge of God. Proverbs 2:1–5

Buried Treasure

Ian's ears were covered with headphones. He held his metal detector close to the sand, sweeping it back and forth.

A beep! He tore off the headphones and dropped to the hot sand. He dug, anxiously hoping that his fingers would connect with something hard and cool.

There, he felt something! Pulling it away from the sand Ian discovered he had found a quarter. Smiling, he stood and added the coin to the other treasures in his pocket.

Today's Bible verses remind us that the greatest treasure we have is not something we can find buried on the beach. The greatest treasure is the free gift of salvation given to us by God through faith in Jesus Christ. Unlike treasure you find buried in the sand, God's treasure is meant to be shared.

____Let's do: Make a list of friends who know about God's treasure. Put a star next to those names. Now make a list of friends who don't know about the treasure. This week see if you can find a chance to tell them about Jesus.

____Let's pray: Father, thank You for Jesus, our greatest treasure. Thank You for all the other treasures You put in our lives too. Amen.

D. L. B.

Which Way?

"What's that, Uncle Raoul?" asked Dominique as she reached out her hand.

"It's a GPS—global positioning satellite," Uncle Raoul answered and handed it to Dominique.

"What does it do?"

"It helps you find out where you are and how long it will take you to get somewhere. If we wanted to walk to St. Louis, we could use this GPS to find out how many steps it would take and how many days we would have to travel." Raoul leaned over Dominique's shoulder. "Let's enter the information and find out."

"Four days! I'd rather ride in a car." Dominique thought for a moment. "Type in heaven, and let's see how long it will take to get there."

Raoul ruffled his niece's hair. "You know there's only one way to get to heaven, Dominique—through Jesus."

"But that's hard, Uncle Raoul. Just believing in Jesus doesn't seem like it will get me to heaven."

"It will. He's the only way there. You can't do anything on your own to get to heaven. Jesus made your journey to heaven possible when you were baptized. If you believe in Jesus as your Savior from sin, you will go to heaven."

Read from God's Word

"And you, my son Solomon, acknowledge the God of your father, and serve Him with wholehearted devotion and with a willing mind, for the LORD searches every heart and understands every motive behind the thoughts. If you seek Him, He will be found by you; but if you forsake Him, He will reject you forever." 1 Chronicles 28:9

_____Let's talk: Do you make it hard to get to heaven? Remember that all the hard work has already been done by God's Son.

_____Let's pray: Heavenly Father, what an awesome God You are! Thank You for making me Your child in Baptism and for giving me salvation through Your Son. Amen.

D. L. B.

One Minute at a Time

"Play it one minute at a time!" yelled a hockey fan. Hockey games move fast, and it takes only a minute to change a losing game into a win.

"In the blink of an eye" is another favorite saying. It means that life can change in an instant.

Can you think of other examples of how things can change quickly? You may think of the time you were carrying a can of soda and dropped it on the carpet. Maybe it was a slice of pizza that landed upside down. Maybe you decided to spend the day with a friend. When you arrived, you discovered that her parents had tickets to take you both to an amusement park.

Because our lives can change at a moment's notice, we need to learn to go to God with everything. He's in charge of our lives. He will provide food for us to eat and a place for us to rest our heads at night. With God in charge, we don't need to be afraid of what the next minute will bring. God's Word in Deuteronomy 31:8 promises that the Lord will always be with us. We can trust that promise.

_____Let's do: Make a list of all the ways God has provided for you today.

_____Let's pray: Father, what a relief to know You will take care of every need. Remind me that You are always with me. Amen.

D. L. B.

Carry Me

Read from God's Word

Even to your old age and gray hairs I am He, I am He who will sustain you. I have made you and I will carry you; I will sustain you and I will rescue you. Isaiah 46:4

How much does God love you? In 1999, at an iron man triathlon, Ricky Hoyt's father showed the world how much he loves his son.

Dave Hoyt transported Ricky through all of the events. He pulled his son through the 2.4-mile swim in a small boat. With Ricky on the front of the bike, Dave pedaled 112 miles. For the final event, he pushed Ricky in a three-wheeled chair while running the 26.2-mile marathon. It took 16 hours to finish the entire race. Why would Dave Hoyt do this?

He did it because he loves his son. Ricky has cerebral palsy and could not do the race by himself. His father wanted to spend time with him. They train together every day. This is the second triathlon Dave and Ricky have entered.

How much does our heavenly Father love us? The Bible reading for today tells us He loves us enough to carry us throughout our entire lives. The next time you think you need to be carried because you're tired, remember God's promise to carry and rescue you. Because of Jesus, He will carry us all the way to our heavenly home.

_____Let's do: Make a collage of people during different times of their lives. Write today's verse across the pictures. Hang it in your room to remind you how much your heavenly Father loves you.

_____Let's pray: Thank You, Father for the love and compassion You have for me. It is comforting to know You will always be there to carry me. Amen.

D. L. B.

Read from God's Word

You will go out in joy and be led forth in peace; the mountains and hills will burst into song before you, and all the trees of the field will clap their hands. Isaiah 55:12

Sing a New Song

Jalissa's hand flew out from under the covers and began swatting at her noisy alarm clock. She hated mornings, especially mornings like this one. She listened to the sound of raindrops beating on the roof. It would be so nice to stay under her warm covers and sleep. If only it wasn't a school day.

Grumbling, she climbed out of bed and stepped on her little brother's plastic car. Sinking to the floor, she sat rubbing her heel. It was going to be a miserable day.

Do you sometimes have mornings like Jalissa's? We all do. Some mornings we start off late or just don't feel right.

What can you do to change those days?

Sing. Yes, sing a song of praise to God! Make one up if you can't remember the words to one. Sing loudly or hum softly. Soon you'll find yourself smiling. It's hard to be miserable when you are praising God in song.

_____Let's do: Start a collection of praise music and plan to listen to a praise song every morning while you get ready for school.

_____Let's pray: Father, I want to praise and thank You for the joy You bring to my life. Amen.

D. L. B.

Are You Ready?

Read from God's Word

It was revealed to them that they were not serving themselves but you, when they spoke of the things that have now been told you by those who have preached the gospel to you by the Holy Spirit sent from heaven. Even angels long to look into these things. 1 Peter 1:12–13

"Dad, did you winterize the lawnmower?" Duane asked. "Ben says his father does that every fall."

"I did get the mower ready for winter, Duane."

"But what does it mean to 'winterize'?"

"For the lawnmower it means to get the engine ready for the cold weather. I make sure the gas tank is empty and I clean the spark plug. Then I clean the dead grass off the blades." Mr. Thorton smiled at his son. "I also sharpened the blades so the mower will be ready for you to use in the spring."

You and I don't need to be winterized, but we do need to be made ready. We need to be ready for Christ's return. We can prepare for that day as we live in God's Word every day.

Today's reading tells us to prepare our minds. Keeping our minds on God, and not on what the world thinks is important, is a step in preparing. God gives us His Spirit to help us read and understand His Word.

_____Let's do: Ask an adult for help in selecting Bible verses to memorize. Pick verses that help you to focus on God.

_____Let's pray: Dear Father, I ask for wisdom in studying Your Word. Help me prepare for the time You send Your Son to bring us home to You. In Jesus' name. Amen.

D. L. B.

Read from God's Word

And we know that in all things God works for the good of those who love Him, who have been called according to His purpose. Romans 8:28

Bendable You

Ashleigh came through the back door and slammed her book bag onto the kitchen floor. "I hate school!" She slid into a kitchen chair and slumped, resting her head on the table.

"Bad day, honey?" her mom asked as she rubbed Ashleigh's back.

"The worst. I understood the game in gym class yesterday, but today the teacher changed the rules."

"Maybe he changed the game to make it more fun." Ashleigh's mom picked up her hand and slipped a rubber band around her wrist.

"What's that for?" Ashleigh stretched the rubber band.

"To remind you that God lets change enter our lives. The rubber band stretches instead of staying the same. It changes to accept what is happening."

Sometimes it's hard to accept changes. God's Word promises us that no matter what changes take place in our lives, God will turn them into good for His children. We can depend on that promise because God always keeps His word.

_____Let's do: Put a rubber band on your wrist. Every time you notice it, think of something in your life that has changed. Then think of the new skills God has given you for dealing with that change.

_____Let's pray: Heavenly Father, sometimes we find changes big and small hard to manage. Please teach us to accept Your will for us. Amen.

D. L. B.

Joy

Christmas is over. The new toys don't seem as exciting as they did a couple of weeks ago. The ornaments and lights have been packed away for another year. The decorations have been taken off light posts and buildings, and the world seems as though it doesn't have as much color.

We may feel joyless because we've forgotten to thank God for the things He has given us. When you woke this morning, did you thank God for the warmth in your house or the bed you slept in? Think how you would feel if your house had no heat.

"Be joyful always; pray continually; give thanks in all circumstances, for this is God's will for you in Christ Jesus" (1 Thessalonians 5:16–18). These verses mean that with everything that happens to us, even things we don't like, we can be thankful. As we give thanks to God for everything, we discover how much He loves us—so much so that He gave His own Son to save us and take us to heaven.

Read from God's Word

May the God of hope fill you with all joy and peace as you trust in Him, so that you may overflow with hope by the power of the Holy Spirit. Romans 15:13

_____Let's do: On the inside cover of a notebook, write five things for which you are thankful. Every day add five more things to the list. God has surely blessed you!

_____Let's pray: Precious Lord, I ask that You fill me with Your joy. Teach me to open my eyes, ears, and heart to the wonderful things You have made for me to discover. Amen.

D. L. B.

Read from God's Word

"Be strong and courageous. Do not be afraid or terrified because of them, for the LORD your God goes with you; He will never leave you nor forsake you."
Deuteronomy 31:6

This Little Light

Turn it off, Jake. You don't need this stupid night-light anymore." David yanked the light out of the socket.

"But now I can't see, and they'll get me!" his younger brother cried.

"You don't have to be afraid of the dark. There isn't anything in this house that will get you. You're old enough not to be afraid anymore." David thought for a moment. "Jake, remember in Sunday school how they told us God is always with us?"

"Yes."

"If you remember that God is always with you, then you won't be afraid of the dark."

The Bible verse for today reminds us of God's promise to always be with us. God's Word tells us that He will never leave us. We can trust in that promise because we know God's Word is true. He will be with us until He takes us to be with Him in heaven.

_____Let's talk: How could you help someone younger than you to remember that God is always with him?

_____Let's pray: Father, teach me to trust You when I am afraid. Show me the light so I won't stumble in my fear. Amen.

D. L. B.

The Gift That Keeps Going!

Read from God's Word

For God did not appoint us to suffer wrath but to receive salvation through our Lord Jesus Christ.
1 Thessalonians 5:9–10

Crack!

"Oops," said Dusty's little brother, Kyle, looking down at the broken toy under his foot.

"Hey," cried Dusty, "you broke my new toy! Mom!"

"That's too bad," said Dusty's mother. "I know you were excited to get that toy for Christmas. But I notice you haven't played with it much since then. Is that why it was left on the floor?"

"I guess so," admitted Dusty, sadly picking up the pieces of the toy. "I just forgot about it."

Some people feel that way about God's gift of a Savior. At Christmas they are happy. They sing carols, go to Christmas parties, attend special worship services, and have fun with their families. When Christmas is over, they forget about Jesus and why He came. They forget to praise God for His great love and daily forgiveness. The amazing gift of a Savior becomes like a forgotten toy.

But of all the gifts in the whole universe, God's gift of a Savior is the very best of all. "Sing to the Lord, praise His name; proclaim His salvation day after day. Declare His glory among the nations, His marvelous deeds among all peoples" (Psalm 96:2–3). Christmas may be over, but God's love for us keeps going!

_____Let's talk: Why do we celebrate Christmas? Why should we want to celebrate every day after that? (Hint: same answer for both questions.)

_____Let's pray: Dear Lord, thank You for Jesus, the greatest gift in the universe! Help me to praise Your name every day. Amen.

K. M.

Read from God's Word

I waited patiently for the LORD; He turned to me and heard my cry. He lifted me out of the slimy pit, out of the mud and mire; He set my feet on a rock and gave me a firm place to stand. He put a new song in my mouth, a hymn of praise to our God. Many will see and fear and put their trust in the LORD. Psalm 40:1–3

What Music Do You Hear?

"Ow," complained Rosa, covering her head. "That music hurts my ears!"

Squeak! Toot! Squeak! Her brother Bill was learning to play the saxophone.

"I can't stand it!" said Rosa, jumping up. "I'm going to another room. I don't want to hear saxophone noise anymore!"

Loud, squeaky music makes most people cringe. As musicians practice, their instruments sound better and better. Some musicians eventually sound so good that listeners don't want the music to stop.

Our sinful lives are like bad music. We are so sinful, rebellious, and selfish that our complaints and whining must make the Lord want to cringe and cover His holy ears. Our sinful nature creates quite a sour symphony for the Lord.

God's musical selections are full of the rich sounds of forgiveness for our sins. Moses and Miriam sang in Exodus 15:2, "The Lord is my strength and my song; He has become my salvation." God assures us through His Word that our sinful noises are drowned out by the beautiful music of His love shown in Jesus, our Savior from sin. May that music never stop!

_____Let's talk: Have you recently complained or whined? What does God do to put His music into your life?

_____Let's pray: O Lord, forgive us when we make sinful noises in our lives. Thank You for surrounding us with Your love and sweet forgiveness. Amen.

K. M.

It's Time for the Jesus Report

Read from God's Word

Blessed are those who have learned to acclaim You, who walk in the light of Your presence, O LORD. They rejoice in Your name all day long; they exult in Your righteousness. Psalm 89:15–16

"It's time to turn on the weather!" announced Will's father. Will plopped onto the couch next to his dad. They liked to watch the weather forecast together.

"A snowstorm is blowing in tonight," warned the announcer. "Be prepared."

"Now we know what kind of plans to make for tomorrow," said Will. "I'm glad we watch the weather report every day!"

How is the spiritual weather in your life? Do you pay attention to it?

As you "watch" the Lord by making time for daily devotions and prayer, you discover that God loves you and wants you to live in Him. He helps you to do that.

God promises that His presence in your life is constant. Unlike television shows, God is always on for you. He covers you with love and abundant forgiveness, preparing you for each day's experiences.

Soon you won't want to miss your daily preparation with Jesus. Paul says in 1 Thessalonians 5:16–18, "Be joyful always; pray continually; give thanks in all circumstances, for this is God's will for you in Christ Jesus."

Now your spiritual weather forecast can always look good!

_____Let's talk: Think of a special time each day when you can pray and learn more about Jesus. Why does the Bible tell us to "be joyful always"?

_____Let's pray: Dear Lord, thank You for watching over me even when I forget to watch You. Help me to pray and give thanks to You at all times. Amen.

K. M.

Read from God's Word

This grace was given us in Christ Jesus before the beginning of time, but it has now been revealed through the appearing of our Savior, Christ Jesus, who has destroyed death and has brought life and immortality to light through the gospel.
2 Timothy 1:9b–10

It's Jesus Time!

Dana drew another X on the calendar. "Only one week until my birthday!" she announced.

"That's seven more days," said her father. "Or we could say 168 hours to go. Or shall we say only about 10,080 minutes left?"

"Dad," groaned Dana, "when you put it that way, it seems a lot longer!" Dana worked on her calculator. "Now I have 1,435 minutes before I can even cross out another day!"

The calendar we use today is similar to one introduced by Julius Caesar, the leader of the Roman Empire, about 50 years before the birth of Christ. But no matter how people name the days or count their years, only the Lord God could invent time in the first place.

He sent His Son, Jesus, into our earthly time, into the first century of Julius Caesar's calendar, and into all the trials and limitations of our sinful human life. Jesus' human time on earth ended with His ascension into heaven.

When Jesus rose again, God gave us a message about another kind of time. When we die, we also will rise again into an eternal time of love and joy in heaven.

_____Let's talk: Why is it helpful to use calendars? What other kind of time do we use?

_____Let's pray: Lord, thank You for sending Jesus into our earthly time to die for our sins. Thank You for the sure hope of eternal life in heaven with You. Amen.

K. M.

Beneath the Surface

Read from God's Word

This then is how we know that we belong to the truth, and how we set our hearts at rest in His presence whenever our hearts condemn us. For God is greater than our hearts, and He knows everything. 1 John 3:19–20

It's a little wooden cat!" exclaimed Sarah, opening her gift.

"That's not all," said Jay. "Take off the head."

Sarah unscrewed the top half of the cat. Inside was another cat! Inside that cat was another and then another. The cats got smaller and smaller. The tiny last cat had an itty-bitty mouse inside it.

"Wow," said Sarah, "when I first saw this cat, I never imagined there were any surprises inside!"

People have surprises inside of them too. We have likes and dislikes, feelings, or ideas that we don't share with everyone. Deep down, we may have fears or doubts that are hard to express. Guilt, anger, or other emotions might hide inside of us just like that mouse hides inside the cat.

There is one thing we know for certain about each human being in God's creation: Each person, and that includes us, needs a Savior from sin. God sent His Son, Jesus, to redeem all humankind. "For Christ died for sins once for all, the righteous for the unrighteous, to bring you to God" (1 Peter 3:18).

No matter what we try to hide deep inside, nothing about us surprises the Lord. He knows us and loves us completely.

_____Let's talk: Why does God care about the feelings we have deep inside? What does every human being need?

_____Let's pray: Dear Jesus, thank You for understanding and forgiving my deepest feelings and fears. Help me to trust in You for my eternal salvation. Amen.

K. M.

Read from God's Word

"Hear, O LORD, and be merciful to me; O LORD, be my help." You turned my wailing into dancing; You removed my sackcloth and clothed me with joy that my heart may sing to You and not be silent. O LORD my God, I will give You thanks forever. Psalm 30:10–12

Pillow Talk

I can't sleep," said Zach to his babysitter, Katie. He held an old blanket in one hand and a stuffed puppy in the other.

"Here, let me hit your pillow!" said Katie. Zach had never heard of anyone who hit pillows. He watched as Katie took his pillow and socked it carefully with her fist. She shook the pillow back and forth to fluff it up. She plopped it back under Zach's head.

"There," said Katie, "is that better?"

Zach nodded and smiled. After Katie said a special prayer with him and sang a song, Zach went right to sleep.

Have you ever been lost? Have you ever needed to talk to someone who wasn't around? People often feel uncertain or afraid. Sometimes you feel uncomfortable or uneasy and something like fluffing a pillow isn't enough to help. What can you do?

Through prayer and Scripture, you can turn to the Lord. He gives you courage when you're afraid and comfort when you're upset. He gives you love and forgives you so you can forgive others.

God says, "So do not fear, for I am with you; do not be dismayed, for I am your God. I will strengthen you and help you; I will uphold you with My righteous right hand" (Isaiah 41:10).

_____Let's talk: Think of a time when you felt uncomfortable or afraid. How did God help you to feel better?

_____Let's pray: Lord, thank You for living in my heart. Help me to live for You so others see that I am Yours. Amen.

K. M.

Aim for God-Power

Read from God's Word

May the God of hope fill you with all joy and peace as you trust in Him, so that you may overflow with hope by the power of the Holy Spirit. Romans 15:13

Phillip pushed the remote button. A different TV program flashed onto the screen. He pushed the button again. On flicked an advertisement for cat food. Phillip's dog whimpered.

Phillip could control all the shows on television. Sometimes he watched two or three shows at once by switching back and forth constantly. Even his dog got confused!

Sometimes we wish we could control our lives as easily. What if we could clean our rooms or do our homework with a remote control? What if a remote control could guarantee good grades or prevent the flu?

But we can't switch off problems or turn off people whenever we please. We can't sit back at a "remote" distance, telling the rest of the world what to do. We can't sit on a couch, or in a pew, and push a button to tell God what to do either.

Instead, God comes near to us. He gets up close and personal with each one of us through His Word, the Bible. He touches us with His forgiving power and helps us through all the troubles that come our way. Through God's grace we can share this power with others.

Save your remote for the TV. Use God-power in your real life!

_____Let's talk: Think of a problem you have that can't be solved with remote control. What can you do to solve it? How can you share God's forgiving power with others?

_____Let's pray: Lord, thank You for being my Savior and for touching me with Your perfect love. Amen.

K. M.

Read from God's Word

When the apostles returned, they reported to Jesus what they had done. Then He took them with Him and they withdrew by themselves to a town called Bethsaida, but the crowds learned about it and followed Him. He welcomed them and spoke to them about the kingdom of God, and healed those who needed healing. Luke 9:10–11

Follow the King of Kings

Naya's uncle collected early American Indian artifacts. He had things made of antlers and of buffalo hide. He had shirts with beads on them. He had a stick with special feathers attached at the top. One day Naya noticed a pair of moccasins.

"Look, Uncle Jose," she said, "these shoes have fringes dragging from the heels."

"When someone walked over a dusty trail," explained Uncle Jose, "the fringe would drag through the dust. This helped erase the footprints."

"Then enemies couldn't follow," said Naya. "That's a good trick."

When Jesus walked the earth, people followed Him wherever He went. Jesus didn't hide His path. He wanted people to follow and hear His Gospel message.

In the Bible, King David said, "I run in the path of Your commands, for You have set my heart free" (Psalm 119:32). When we read God's Word, we learn that Jesus guides us along His path of love and forgiveness. At the end of this path is eternal life with Him in heaven. How wonderful to have a Lord who helps us to follow Him!

____Let's talk: Why is Jesus glad when people follow Him? How can we follow Jesus' path today? Why do we need Jesus as our guide?

____Let's pray: Thank You for forgiving us when we lose our way, dear Lord. Help us to trust and obey You as we follow in Your steps. Amen.

K. M.

True Value

Read from God's Word

But because of His great love for us, God, who is rich in mercy, made us alive with Christ even when we were dead in transgressions—it is by grace you have been saved. Ephesians 2:4–5

"Grandpa," shouted Valerie, "look at my new book!" She held up a book with a shiny cover and beautiful pictures. "Mom says it was expensive so I have to take good care of it. It might be valuable someday!"

"I also have a book that's valuable," said Grandpa, reaching for an old, tattered Bible. When he held it up, two pages fell out and the back cover hung loose.

"That doesn't *look* valuable," frowned Valerie.

"Oh," said Grandpa, tenderly putting it back together, "inside this book is real treasure. I have been learning about it all my life!"

The Bible is God's Word. When we read and study it, we discover something that's eternally valuable. We learn about the valuable treasure that is God's perfect love for us.

God's gift of His Son, Jesus, who died for our sins, was more expensive than jewels or fancy houses.

God's gift of eternal life in heaven is a priceless treasure that we don't deserve.

God's gift of the Holy Spirit in our hearts is more precious than silver or gold. Through the Holy Spirit we believe in the truth of God's treasures and in how much God wants to give them to us.

Why? Because through God's love, we are His treasures!

____Let's talk: Why is the Bible valuable? Why does God want us to have His treasures?

____Let's pray: Dear Lord, thank You for all the undeserved riches You offer to us. Help us to praise and thank You every day! In Jesus' name. Amen.

K. M.

Read from God's Word

Great is the LORD and most worthy of praise; His greatness no one can fathom. One generation will commend Your works to another; they will tell of Your mighty acts. They will speak of the glorious splendor of Your majesty, and I will meditate on Your wonderful works. They will tell of the power of Your awesome works, and I will proclaim Your great deeds. They will celebrate Your abundant goodness and joyfully sing of Your righteousness. Psalm 145:3–7

Sharing Christ through the Ages

Jeremy's fingers typed a message that appeared on his computer screen. He pushed the Send key. Seconds later and thousands of miles away, his words appeared on a computer screen in the home of Jeremy's missionary friends in Venezuela!

His message read, "The Lord be with you."

In Jesus' day, computers hadn't been invented. Videos, fax machines, and telephones didn't exist. So how did people communicate? In those days, teachers, travelers, shepherds, and kings told others about Jesus and shared His love with them. In the Bible we see that since the days of Adam and Eve, God's people have communicated their belief in God through their words and actions.

With or without technology, Satan and a sinful world try to place obstacles in the way of God's Word. But nothing can stop the Holy Spirit from working in people's hearts. 2 Peter 1:21 says, "For prophecy never had its origin in the will of man, but men spoke from God as they were carried along by the Holy Spirit."

The Holy Spirit continues to work through people—that's us!—to spread the Gospel in many ways. As He did in Bible times, God still uses people to make the difference!

____Let's talk: Name a traditional way of spreading God's Word. Name a modern method. Why does God want His Gospel to be spread?

____Let's pray: Thank You, Lord, for all the opportunities You give people around the world to learn about You. Use me, too, to share Your love. Amen.

K. M.

I Can't Do It

Juan often gave up easily. He'd complain that the job was too hard and he couldn't do it. One day, Juan's father told him to get a board, pocketknife, and pencil. Juan asked, "Now what?"

"Just put them on the shelf," said Mr. Lopez.

The next day Mr. Lopez told Juan to draw a line across the board then put everything away. Each day after that, Mr. Lopez had Juan use the pocketknife to make three cuts along the line. This went on for weeks. Finally, the board had been cut in half. "Now what?" asked Juan.

Mr. Lopez replied, "Nothing. If I'd told you to cut the board in half with a pocketknife, you would have given up. You would have said it was impossible."

Mr. Lopez taught his son that sometimes it takes a lot of time and hard work to get something done. That doesn't mean we can do anything. Some things are impossible for us to do. We can't lead a perfect life. We can't take away our own sins. We can't be good enough to go to heaven.

The wonderful news is that these impossible things have been done for us. Jesus lived a perfect life and died on the cross for our sins. Because of Jesus' death and resurrection, our sins are forgiven. When we die, we can live forever in heaven because of Christ.

Read from God's Word

Jesus looked at them and said, "With man this is impossible, but not with God; all things are possible with God." Mark 10:27

"For nothing is impossible with God." Luke 1:37

Jesus replied, "What is impossible with men is possible with God." Luke 18:27

_____ Let's do: Think of something you'd like to do in the next month. Then write on a calendar what you will do each day to accomplish your goal.

_____ Let's pray: Jesus, thank You for doing the impossible for me. Thank You for dying for my sins and giving me eternal life. Amen.

J. A. D.

Nothing Stopped Him

Read from God's Word

Are they servants of Christ? ... I am more. I have worked much harder, been in prison more frequently, been flogged more severely, and been exposed to death again and again. Five times I received from the Jews the forty lashes minus one. Three times I was beaten with rods, once I was stoned, three times I was shipwrecked, I spent a night and a day in the open sea, I have been constantly on the move. I have been in danger from rivers, in danger from bandits, in danger from my own countrymen, in danger from Gentiles; in danger in the city, in danger in the country, in danger at sea; and in danger from false brothers. I have labored and toiled and have often gone without sleep; I have known hunger and thirst and have often gone without food; I have been cold and naked.
2 Corinthians 11:23–28

The weather was terrible—ice, snow, and bitter-cold winds. Yet outside someone was walking up to the door. It was the mail carrier.

The United States Post Office delivers the mail—no matter what. Nothing stops them.

The apostle Paul delivered news too. His news was a thousand times more important than the mail. Paul spread the Good News that Jesus brought salvation to the world. Paul wanted to tell people that their sins were forgiven and they had eternal life.

Paul went through much more than bad weather to spread the Gospel. He tells about some of the hardships he endured in 2 Corinthians 11:24–26. Read the passage again, then add the missing words below.

"Five times I received from the Jews the forty ________ minus one. Three times I was ________ with rods, once I was ________ , three times I was ____________ , I spent a night and a day in the open __________ , I have been constantly on the ________ . I have been in danger from ________ , in danger from __________ , in danger from my own ____________ , in danger from __________ ; in danger in the __________ , in danger in the _________ , in danger at __________ ; and in danger from false ___________ ."

_____Let's do: Think of someone who doesn't know about Jesus. Practice what you could say to him or her.

_____Let's pray: Thanks, Lord, for Paul, who endured great hardships to spread the Gospel. Help me tell others about Jesus too. Amen.

J. A. D.

Each One Is Special

Tasha shouted, "It's snowing!"

The rest of the class ran to the windows. "Ooh, the snowflakes look like feathers," Alex declared.

The teacher laughed. "Let's bundle up and go outside for a closer look at those snow feathers."

Soon the kids were running into the snow. Mrs. Campbell handed each child a piece of dark paper and told them to catch snowflakes on it. Then she gave them magnifying glasses to examine the flakes more closely.

"Look at your snowflakes," Mrs. Campbell said. "Each one has six sides, but no snowflake is exactly like another. Each one is special."

God chose to make each snowflake different. They are God's creations. But an even more amazing creation of God is people. We're all different from one another too. Unfortunately, there is one way we are all alike. We all sin. But God loves us. He made each of us special, and we're very important to Him.

Read from God's Word

"The man who enters by the gate is the shepherd of his sheep. ... He calls his own sheep by name and leads them out. When he has brought out all his own, he goes on ahead of them, and his sheep follow him because they know his voice. But they will never follow a stranger; in fact, they will run away from him because they do not recognize a stranger's voice. ... I am the good shepherd; I know My sheep and My sheep know Me." John 10:2–5, 14

"Are not five sparrows sold for two pennies? Yet not one of them is forgotten by God. ... Don't be afraid; you are worth more than many sparrows." Luke 12:6–7

We're so important to God that He sent His Son to take away our sins. Because Jesus died and rose again, our sins are forgiven. Now we know that we'll live forever in heaven with Jesus after we die. Isn't it great to be so special?

____Let's do: Draw a snowflake picture. Write "Each One Is Special" on the picture.

____Let's pray: Thank You, God, for making each of us special. Help me live as Your special child and obey You. In Jesus' name. Amen.

J. A. D.

Tell It Like It Is

Read from God's Word

So the king of Israel brought together the prophets—about four hundred men—and asked them, "Shall I go to war against Ramoth Gilead, or shall I refrain?" "Go," they answered, "for the Lord will give it into the king's hand." But Jehoshaphat asked, "Is there not a prophet of the LORD here whom we can inquire of?" The king of Israel answered Jehoshaphat, "There is still one man through whom we can inquire of the LORD, but I hate him because he never prophesies anything good about me, but always bad. He is Micaiah son of Imlah." "The king should not say that," Jehoshaphat replied." 1 Kings 22:6–8

James sneaked through the door and tiptoed to his room. He was trying to delay talking to Mom as long as possible because he knew Mom would ask how he'd done on his big test. How could he tell her he'd really bombed?

James had played video games instead of studying. That was not what Mom wanted to hear! Sometimes it's really tough to "tell it like it is." We'd rather tell it like we wish it were or maybe like someone wants to hear it.

Israel's King Ahab wasn't obedient to God. He used false prophets to predict the outcomes of his battles. Many of these prophets simply said what they thought Ahab wanted to hear.

One time Ahab and the king of Judah, who obeyed God, were joining forces in a battle. The king of Judah called in Micaiah, a prophet of God. Micaiah told it like it was. He prophesied that Ahab would be defeated if he went to battle. Disregarding Micaiah's words, Ahab fought and was killed.

God always "tells it like it is." God tells us we're sinners and deserve to be punished. But He also tells us He "so loved the world that He gave His one and only Son, that whoever believes in Him shall not perish but have eternal life" (John 3:16).

____Let's talk: How do you feel when someone isn't honest with you? Why is honesty "the best policy"?

____Let's pray: Dear God, thanks for always being completely honest and for sparing me from Your just punishment. Help me "tell it like it is" and be honest in all I say and do. Amen.

J. A. D.

Promises You Can Count On

Mr. and Mrs. Cromwell had been saving money for two years until they had enough to take a wonderful vacation. They wanted to go to a tropical island.

"You will stay at a luxurious hotel right by the ocean," promised the travel agent. "The people are so friendly and helpful. The food is absolutely delicious."

When they arrived, Mr. and Mrs. Cromwell found that the hotel employees weren't friendly at all. The food was tasteless. If they stood on their bed and pressed their noses against the window, they could see a small speck of the ocean. To actually get to the water, they had to walk seven blocks. The vacation was not what the travel agent had promised.

We may meet people who don't keep their promises. They say they'll do something but they don't. They forget or they're too busy or they're just not reliable. When this happens, we're sad and disappointed.

We can count on God because He always keeps His promises. God promises to love and care for us, and He does. God promised to send a Savior to save people from their sins, and He did. Jesus guaranteed His promises with His life. Now our sins are forgiven and we have eternal life—just like God promised. Isn't He super?

Read from God's Word

Your kingdom is an everlasting kingdom, and Your dominion endures through all generations. The LORD is faithful to all His promises and loving toward all He has made. The LORD upholds all those who fall and lifts up all who are bowed down. ... The LORD is righteous in all His ways and loving toward all He has made. The LORD is near to all who call on Him, to all who call on Him in truth. He fulfills the desires of those who fear Him; He hears their cry and saves them. The LORD watches over all who love Him, but all the wicked He will destroy. My mouth will speak in praise of the LORD. Let every creature praise His holy name forever and ever. Psalm 145:13–21

_____Let's do: Read Psalm 145. On a sheet of paper, list things God gives you or does for you. Write the words of Psalm 145:13b across the bottom of the paper.

_____Let's pray: Thank You, Lord, for always keeping Your promises. Help me always to trust You and Your Word. In Jesus' name I pray. Amen.

J. A. D.

Read from God's Word

Blessed is the man who perseveres under trial, because when he has stood the test, he will receive the crown of life that God has promised to those who love Him. James 1:12

By faith Moses, when he had grown up, refused to be known as the son of Pharaoh's daughter. He chose to be mistreated along with the people of God rather than to enjoy the pleasures of sin for a short time. He regarded disgrace for the sake of Christ as of greater value than the treasures of Egypt, because he was looking ahead to his reward. ... By faith he kept the Passover and the sprinkling of blood, so that the destroyer of the firstborn would not touch the firstborn of Israel. Hebrews 11:24–28

1-2-3, Boom!

Everyone was watching. 1-2-3, boom! Step, step, boom! 1-2-3-4, boom!

Little Madeline was learning to walk. She was down more than she was up, but Madeline didn't give up. She kept right on trying and soon she was walking everywhere. One-year-old Madeline persevered.

Many people in Bible times persevered even when things looked hopeless.

Moses asked Pharaoh to let the Israelites go. Five times Pharaoh said they could go and then changed his mind. With God's help, Moses kept asking and finally the Israelites were freed.

Job lost everything—money, family, and health. But Job persevered in his faith and trust in God. God helped Job and eventually He gave Job even more than he had lost.

And how about Jesus? The reason He had come to earth was to pay for the sins of all people. Jesus could have said, "Forget it. That's too hard. I won't do it." But He didn't. Jesus suffered the full punishment for every wrong we have ever done. He loved us so much that He persevered all the way to the cross.

Now our sins are forgiven, and we can live with our Savior forever. May we persevere in faith as long as we live!

____Let's talk: To find out more about Moses' perseverance, read Exodus 7–11. According to today's Bible reading, why did Moses choose to suffer ill treatment?

____Let's pray: Dear Jesus, thank You for persevering in Your work on earth. Thank You for forgiveness and eternal life. Amen.

J. A. D.

The God Squad

Brian loved basketball. There was only one problem—Brian wasn't a very good player. Brian joined his school's basketball team anyway.

During a tournament, the team was playing in a very close game. Brian could hardly believe it when Coach Davis put him in. It was even more unbelievable when he stole the ball at midcourt and made a beautiful lay-up. It was a great shot—but in the wrong basket. He'd scored two points for the other team!

Brian wished he could disappear. Coach Davis called a time-out and put his arm around Brian. "It's okay," Coach said. "Everyone makes mistakes. Now go back out there and do your very best." Coach Davis didn't pull Brian out of the game or yell at him. He let him go on playing.

We are like Brian. We make many mistakes. These mistakes are called sins. Lying, being unkind, gossiping, and disobeying our parents are some of our sins.

But God doesn't give up on us. God loves us so much that He sent His own Son, Jesus, to be our substitute. Jesus obeyed all of God's laws for us and even died to make up for our disobedience. Jesus makes us fully accepted members of "God's squad." What a great sub to have in the game of life!

Read from God's Word

But because of His great love for us, God, who is rich in mercy, made us alive with Christ even when we were dead in transgressions—it is by grace you have been saved. And God raised us up with Christ and seated us with Him in the heavenly realms in Christ Jesus. Ephesians 2:4–6

_____Let's talk: Think of a time you felt really terrible about something you did. Read what God says in Romans 4:7–8. Why do these words make you glad?

_____Let's pray: Chief of sinners though I be, Jesus shed His blood for me, Died that I might live on high, Lives that I might never die. As the branch is to the vine, I am His, and He is mine. (*Lutheran Worship* 285:1)

J. A. D.

Read from God's Word

Though my father and mother forsake me, the LORD will receive me. Teach me Your way, O LORD; lead me in a straight path because of my oppressors. Do not turn me over to the desire of my foes, for false witnesses rise up against me, breathing out violence. I am still confident of this: I will see the goodness of the LORD in the land of the living. Wait for the LORD; be strong and take heart and wait for the LORD. Psalm 27:10–14

When God Says "Wait"

Jennifer works for a large company. One day she saw a job opening in another department. It seemed perfect for her and she immediately applied for the job—along with 20 other people!

After three interviews the choice came down to Jennifer and one other person. She'd been praying the whole time to get the job. But the job went to the other person. Didn't God hear Jennifer?

She was disappointed, but she went on with the job she had. Three years passed. One day the boss Jennifer had talked to three years earlier said, "We need another person in our department. You're just right for it. Would you like the job?"

God did hear Jennifer's prayers. He just said, "Wait," the first time she asked for the job.

God knows what's best for each of us. So sometimes He says, "Wait." But there are some prayers that God never answers with "Not now." God always answers yes when we ask for His guidance, love, and care. God doesn't make us wait when we confess our sins and ask for forgiveness. Jesus sacrificed His life for the sins of all people. He also came back from the dead to give us life without end. So all believers have forgiveness and eternal life—right now!

_____Let's do: Write the words of Psalm 27:14 at the top of a sheet of paper. Then, under the Bible verse, list some things you're waiting for.

_____Let's pray: Dear God, thank You for hearing my prayers. Help me be patient when Your answer is "Wait." I'm glad You always love me. Amen.

J. A. D.

Guilty or Not Guilty?

I had been in a minor accident and had to go to traffic court. About 100 people were there. The judge explained our rights and the penalties that could be given. Everyone, including me, seemed nervous and a little scared.

The judge read each charge and asked each person, "How do you plead—guilty or not guilty?" Many pleaded not guilty or tried to excuse what they had done. Then the judge gave her decision. Most people had to pay a fine. Some also had to go to driving school. Others would have a trial before a jury.

Finally, the judge read my name in a loud voice and stated when and where the accident had happened. I pleaded not guilty. Then she asked, "Does anyone here have a complaint in this case?"

No one answered. I was free—no penalty, no fine, nothing!

Before God, we all have to plead guilty since "all have sinned and fall short of the glory of God" (Romans 3:23). But we don't suffer the punishment. Jesus did that when He died for our sins.

When we believe in Jesus as our Savior, our sins are forgiven and forgotten. Now we are free from sin and eternal death. God declares our penalty "paid in full." Hallelujah!

Read from God's Word

But now a righteousness from God, apart from law, has been made known, to which the Law and the Prophets testify. This righteousness from God comes through faith in Jesus Christ to all who believe. There is no difference, for all have sinned and fall short of the glory of God, and are justified freely by His grace through the redemption that came by Christ Jesus. God presented Him as a sacrifice of atonement, through faith in His blood. … He did it to demonstrate His justice at the present time, so as to be just and the one who justifies those who have faith in Jesus. Romans 3:21–26

_____ Let's do: Read the parable of the lost son (Luke 15:11–24). Substitute your name for the younger son and God for the father.

_____ Let's pray: Lord, thank You for paying my penalty so I can be found "not guilty." Amen.

J. A. D.

Read from God's Word

But as for you, continue in what you have learned and have become convinced of, because you know those from whom you learned it, and how from infancy you have known the holy Scriptures, which are able to make you wise for salvation through faith in Christ Jesus. All Scripture is God-breathed and is useful for teaching, rebuking, correcting and training in righteousness, so that the man of God may be thoroughly equipped for every good work. 2 Timothy 3:14–17

Soul Food

"There's another one," said Stuart, looking out the window.

"I've seen four in this one town!" replied his sister, Tia.

Mom had been listening to this conversation from the front seat of the car. "What are you talking about?" she asked.

"Signs advertising soul food," said Stuart.

Mom explained, "The signs advertise a certain kind of cooking—ham hocks, collard greens, corn bread, sweet potatoes, and cobbler. Some people say soul food is the best in the world."

"All this food talk has made me hungry," said Stuart. "Why don't we stop and have a soul food taste test?"

Signs could be put in front of churches that say "God's Soul Food—Free!" Of course, this wouldn't be food to fill your stomach. It's much more important than that. God's soul food is in the Bible. As we read and study it, we learn about God and how He loves and cares for us.

The Bible tells us that God loves us so much that He sent Jesus to rescue everyone. Because He died and rose again, all our sins are forgiven, and we can live joyfully as God's children. Now that's true soul food!

_____Let's talk: What's your favorite food? How is God's soul food better than anything else in the world?

_____Let's pray: Heavenly Father, thanks for giving us Your Word and the great news of salvation. Help us tell others of Your wonderful soul food. Amen.

J. A. D.

Out of Control!

It was a perfect day for a drive in the country. We were all enjoying the scenery when suddenly I felt the car lurch and leave the road.

The next thing I remember is waking up with injured relatives all around me. My husband was seriously injured with a broken back. We'd gone from a great country ride to what looked like a battlefield. I was hurt and very scared as I prayed to God for help.

God was already helping even before I prayed. An emergency room nurse who was driving by saw the crash. She immediately knew what to do. Six men who'd been hunting came running, and one was a paramedic. Another man called for an ambulance on his cell phone. God sent people to help us.

My husband had surgery and went through months of pain and rehabilitation. God was always with us—loving, caring, and comforting.

God is never out of control. He loves and cares for us. God loves us so much that He sent His Son, Jesus, to take away the sins of all people. Every day He richly blesses us with mercy and grace. When we die, we will go to heaven to live forever with the Lord.

It's wonderful to know that God is always in control no matter what!

Read from God's Word

"Therefore I tell you, do not worry about your life, what you will eat or drink; or about your body, what you will wear. Is not life more important than food, and the body more important than clothes? Look at the birds of the air; they do not sow or reap or store away in barns, and yet your heavenly Father feeds them. Are you not much more valuable than they? Who of you by worrying can add a single hour to his life? … Therefore do not worry about tomorrow, for tomorrow will worry about itself. Each day has enough trouble of its own." Matthew 6:25–27, 34

_____Let's talk: Think of times when you were scared or worried. How did God help you? How did you know God was in control?

_____Let's pray: God, thank You for always being in control. Help us not to worry but always to trust in Your love and care. Amen.

J. A. D.

february

Contributors for this month:

Jim Hahn

Carol Delph

Suzanne Marvosh

Garth D. Ludwig

Kenneth J. Braun

Annette Schumacher

A Sure Hope!

Read from God's Word

For in this hope we were saved. But hope that is seen is no hope at all. Who hopes for what he already has? But if we hope for what we do not yet have, we wait for it patiently. Romans 8:24–25

Now faith is being sure of what we hope for and certain of what we do not see. Hebrews 11:1

Birthdays are very special for the Hahn family. Mom always asks what the birthday boy or girl would like for supper and what kind of cake she should bake. Jimmy always chooses the same—round steak, mashed potatoes and gravy, and corn. The birthday cake is chocolate with chocolate icing. And it is always so good!

But the best part is making a wish, blowing out the candles, and opening presents. Jimmy crosses his fingers, hoping to get what he wants. He is often pleased with his gifts, but sometimes he is disappointed that he doesn't get exactly what he wants. Crossing his fingers doesn't guarantee getting what he hopes for.

Christians have the hope of heaven. This hope is different from the hoped-for birthday presents. Our hope of one day going to heaven is a sure thing.

Christ paid the price for us to enter heaven through His life, death, and resurrection. We have this sure hope by faith, which is His gift to us. God never disappoints us.

_____Let's talk: What are some gifts you have hoped for and received? Have you ever been disappointed? How does God never disappoint us? (See Romans 8:28.)

_____Let's pray: Dear God, forgive me when I am disappointed with gifts, especially when I remember all gifts come from You. Thank You for the gift You gave in Jesus, who gives me the sure hope of eternal life. Amen.

J. H.

Read from God's Word

But God demonstrates His own love for us in this: While we were still sinners, Christ died for us. Since we have now been justified by His blood, how much more shall we be saved from God's wrath through Him! Romans 5:8–9

Fire Ants!

Moving to Florida can teach you many things. The climate, plants, and animals are certainly different from the rest of the country. If you plan to be outside, sunscreen is essential. Another thing people learn about Florida is never walk barefoot in the grass.

In Florida, as in other southern states, small insects called fire ants live in the grass. You can recognize a large colony of fire ants by the mound of dirt they create. But until those mounds are visible, fire ants are so small you don't notice them until it is too late. If they contact your skin, they immediately bite and then painful little blisters appear.

There are things we all need to avoid. Those are the things that would lead us to sin. The devil's temptations, like fire ants, aren't always seen until it is too late and we have given in to temptation. We all sin daily, but thankfully we've learned where to go to receive treatment. Because Jesus loves us, He is ready to forgive us as we confess our sins and ask for His forgiveness. Thank God that He has removed the pain of our sins!

_____Let's talk: What kind of pain or hurt have you experienced? What was done to relieve the pain? How can you help someone with his or her pain?

_____Let's pray: Father, forgive me for the times I have done things that hurt You. Help me to say no to the devil and temptation. Thank You that I am forgiven because of the work of Jesus, in whose name I pray. Amen.

J. H.

A Free Lunch

When Danny was very young, his family went on vacation. They stopped to eat at a cafeteria. They didn't eat out much, so a cafeteria was something new to him. Danny's dad told him as they walked in, "Just tell them what you want, and they will give it to you." When he reached the end of the line, the woman at the cash register smiled and said, "Okay." Danny didn't have to pay a thing!

Danny thought it was so nice that he had received a free lunch. But a cafeteria wouldn't stay in business very long if they gave everyone free lunches. Later he learned that his dad paid for the meal.

The Bible reading for today says that if parents know how to give good things to their children, how much more will our heavenly Father give us if we only ask Him. God gives us good gifts even without our asking. Everything we have comes as a gift from God.

The greatest gift He gives us is the forgiveness of sins. We are free because God paid the price. That price was giving up His own Son, Jesus, to die on a cross and rise again. The price was paid once and for all. Thank God for His wonderful gift!

Read from God's Word

"Which of you, if his son asks for bread, will give him a stone? Or if he asks for a fish, will give him a snake? If you, then, though you are evil, know how to give good gifts to your children, how much more will your Father in heaven give good gifts to those who ask Him!" Matthew 7:9–11

_____Let's talk: What are some things for which you are thankful? How might you show God and others that you are thankful for the gifts you've received?

_____Let's pray: God, You give me so much although I'm undeserving. Help me to appreciate all Your gifts and also to share them with others. Thank You for the gifts of Jesus, the forgiveness of sins, and eternal life. In His name. Amen.

J. H.

Read from God's Word

Praise be to the God and Father of our Lord Jesus Christ, who has blessed us in the heavenly realms with every spiritual blessing in Christ. For He chose us in Him before the creation of the world to be holy and blameless in His sight. In love He predestined us to be adopted as His sons through Jesus Christ, in accordance with His pleasure and will—to the praise of His glorious grace, which He has freely given us in the One He loves. In Him we have redemption through His blood, the forgiveness of sins, in accordance with the riches of God's grace that He lavished on us with all wisdom and understanding. Ephesians 1:3–8

Almost Good Enough

It had happened again! Tryouts for the school musical were underway. Sarah hoped to be chosen as one of the lead singers. She enjoyed singing and had a pretty voice. She practiced every free minute so she could do her best.

Tryouts continued until only two finalists were left—Sarah and Susan. The final tryout was held. Susan was selected because her voice was just a little stronger. Sarah cried. She had come so close—she had *almost* been good enough.

The Bible tells us that we were chosen by God even before the creation of the world. Not only did He choose us, He chose us to be holy and blameless in His sight. We didn't have to try out. We didn't have to prove anything.

So great is God's love for us that He chose us even while knowing our sinfulness. Through Jesus, God made us His sons and daughters. God did all of that out of grace—we certainly aren't good enough to deserve it. Being chosen by Him is far better than being chosen for anything else. You are chosen because of Jesus.

____Let's talk: Why do you feel good when you are chosen and sad when you are not? Share a time when you received something good even if you didn't deserve it.

____Let's pray: Dear God, thank You for choosing me and making me one of Your children. Help me to live a life that shows I've been chosen by You. In Jesus' name. Amen.

J. H.

Unsinkable!

I was excited—the day had finally arrived. I was going ocean fishing. I had visions of catching a bigger fish than I had ever caught before. My friend picked me up before sunrise, and it looked like it was going to be a beautiful, sunny day.

We launched the boat and headed through the channel toward the Gulf of Mexico. At first the water was calm and smooth, but the farther out into the gulf we went, the larger the waves became. A look of panic on my face caused my host to smile. He reassured me that I had nothing to fear; the boat was unsinkable.

The Bible reading says that as Jesus and the disciples crossed the sea, the wind and waves increased. The boat began to fill with water; the disciples panicked. They forgot their boat was "unsinkable"— not because of the way the boat was built but because Jesus was with them. After Jesus calmed the storm, the disciples began to realize His power.

Thanks be to God that He makes us "unsinkable" too. Through the life, death, and resurrection of Jesus, we are saved from the storm of eternal death.

Read from God's Word

That day when evening came, He said to His disciples, "Let us go over to the other side." Leaving the crowd behind, they took Him along... in the boat. ... A furious squall came up, and the waves broke over the boat, so that it was nearly swamped. Jesus was in the stern, sleeping on a cushion. The disciples woke Him and said to Him, "Teacher, don't you care if we drown?" He got up, rebuked the wind and said to the waves, "Quiet! Be still!" Then the wind died down and it was completely calm. He said to His disciples, "Why are you so afraid? Do you still have no faith?" They were terrified and asked each other, "Who is this? Even the wind and the waves obey Him!" Mark 4:35–41

_____Let's talk: What is something you've worried about? How did going to God in prayer help you?

_____Let's pray: Dear God, I am thankful that You are all powerful, and with You nothing is impossible. Thank You for Your care and protection. Help me to trust You at all times and in all things. In Jesus' name I pray. Amen.

J. H.

Read from God's Word

Now there was a man in Jerusalem called Simeon, who was righteous and devout. ... It had been revealed to him by the Holy Spirit that he would not die before he had seen the Lord's Christ. Moved by the Spirit, he went into the temple courts. When the parents brought in the child Jesus to do for him what the custom of the Law required, Simeon took him in his arms and praised God, saying: "Sovereign Lord, as You have promised, You now dismiss Your servant in peace. For my eyes have seen Your salvation, which You have prepared in the sight of all people, a light for revelation to the Gentiles and for glory to Your people Israel." Luke 2:25–32

Worth Waiting For!

Dan had been a little disappointed at Christmas because he didn't get the one gift he really wanted. His parents told him he would have to be patient and just wait.

But today was Dan's birthday. Following dinner, his family sang "Happy Birthday" and gave Dan his presents. One by one he opened his gifts and thanked everyone. As Dan opened the last gift his face showed his surprise and pleasure. Inside the box were in-line skates, the gift he had wanted at Christmas. They were even better than what he had hoped for!

In our Bible reading, Simeon had also been waiting. He was waiting for God's promise of the Messiah to be fulfilled. Mary and Joseph brought Jesus to the temple when He was only eight days old. Simeon held Jesus—the promised Savior—in his arms. He thanked God. Simeon told God there was nothing more he needed; he was ready to die and go to heaven.

Like Simeon, we too have a gift worth waiting for. Jesus has promised to return to take us to heaven and be with Him forever. God Himself has promised this gift—our salvation—through Jesus, our Savior.

_____Let's talk: Why is it sometimes good to have to wait for something special? What is something you've received that was worth waiting for?

_____Let's pray: God, thank You for keeping Your promise, for sending Jesus. As we wait for Jesus to come again to take us to heaven, help our faith in You to grow. In His name we pray. Amen.

J. H.

The "Undo" Key

Computers are amazing machines that can do many different things. Learning how to properly use software helps us work better, but sometimes we still have problems. There are times when we push a wrong key and something happens that we didn't want.

It's easy to be frustrated unless we "undo" the action. By clicking undo, the computer goes back to the previous screen, letting us continue as we want.

How great it would be if we could take back the hurtful things we've said or done—if we could somehow undo our sins. Paul tells the Romans that the good he wants to do, he doesn't do. And the evil he doesn't want to do is what he does instead.

You and I are no different from Paul. We are unable to help ourselves—unable to undo the sins we've committed. But God provided for us. He rescued us so we could continue in the right way. Jesus Christ, by His death and resurrection, has paid for our sins. Jesus did what we were unable to do.

Read from God's Word

I do not understand what I do. For what I want to do I do not do, but what I hate I do. And if I do what I do not want to do, I agree that the law is good. As it is, it is no longer I myself who do it, but it is sin living in me. I know that nothing good lives in me, that is, in my sinful nature. For I have the desire to do what is good, but I cannot carry it out. For what I do is not the good I want to do; no, the evil I do not want to do—this I keep on doing. ... What a wretched man I am! Who will rescue me from this body of death? Thanks be to God—through Jesus Christ our Lord! So then, I myself in my mind am a slave to God's law, but in the sinful nature a slave to the law of sin. Romans 7:15–20, 24–25

_____Let's talk: Identify something you cannot do. Who or what can do it for you? Who had to pay the cost for your sins?

_____Let's pray: Dear Father, forgive me for not always doing what You want me to do. Thank You for sending Jesus to undo what I've done so I can have forgiveness and eternal life. Help me to resist the devil and his temptations. In Jesus' name. Amen.

J. H.

Read from God's Word

"Behold, I am coming soon! My reward is with Me, and I will give to everyone according to what he has done. I am the Alpha and the Omega, the First and the Last, the Beginning and the End. … I, Jesus, have sent My angel to give you this testimony for the churches. I am the Root and the Offspring of David, and the bright Morning Star." Revelation 22:12–13, 16

Reversed!

The letters were ready and the children were ready. As each letter was held up, the children were to identify what the letter stood for: S is for Savior, T is for tender, A is for amazing, and R is for royal. The letters would spell STAR, a reminder of Jesus, who is called the "bright Morning Star."

The letters were supposed to spell STAR, but there was a problem. The letters had accidentally gotten out of order when they were handed to the children. So instead of spelling STAR, the letters spelled RATS. People chuckled as the teacher quickly corrected the error.

This funny story has an important message. Jesus was the Star, the promised Messiah, about whom the angels sang to the shepherds. The angels said Jesus would bring great joy to all people.

When the devil saw the Star, he didn't rejoice. He said, "Rats!" This Star, Jesus, was the One whom God had promised would defeat the devil and pay the price for the sins of the whole world. Thank God that this Star came and still shines today!

_____Let's talk: How can you shine like a star, reflecting Christ's love at home? at school? in your neighborhood? What can you do to make a difference?

_____Let's pray: Dear Father, thank You for sending Your Son to defeat the devil so I can have forgiveness of my sins and eternal life. May the light of Jesus shine in my life and reflect His love to others. I ask this in His name. Amen.

J. H.

God Pleasing

Today's Bible reading was the Gospel lesson for a worship service one Sunday. Since most children don't remember their Baptism, the pastor asked permission to put water in the baptismal font as part of the children's message. As the children came forward for the message, the pastor invited them to put their hands in the water and feel it.

There was nothing special about the water; it came from the faucet in the workroom. What gives Baptism power is when the water is combined with God's Word. As the pastor baptized you in the name of the triune God, your sins were forgiven, the Holy Spirit put faith in your heart, and you became a child of God.

At Jesus' Baptism, a voice from heaven said, "You are My Son, whom I love; with You I am well pleased." Because of Jesus' life, death, and resurrection on your behalf, God says these same words to you too. He says, *"You are My child, whom I love; with you I am well pleased."*

Read from God's Word

And so John came, baptizing in the desert region and preaching a baptism of repentance for the forgiveness of sins. The whole Judean countryside and all the people of Jerusalem went out to him. Confessing their sins, they were baptized by him in the Jordan River. … And this was his message: "After me will come one more powerful than I. … I baptize you with water, but He will baptize you with the Holy Spirit." At that time Jesus came from Nazareth in Galilee and was baptized by John in the Jordan. As Jesus was coming up out of the water, He saw heaven being torn open and the Spirit descending on Him like a dove. And a voice came from heaven: "You are My Son, whom I love; with You I am well pleased." Mark 1:4–11

_____Let's talk: When is your baptismal birthday? How old were you when you were baptized? Who were your Godparents? How can you celebrate your Baptism daily?

_____Let's pray: Thank You, God, for Christian parents who brought me to be baptized so I could be forgiven and receive new life. Thank You that I am Your child. Continue to strengthen me in my faith and help me to lead a life pleasing to You. I pray for the sake of Your Son, Jesus. Amen.

J. H.

Read from God's Word

Praise the LORD, O my soul; all my inmost being, praise His holy name. Praise the LORD, O my soul, and forget not all His benefits—who forgives all your sins and heals all your diseases, who redeems your life from the pit and crowns you with love and compassion, who satisfies your desires with good things so that your youth is renewed like the eagle's. The LORD works righteousness and justice for all the oppressed. He made known His ways to Moses, His deeds to the people of Israel: The LORD is compassionate and gracious, slow to anger, abounding in love. He will not always accuse, nor will He harbor His anger forever; He does not treat us as our sins deserve or repay us according to our iniquities. For as high as the heavens are above the earth, so great is His love for those who fear Him; as far as the east is from the west, so far has He removed our transgressions from us. Psalm 103:1–12

Spot Remover

The holidays had been over for weeks. The party was done. The guests had all gone home. And although the house was clean, there were noticeable spots in the carpeting.

Stores offer a variety of spot removers. Each one claims to be the best. And although all the products guaranteed to clean the carpeting of spots, each one worked differently. One said to spray the spot, let it dry, then vacuum. Directions on another cleaner were to spray the spot, gently brush in the product, then vacuum after drying. Still another product called for spraying, scrubbing, and rinsing. Besides all of these cleaners, another option is to hire a professional carpet cleaner to remove the spots.

The "spots" in our lives are the sins we commit. Once done there is no way we can remove the hurt and damage they cause. There is only one way for our sins to be removed and forgiven, and that is through Jesus Christ. When we come to Him in repentance and ask for forgiveness, He removes our sins from us "as far as the east is from the west." Because our sins are removed, one day we will be with Him forever in our heavenly home.

_____Let's talk: When is it hardest for you to forgive someone? Why do we need to forgive others? (See Colossians 3:13.)

_____Let's pray: Dear God, thank You for not treating me as I deserve but for forgiving my sins. Help me to forgive others as You forgive me. For Jesus' sake I ask it. Amen.

J. H.

Dare to Be Different

Have you ever worn wooden shoes? Since the 1300s, the people of the Netherlands have worn them. Wooden shoes insulate their feet, guard against injury, improve circulation, and give excellent support. The Dutch people dare to be different than the rest of the world.

As baptized Christians, we dare to be different because we know the benefits of God's grace. The world doesn't understand when we say that God gives us His grace in the water of Baptism and in the bread and wine of the Lord's Supper. They wonder at us when we believe that God uses our pastor to share His grace.

Sometimes we wonder too. We wonder if all this Word and Sacrament talk looks foolish to the world.

But God uses His Word to remind us, "Be still, and know that I am God; I will be exalted among the nations" (Psalm 46:10). We exalt, or lift up, God when we exalt the places where He is present—His Word and Sacraments.

We are different because God is different. We come to church to get away from the world and be with our Lord. He washes our sins away, gives us Himself, and sends us out into the world again to share His love.

Read from God's Word

"I no longer call you servants, because a servant does not know his master's business. Instead, I have called you friends, for everything that I learned from My Father I have made known to you. You did not choose Me, but I chose you and appointed you to go and bear fruit—fruit that will last. Then the Father will give you whatever you ask in My name. This is My command: Love each other. If the world hates you, keep in mind that it hated Me first. If you belonged to the world, it would love you as its own. As it is, you do not belong to the world, but I have chosen you out of the world. That is why the world hates you." John 15:15–19

_____Let's talk: Do you know someone who has dared to be different in God's eyes? Say a prayer of thanksgiving for them.

_____Let's pray: Lord, give me Your courage and the boldness to be different from the world. In Jesus' name. Amen.

C. D.

Read from God's Word

In those days Hezekiah became ill and was at the point of death. The prophet Isaiah son of Amoz went to him and said, "This is what the LORD says: Put your house in order, because you are going to die; you will not recover." Hezekiah turned his face to the wall and prayed to the LORD, "Remember, O LORD, how I have walked before You faithfully and with wholehearted devotion and have done what is good in Your eyes." And Hezekiah wept bitterly. Then the word of the LORD came to Isaiah: "Go and tell Hezekiah, '… I have heard your prayer and seen your tears; I will add fifteen years to your life. … This is the LORD's sign to you that the LORD will do what He has promised: I will make the shadow cast by the sun go back the ten steps it has gone down on the stairway of Ahaz.'" … Lord, by such things men live; and my spirit finds life in them too. You restored me to health and let me live. Isaiah 38:1–8, 16

God's Will

Samantha looked at her friend Raquel through tears. "I'm so sick of hospital gowns, needles, and mushed-up food," she said. "But most of all, I'm just sick of feeling sick."

"I'm praying for you, Sam," Raquel whispered. "I hope you get better soon."

Samantha replied with a tiny smile, "I'm willing!"

Samantha had a great desire to get well. In our Bible reading, Hezekiah wanted to get well too. God had told him through the prophet Isaiah that he would soon die. Hezekiah cried and pleaded with God to let him live.

God heard Hezekiah's prayer and promised to let him live longer. God gave Hezekiah a sign—something he could see—to help him believe the promise. The sun's shadow went back 10 steps. Hezekiah got better. God kept His promise!

Many of us have family and friends who face sickness and death. God hates the diseases and sins we battle. He sent Jesus to deliver us from death by dying for us.

As we confess our sins, we remember God's promise to forgive us for Jesus' sake. His forgiveness restores our broken bodies, our broken spirits, and our broken lives. His will is to make us whole again, preparing us to live forever with Him in heaven.

____Let's talk: Do you know someone who suffers with a long-term sickness? How can you share the message of God's good will with them?

____Let's pray: Thank You, Lord, for eternally mending my life for the sake of Jesus. Amen.

C. D.

The Promised Land

God designed everything so uniquely. Just think of how many shapes and colors of fruit God gives us: apples, bananas, grapes, peaches, pomegranates ... Pomegranates?

A pomegranate has thick skin that hides fleshy fruit and lots of seeds. Inside are sacs of sweet juice. The blood-red juice stains everything it touches. The top of this fruit looks like a crown.

When Adam and Eve fell into sin, God's perfectly created world became blighted, wormy, and rotten. Cast out of Paradise, man had to work long hours fighting the weeds and thorns of the fallen world just for food.

God promised His people a Savior and another special place to live. Milk, honey, and fruit would be abundant in this Promised Land. It would be a Holy Land, for God would dwell with them there.

All of God's promises concerning the Promised Land are fulfilled in Christ. In Him, we find God in the flesh. His blood shed for us on the cross washes away our sins. God is with us in His Word and Sacraments in the land of believers, His church.

The pomegranate can remind us of Christ—seed of promise, flesh, blood, and kingly crown. Christ saves us and gives us the promise of heaven, our new Promised Land. There we will be with Him forever.

Read from God's Word

Observe the commands of the LORD your God, walking in His ways and revering Him. For the LORD your God is bringing you into a good land—a land with streams and pools of water, with springs flowing in the valleys and hills; a land with wheat and barley, vines and fig trees, pomegranates, olive oil and honey; a land where bread will not be scarce and you will lack nothing; a land where the rocks are iron and you can dig copper out of the hills. When you have eaten and are satisfied, praise the LORD your God for the good land He has given you. Deuteronomy 8:6–10

_____Let's talk: If you could design a fruit, what shape would you make it? What color? How would it taste?

_____Let's pray: Thank You, God, for keeping all of Your promises in Christ. In His name I pray. Amen.

C. D.

Read from God's Word

After He had said this, Jesus was troubled in spirit and testified, "I tell you the truth, one of you is going to betray Me." His disciples stared at one another, at a loss to know which of them He meant. One of them, the disciple whom Jesus loved, was reclining next to Him. Simon Peter motioned to this disciple and said, "Ask Him which one He means." Leaning back against Jesus, he asked Him, "Lord, who is it?" Jesus answered, "It is the one to whom I will give this piece of bread when I have dipped it in the dish." Then, dipping the piece of bread, He gave it to Judas Iscariot, son of Simon. As soon as Judas took the bread, Satan entered into him. "What you are about to do, do quickly," Jesus told him, but no one at the meal understood why Jesus said this to him. John 13:21–28

Loved

The author of the Gospel of John never used his name while writing the book. Many scholars think the writer who called himself "the disciple whom Jesus loved" is John. Do you think John was bragging about how lovable he was?

John sat in a place of honor next to Jesus at the Last Supper. During the meal, Jesus said one of the disciples would betray Him. Peter told John to ask who it would be. Jesus told John how to identify the betrayer.

The disciple whom Jesus loved knew the identity of Jesus' betrayer but didn't try to stop him. John didn't understand what was going on.

Later, the disciple whom Jesus loved stood near the cross. John must have felt guilt and shame as he looked at the dying Savior. Instead of accusing him, Jesus honored John with the task of caring for Mary, His mother.

Jesus removed John's sin and guilt. In deep humility, John gave up his name to point others to the name of Jesus.

On this Valentine's Day we remember Jesus' love for us. Our Lord washed away our sins in Baptism. He names us children of God! Now we are disciples whom Jesus loves.

_____Let's talk: John later became a leader in the early church. He wrote four more books of the Bible. Can you name them?

_____Let's pray: Thank You, loving Savior, for washing away my sins. Help me share Your love with others. Amen.

C. D.

The Color of Love

Little Roberto sifted through the crayons. He picked up a green crayon then a purple one. Finally he said, "I'll color Jesus flesh-colored!"

It makes no difference what color Jesus' skin was. The important thing to remember is that Jesus had real skin. He's a real person. He got goose bumps. His skin bled and hurt when He cut Himself. He knows how hard life is.

Jesus relied on His heavenly Father, especially during times of suffering. He prayed "with loud cries and tears to the One who could save Him from death" (Hebrews 5:7).

One Sunday at the end of the worship service, Roberto could be heard quietly spelling J-E-S-U-S. "That spells God!" he said.

Through the faith of a child, we see Jesus is both true God and true man. He knows our needs and provides for them. He knows how Satan tempts us to sin; He is our Savior from sin. He knows how much we need to hear God's Word; He *is* the Word.

In our Baptism, our Lord washed us with His Word of forgiveness and gave us faith. We pray in Jesus' name, trusting Him for all our needs. Jesus sits beside God's throne, pleading for us. Our Father looks at Jesus and loves us.

Read from God's Word

In bringing many sons to glory, it was fitting that God, for whom and through whom everything exists, should make the author of their salvation perfect through suffering. Both the One who makes men holy and those who are made holy are of the same family. So Jesus is not ashamed to call them brothers. … He too shared in their humanity so that by His death He might destroy him who holds the power of death—that is, the devil—and free those who all their lives were held in slavery by their fear of death. … For this reason He had to be made like His brothers in every way, in order that He might become a merciful and faithful high priest in service to God, and that He might make atonement for the sins of the people. Because He Himself suffered when He was tempted, He is able to help those who are being tempted. Hebrews 2:10–18

_____Let's do: Think of someone whose world is colored with hatred. Share God's rich words of love with them.

_____Let's pray: Father, thank You that You show me Your love through the work of Christ on my behalf. In Jesus' name. Amen.

C. D.

Read from God's Word

Fix these words of mine in your hearts and minds; tie them as symbols on your hands and bind them on your foreheads. Teach them to your children, talking about them when you sit at home and when you walk along the road, when you lie down and when you get up. Write them on the doorframes of your houses and on your gates, so that your days and the days of your children may be many in the land that the LORD swore to give your forefathers, as many as the days that the heavens are above the earth. Deuteronomy 11:18–21

Remember Me

Children attending Christian day schools are often assigned Bible passages, stanzas of hymns, and parts of the catechism to memorize.

Emma attended a Christian day school and had lots of memory work. She lives in a nursing home now. She has an illness called Alzheimer's disease. This disease attacks her brain and results in loss of memory and unusual behavior.

Even with this terrible disease, God's Word is with her. Emma still remembers many of the Bible verses and hymns she learned as a child. The words she memorized long ago are still with her. With help, she can sing beautifully most of the church's liturgy. As this disease advances, God's Word continues to link Emma with her family and church.

Our Lord's Word is powerful. It molds and shapes His children and gives them a lifetime of guidance, comfort, and strength.

Emma's family takes comfort in the fact that her faith remains strong. And even if Emma can't remember, God remembers His promise to take Emma and all who believe in Him to heaven. He will keep His Word.

_____Let's do: Do you know anyone who lives in a nursing home? Share a hymn or psalm with them.

_____Let's pray: I am trusting You, Lord Jesus, Trusting only You; Trusting You for full salvation, Free and true. (*Lutheran Worship* 408:1)

C. D.

Break-fast

To "fast" means not to eat. Every morning we break the fast of our sleeping hours. We eat breakfast. Nutritionists tell us not to skip breakfast. Some call it the most important meal of the day.

The Old Testament people of God fasted and prayed in times of trouble. God sent Jonah to tell the people of Nineveh to repent. Their city would be destroyed in 40 days because of their sin. The Ninevites believed God. The King of Nineveh ordered the people not to eat or drink and to wear sackcloth as a sign of repentance.

The Ninevites knew they had sinned and deserved God's wrath. They prayed for God's mercy. He saw their repentant hearts and heard their prayers. He had compassion on them and spared them and their city.

God's Holy Word convinces us we have sinned. He calls us to repentance. Christ paid for our sin on Calvary's cross. He rose from the grave to tell us about His victory over sin, death, and the devil. He gives us His Word of forgiveness in Holy Baptism.

Instead of God's wrath, we have God's great mercy. We rejoice in His compassion, goodness, and love given to us for Christ's sake.

Read from God's Word

Jonah obeyed the word of the LORD and went to Nineveh. ... He proclaimed: "Forty more days and Nineveh will be overturned." The Ninevites believed God. ... When the news reached the king of Nineveh, he...issued a proclamation in Nineveh: "By the decree of the king and his nobles: Do not let any man or beast, herd or flock, taste anything; do not let them eat or drink. But let man and beast be covered with sackcloth. Let everyone call urgently on God. Let them give up their evil ways and their violence. Who knows? God may yet relent and with compassion turn from His fierce anger so that we will not perish." When God saw what they did and how they turned from their evil ways, He had compassion and did not bring upon them the destruction He had threatened. Jonah 3:3–10

_____Let's talk: What signs of repentance does God see in your life?

_____Let's pray: Lord, convince me of my sins and help me to repent and live as Your forgiven child. For Jesus' sake. Amen.

C. D.

Read from God's Word

All who rely on observing the law are under a curse, for it is written: "Cursed is everyone who does not continue to do everything written in the Book of the Law." Clearly no one is justified before God by the law, because, "The righteous will live by faith." The law is not based on faith; on the contrary, "The man who does these things will live by them." Christ redeemed us from the curse of the law by becoming a curse for us, for it is written: "Cursed is everyone who is hung on a tree." He redeemed us in order that the blessing given to Abraham might come to the Gentiles through Christ Jesus, so that by faith we might receive the promise of the Spirit. Galatians 3:10–14

Lightning Strikes!

When he was 21, a thunderstorm and a bolt of lightning knocked Martin Luther to the ground. Martin prayed. He promised he would become a monk if he were saved from the storm.

Martin was saved from the storm. He kept his promise and became a monk. In the monastery, Martin was tortured by his sins. He beat his body, fasted, prayed for long hours, and slept on the floor—hoping by all his actions to earn God's forgiveness.

An old monk said to him, "I believe in the forgiveness of sins." Martin thought about those words and tirelessly studied the Bible. Martin found that in Christ, the Law's demands were kept perfectly. Christ suffered the penalty for our sins by dying. God raised Him from the grave to live forever. He lives today, and in the Word of God, Baptism, and the Lord's Supper He gives us forgiveness for our sins.

God's Law works like a lightning bolt to accuse us of our sin and show us our need for a Savior. God's Gospel lifts us up with His gifts of grace. Faith receives God's gifts of forgiveness and new life in Christ.

We thank God for using Martin Luther to rediscover the Gospel light. We rejoice in God's peace, found in Christ Jesus.

_____Let's talk: Think about all the people you know. Who can you share the Gospel with this week?

_____Let's pray: O Lord, guard our church's teachings. Help me share the Gospel's truth for Jesus' sake. Amen.

C. D.

Cave Dwellers

There are many caves in the rugged mountains of the Holy Land. During Old Testament times, these caves were places of refuge for people. David wrote Psalm 57 while hiding from King Saul in a cave.

While reading this psalm, we sense the cool darkness of the cave as well as David's fear and loneliness. Evil people plot to get him. God is his only refuge. He has no clue how God will get him out of this tight spot. But he knows God will save him.

Can you remember being in a tight spot? Maybe the situation happened because of something you did. Maybe someone accused you falsely.

Like David, we know that God is our only refuge. We pray for God to rescue us, to make everything right again. God comes to us in our suffering, trials, and persecution. He uses the darkness of our situation to help our faith and trust in Him to grow. We wait for the light of Christ's love to appear.

Through His blood-bought forgiveness, our Savior rescues us from our tight spot. The darkness leaves. We live freely in Christ's light, rejoicing in our sufferings. In the cave we find the depth of His wisdom and undeserved love.

Read from God's Word

Have mercy on me, O God, have mercy on me, for in You my soul takes refuge. I will take refuge in the shadow of Your wings until the disaster has passed. I cry out to God Most High, to God, who fulfills His purpose for me. He sends from heaven and saves me, rebuking those who hotly pursue me; God sends His love and His faithfulness. … Be exalted, O God, above the heavens; let your glory be over all the earth. They spread a net for my feet—I was bowed down in distress. They dug a pit in my path—but they have fallen into it themselves. My heart is steadfast, O God, my heart is steadfast; I will sing and make music. Awake, my soul! Awake, harp and lyre! I will awaken the dawn. Psalm 57:1–8

_____ Let's talk: Do you know someone who is in a tight situation? How can you help?

_____ Let's pray: Thank You, Jesus, for suffering for me and meeting me in my suffering. I look forward to meeting You someday in glory. Amen.

C. D.

Read from God's Word

Now I want you to know, brothers, that what has happened to me has really served to advance the gospel. As a result, it has become clear throughout the whole palace guard and to everyone else that I am in chains for Christ. Because of my chains, most of the brothers in the Lord have been encouraged to speak the word of God more courageously and fearlessly. It is true that some preach Christ out of envy and rivalry, but others out of goodwill. The latter do so in love, knowing that I am put here for the defense of the gospel. Philippians 1:12–16

Victory Lane

Children learn a valuable lesson in school. To succeed in their classes, they try to figure out how their teacher thinks, teaches, and tests.

At times, it's hard for Christians to figure out our Master Teacher. His ways are unsearchable; His works are miraculous.

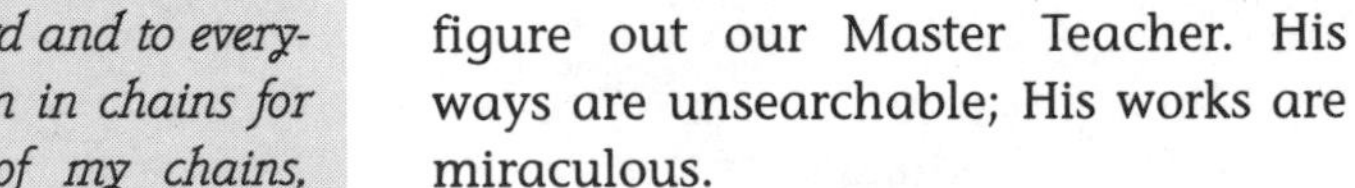

In our Bible reading, the Romans had placed the apostle Paul in chains for spreading the Gospel of Christ. The Romans thought that putting Paul in chains and keeping him in prison would stop the Gospel. But God doesn't work that way. People caring for Paul while he was in chains heard him preach about Christ and they became believers. The Gospel was shared!

Our Lord's church grows as it both proclaims and defends the truth of the Gospel. The world may laugh at us for believing that a tiny baby has faith or that Christ is truly present with us in Holy Communion. But we believe and defend what God tells us in His Word.

Unbelievers see our faith. They see that our church believes in Christ's means of grace. They see that we aren't afraid to suffer to defend our Savior. Unbelievers see and they believe.

We walk in Christ's way, His truth. His cross leads us forward in eternal victory!

_____Let's do: Pray for the people who are working in the world to share the Gospel. They may be missionaries in other countries or people who work in prison ministry.

_____Let's pray: Lord Jesus, help me to see that You are the way, the truth, and the life. Amen.

C. D.

A Case of the Slows

Matthew slumped at his desk. "I've got a clase of the slows today," he complained.

We all have slow days. We drag throughout the day, wondering how we'll ever make it.

Do you think our Lord has slow days? When our prayers aren't answered, do we suspect that God has a "case of the slows"?

At times we find it hard to wait for God to act. Maybe we try to nudge Him along with our prayers. We worry and fuss. Perhaps we even give up and try to answer the prayers ourselves.

God asks us to depend on Him. God shows His goodness and love for us by giving up His Son to pay for our sins. He forgives us and gives us His Son's life in Baptism. He wants only the best for us.

Although we are God's children, we live in a sinful world. We share in Christ's sufferings. We can be certain our heavenly Father sees our tears. He hears our cries. His heart goes out to us—wanting to act but sometimes waiting for our good.

God teaches us how to trust in Him. He comes to us in His Word, strengthening us to rest in Him. At just the right time, He acts swiftly and powerfully to help us.

Read from God's Word

I wait for the LORD, my soul waits, and in His word, I put my hope. My soul waits for the LORD more than watchmen wait for the morning, more than watchmen wait for the morning. O Israel, put your hope in the LORD, for with the LORD is unfailing love and with Him is full redemption. He Himself will redeem Israel from all their sins. Psalm 130:5–8

_____Let's talk: Tell of a time God slowly but surely answered your prayer. Were you quick to thank Him?

_____Let's pray: Dear Lord God, in Your Word I put my hope. I wait for Your unfailing love. In Jesus' name. Amen

C. D.

Read from God's Word

"This is what the LORD says: 'In the same way I will ruin the pride of Judah and the great pride of Jerusalem. These wicked people, who refuse to listen to My words, who follow the stubbornness of their hearts and go after other gods to serve and worship them, will be like this belt—completely useless! For as a belt is bound around a man's waist, so I bound the whole house of Israel and the whole house of Judah to Me,' declares the LORD, 'to be My people for My renown and praise and honor. But they have not listened.'" Jeremiah 13:9–11

Being Different

Chris, you don't need a new winter coat," said Mrs. Alexander. "And this one is so expensive."

"But Mom, everyone at school has a coat like this. I don't want to be different." Chris was almost in tears.

Why do some people want to dress or act as others do? One reason is to be accepted or to fit in. Chris thinks if he has a coat like the others, they might include him in their activities.

If you sometimes feel this way, remember that God created each of us to be different. He gave each of us a unique body, smile, personality, and brain. Do you think He wants us to be just like someone else?

Many people in the Bible were "different." David stepped out of the crowd and confronted the giant Goliath. John the Baptizer was unconventional. He wore animal skins and ate bugs. Each of them accepted themselves as God had created them. They used their God-given talents to glorify the Lord.

God created us individually and He loves each of us personally. Jesus came to rescue every person, including each of us. Through the power of His Spirit, we can be what God wants us to be. We can dare to be different for Him.

_____Let's talk: How might you help Chris realize it isn't important to be like everyone else? Why is it important to do the best you can with what God has given you?

_____Let's pray: Dear Lord, what a magnificent God You are! You made each of us special. Help us discover our talents and use them to glorify Your name. For the sake of Jesus we ask it. Amen.

S. M.

Heavenly Control Center

Many people influence us. They tell us how to manage our lives. Parents set guidelines to keep us safe. Teachers tell us to study so we will learn. Dentists remind us to floss and brush regularly for healthy teeth. Doctors suggest good nutrition and regular exercise to keep us healthy.

All of this is good advice. But it takes a lot of self-control to follow healthy habits. We aren't always in control. We are sinners. We often fail. We feel life is out of control sometimes.

The great news is that God is in control. When we keep our focus on Him, we don't feel out of control. He is always there to lead us.

God has a plan for our lives. In it, He is in the controller's seat. He promises always to watch out for us and take care of us.

The Bible teaches that we are saved by God's grace, through faith alone. To live in eternity, we need only believe in our Jesus as our Savior. Even faith is a free gift. Jesus was obedient unto death so we could belong to God forever.

No matter how afraid we may get that life seems out of control, we needn't panic. Our God is never out of control. What a comforting thought!

Read from God's Word

Those who live according to the sinful nature have their minds set on what that nature desires; but those who live in accordance with the Spirit have their minds set on what the Spirit desires. The mind of sinful man is death, but the mind controlled by the Spirit is life and peace; the sinful mind is hostile to God. It does not submit to God's law, nor can it do so. Those controlled by the sinful nature cannot please God. You, however, are controlled not by the sinful nature but by the Spirit, if the Spirit of God lives in you. And if anyone does not have the Spirit of Christ, he does not belong to Christ. Romans 8:5–9

_____Let's talk: What might happen to our lives if God were not in control? How does it help you to remember that God never loses control?

_____Let's pray: Dear God, send Your Holy Spirit to us. Comfort us when life seems out of control. Remind us that You have a plan for our lives. Thank You for caring enough to be in control. In Your Son's name we pray. Amen.

S. M.

Read from God's Word

"Do not judge, or you too will be judged. For in the same way you judge others, you will be judged, and with the measure you use, it will be measured to you. Why do you look at the speck of sawdust in your brother's eye and pay no attention to the plank in your own eye? How can you say to your brother, 'Let me take the speck out of your eye,' when all the time there is a plank in your own eye? You hypocrite, first take the plank out of your own eye, and then you will see clearly to remove the speck from your brother's eye." Matthew 7:1–5

Judge Not

A man and his friend had just visited a reservation in the southwestern United States. They were driving home and were discussing what they had seen.

The friend said, "I really enjoyed my visit to the reservation. But one thing bothers me."

"What's that?" asked the man.

"The Native Americans seemed cold and unfriendly," the friend said. "Whenever I asked them a personal question, they just looked at me or walked away."

The man said, "For them it's bad manners to ask about things that are private. They weren't being unfriendly to you."

Sometimes we form opinions about people of other cultures before we know much about them. We judge them as strange only because they're different from us.

Jesus taught us not to judge people but to love them. He Himself loved people of all races and accepted them for what they were. The color of people's skin or their customs didn't stop Jesus. His mission was to bring God's forgiveness to everyone. "He died for all," said St. Paul (2 Corinthians 5:15).

The best way to understand people is to love them. Think how Jesus would treat a person of another race or culture. Then ask God to help you show His love to others by talking about it.

_____Let's talk: Why do people of other races sometimes seem different to us? How can we keep from judging people who live differently than we do?

_____Let's pray: Lord Jesus, help me be kind and loving to all people I meet, no matter who they are. Show me how to love them just as You love me. Amen.

G. D. L.

Preparing to Serve

ain't goin' to school," Mark shouted. "Gimme one good reason why I should."

Mark had a hundred reasons why he didn't want to go to school. School was hard. There was always homework. Studying was boring.

Mark had been listening when his parents went to the last conference with his teacher. He heard Miss March use phrases like "attitude problem" and "working below potential." Mark decided he wasn't going back to school.

Mark's parents had tried to reason with him. They told him he would get a better job later on. He could go to college. They even tried the hard line: "It's the law—you have to go!" Nothing worked.

Pastor Frank was their last hope. Pastor Frank told Mark, "You go to school because you belong to a loving God and you want to serve Him. God gave His Son to serve you with His life. He gives everyone at least one talent; some get even more. It's up to each person to develop and use that talent to serve others. Going to school is the time when you find your talent and get it ready so you can help others in life."

What Pastor Frank said made sense to Mark. He decided he'd go to school after all.

Read from God's Word

The man who had received the five talents brought the other five. 'Master,' he said, 'you entrusted me with five talents. See, I have gained five more.' His master replied, 'Well done, good and faithful servant! You have been faithful with a few things; I will put you in charge of many things. Come and share your master's happiness!' ... For everyone who has will be given more, and he will have an abundance. Whoever does not have, even what he has will be taken from him. ..." Matthew 25:20–30

_____Let's talk: Name your talent or talents (if you have more than one). Ask the Holy Spirit for help to develop your talent so you can serve others with it as Jesus served you.

_____Let's pray: Lord God, thank You for giving me my abilities. Help me develop them as I go to school each day and prepare to serve You with my life. Bless my school, my teachers, and my classmates. For Jesus' sake. Amen.

K. J. B.

Read from God's Word

"But Zion said, "The LORD has forsaken me, the Lord has forgotten me." "Can a mother forget the baby at her breast and have no compassion on the child she has borne? Though she may forget, I will not forget you! See, I have engraved you on the palms of My hands; your walls are ever before Me." Isaiah 49:14–16

God Never Forgets Us

The wrench slipped for the fifth time and clattered to the floor. Krista was totally frustrated and shoved the bike in anger.

Krista's mom came out to see what was up. She saw Krista with a bleeding knuckle and a bike with no front wheel.

"I just can't fix this," Krista cried. "Why can't Dad be here to help? I need him. I feel so alone without him."

Mom hugged her hard. "I feel lonely without him too. But I keep going because I know our heavenly Father is always with us. He never forgets us."

When Isaiah was alive, things went from bad to worse for the people of Judah. Enemies attacked. They were defeated and taken captive. They felt alone and forsaken. But God said, "I have engraved you on the palms of My hands." If we write someone's name on our hands, we see it constantly. We don't forget it. So we can know that God never forgets us.

Jesus said the same thing: "I am with you always" (Matthew 28:20). He is with us every moment of every day. He loves us and forgives us.

Together Krista and her mom repaired her bike. Then Krista went for a ride, giving thanks for Jesus, her Friend forever.

_____Let's talk: Think of a time when you felt alone. How might things have been different if you had remembered that God was there with you? Make a promise that in your lonely times you will trust God's words "I will not forget you."

_____Let's pray: Good Father, how comforting to know that You are with me! Help me turn to You in every lonely time of my life. Thank You for being here right now to hear my prayer for Jesus' sake. Amen.

K. J. B.

Peace through Forgiveness

“I hate you!” Heather screamed. “I never want to talk to you again.” She ran into her room and slammed the door.

It’s hard being a brother or a sister. Living so close in the family offers lots of opportunities for hurt feelings and outright anger. That closeness offers many opportunities to sin. And sin always separates.

Joel wondered what he should do. His teasing had gone too far this time. He was sorry, but what could he do?

Perhaps Joel could take a clue from God. Every time we separate ourselves from Him by some sin, He is willing to forgive. When we come to God and ask for forgiveness, He lovingly takes us back. Because of Jesus’ death on the cross, He brings us together with Himself again. He doesn’t allow the sin to stand between us and Him.

Joel tried the Christian way. He knocked on Heather’s door. An angry “Go away!” was her response.

“Heather, I’m sorry,” Joel said. “Please forgive me. I’ve asked God to, and now I’m asking you.”

Heather opened the door. Tearfully but with a smile she said, “I forgive you, Joel.”

The separation was over. There was peace through the cross of Jesus, their Lord.

Read from God’s Word

For God was pleased to have all His fullness dwell in Him, and through Him to reconcile to Himself all things, whether things on earth or things in heaven, by making peace through His blood, shed on the cross. Once you were alienated from God and were enemies in your minds because of your evil behavior. But now He has reconciled you by Christ’s physical body through death to present you holy in His sight, without blemish and free from accusation—if you continue in your faith, established and firm, not moved from the hope held out in the gospel. This is the gospel that you heard and that has been proclaimed to every creature under heaven, and of which I, Paul, have become a servant. Colossians 1:19–23

_____Let’s talk: Think about the last time you had a disagreement with someone. How did you handle it? Is there still separation between you and that person? Is it time to say, “I’m sorry; please forgive me”?

_____Let’s pray: Father, I cause so much separation because of my sin. I don’t want to be separated from You. In Jesus’ name, forgive me. Please heal any separation between me and anyone else. Help me to ask for forgiveness. And when others ask for my forgiveness, help me give it as freely and eagerly as You forgive me. Amen.

K. J. B.

Read from God's Word

The body is a unit, though it is made up of many parts; and though all its parts are many, they form one body. So it is with Christ. For we were all baptized by one Spirit into one body … and we were all given the one Spirit to drink. … God has arranged the parts in the body, every one of them, just as he wanted them to be. If they were all one part, where would the body be? As it is, there are many parts, but one body. … If one part suffers, every part suffers with it; if one part is honored, every part rejoices with it. Now you are the body of Christ, and each one of you is a part of it. 1 Corinthians 12:12–20, 26–27

Working Together

Jamal was a member of Boy Scout Troop 141. The meetings on Tuesday nights were fun enough, but the camping trips were what he really liked.

On the campouts everybody had a job to do. One scout made the fire, a couple of guys cooked, and others cleaned up. *What makes camping so much fun*, Jamal thought, *is that everyone helps out.*

Then a new kid, Ashanti, joined the troop. Ashanti was unwilling to do his share. He did anything to get out of his assigned task. Worse, he cost them a badge when points were taken off because he didn't clean up the campsite.

For Jamal, scouting wasn't as much fun now because Ashanti didn't do his share.

In our Bible reading, St. Paul compares the church to a body. Every Christian is part of this body. When all the parts work together, everything goes well and blessings abound. When a part of the body doesn't work, the whole body is hurt.

Christ is the head of the church. He loved the church so much that He gave Himself up for all of us, to make us holy and blameless before God.

Working together is God's plan for us. Willingness to serve and pitching in to do whatever we do best helps build up the body of Christ.

_____Let's talk: Name the groups that you are in. How do you fit into those groups? How are you using your God-given abilities to help the groups grow and get their job done?

_____Let's pray: Dear Father, thank You for placing me in groups. Help me use my special gifts from You to help every group I'm in work well. Take away my sinful attitudes and selfish actions and replace them with Your Spirit-inspired willingness and love. In Jesus' name. Amen.

K. J. B.

A Good Laugh

Read from God's Word

A happy heart makes the face cheerful, but heartache crushes the spirit. Proverbs 15:13

Sean's dad liked to play practical jokes on his wife. One morning he left a phone number and message to "Please call Jerry Raff."

Sean's mom called the number and asked to speak with Jerry Raff. The person who answered the phone laughed. "I think someone's playing a joke on you. This is the zoo!"

Most people like to laugh. We laugh at funny stories and jokes. Maybe you have a teacher, friend, or relative who tells a joke well. We enjoy funny books, movies, television shows, and cartoons. Many people like the "funnies" better than any other section of the newspaper.

A good sense of humor is a blessing from God. It frees us up to relax and have fun. Laughter sometimes changes a sad mood to a glad mood. Many doctors even consider laughter to be healthy.

Our Bible reading today says, "A happy heart makes the face cheerful." If our hearts are happy, we will show that joy with our smiles. God has given us so much to fill our hearts with happiness. He even gave His only Son, Jesus, so we will have happiness forever in heaven.

God must also have a sense of humor. He created some funny-looking animals. One of them is the giraffe!

_____Let's do: Name some other funny-looking animals. Find a joke book in your school library and read some jokes to your family and friends. Have some good laughs.

_____Let's pray: Dear God, thank You for the gift of humor. May it brighten our lives with the sparkle of that special gift of love from You. In Jesus' name. Amen.

A. S.

m a r c h

Contributors for this month:

Dawn Napier

Doris Schuchard

Donna Rathert

Cheryl Thompson

Glenda Schrock

Staying on Top

Read from God's Word

I am sending you out like sheep among wolves. Therefore be as shrewd as snakes and as innocent as doves.
Matthew 10:16

"I need two volunteers," Mr. Hernandez said.

"Nick, will you stand on this table? And Jason, please stand next to it." The other students giggled as the boys took their places.

"Now Nick," said Mr. Hernandez, "try to pull Jason onto the table with you. Jason, you try to pull Nick off the table."

After a few moments of pushing and pulling, Nick jumped off the table to the floor.

"What just happened?" the teacher asked.

"Jason had gravity helping him pull Nick down," said Amy. "Nick never had a chance."

Mr. Hernandez nodded. "Sometimes Christians find themselves in situations like that. They believe they can be with people who are headed for trouble and still resist temptation themselves. They might even believe they can change things for the better. But when you're with someone who is involved in sinful things, it's like being on the table. It's easier to be pulled down into sin than to pull someone up out of it."

Today's verse tells us to "be shrewd [wise] as snakes and as innocent as doves." We can't always avoid people who are trapped in sinful living. And God wants us to tell everyone about Jesus. But we also need to be with people who love God. They help us keep His Word in our hearts and lives.

_____Let's talk: How can you be innocent as a dove around others who may not know Jesus? Why is it important to also be as wise or as clever as a snake in those situations?

_____Let's pray: Heavenly Father, plant Your Word and wisdom in me that I may know right from wrong, obey You, and witness to others of Your glory. In Jesus' name. Amen.

D. N.

Read from God's Word

"Forget the former things; do not dwell on the past. See, I am doing a new thing! Now it springs up; do you not perceive it? I am making a way in the desert and streams in the wasteland. The wild animals honor Me, the jackals and the owls, because I provide water in the desert and streams in the wasteland, to give drink to My people, My chosen, the people I formed for Myself that they may proclaim My praise." Isaiah 43:18–21

Water in the Desert

Read today's Bible verses aloud. Like poetry, they contain picture language.

Think about Moses leading the Israelites out of slavery. Soon after they left Egypt, Pharaoh changed his mind about letting them go. As Pharaoh's soldiers chased them, God saved His people in a miraculous way. God parted the water of the Red Sea so they could cross to the other side. When the soldiers tried to follow, God released the water. The soldiers and their horses drowned. Today's reading tells us that God can make water in a desert, just as He can make a dry path in a sea.

God created each person to be different and special. He faithfully loves us even though we sin. He sent His own Son to redeem us from sin. He promises never to leave us. He hears every prayer and knows what we need before we even ask. He has prepared a home for us in heaven.

God can make rivers in the desert and He can bring good out of bad situations. We can trust Him with every moment of our lives. He blesses our service to His glory. He is worthy of our praise.

_____Let's do: Try to remember a time when you were really thirsty. What did you feel like when you finally got a drink of water? God refreshes us through His Word and the waters of Baptism.

_____Let's pray: Lord, help us to remember how much You care for us. Thank You for loving us even when we are unfaithful. In Jesus' name. Amen.

D. N.

Made New in Christ

Read from God's Word

Therefore, if anyone is in Christ, he is a new creation; the old has gone, the new has come! All this is from God, who reconciled us to Himself through Christ and gave us the ministry of reconciliation. 2 Corinthians 5:17–18

One night Jeremy and his friends stole a car. His friends laughed as he drove faster and faster. Suddenly there was a crash and everything went black.

When Jeremy woke up in the hospital, he learned he had hit another car. The woman driving that car would be in a wheelchair for the rest of her life. Jeremy had to go to jail.

In jail Jeremy met Pastor Colton, who visited the inmates. Pastor Colton told him about Jesus, who came to take away our sins. Jeremy studied God's Word and learned that Jesus died and rose again for him. He prayed, and he knew God forgave him because of Jesus.

When Jeremy got out of jail, Pastor Colton took him out for lunch. At the restaurant Jeremy noticed a man in a wheelchair. This was a painful reminder that someone was in a wheelchair because of what he had done. Jeremy ran out the door in tears.

Pastor Colton followed and gently said, "Although God forgives you there are still consequences for sin. Seeing someone in a wheelchair may always remind you of your sin. But it can also remind you of what God has done for you. Each time you see a wheelchair, praise God for the victory He gave you over your sin."

_____Let's talk: What things remind you of your sins? How can these same things make you think of God's goodness? How does the cross remind us of both terrible and wonderful things?

_____Let's pray: Father, let my sins remind me of what Jesus has done for me. Thank You for Your forgiveness and for my new life in Jesus. Amen.

D. N.

Read from God's Word

Therefore confess your sins to each other and pray for each other so that you may be healed. The prayer of a righteous man is powerful and effective. James 5:16

Praying in God's Will

One Sunday afternoon Grandma went into the hospital with a bad infection.

"Let's pray that God will heal Grandma," Mom said to the children.

Haley took Mom's hand and bowed her head as the family prayed together. Then she looked up and said, "If God knows everything, then He knows if Grandma will get better, doesn't He?"

"Yes," Mom said quietly.

"Then why should we pray? Will praying change anything?"

"Oh, yes!" Mom said. "There are places in the Bible that tell of people who prayed and how God changed His mind because of those prayers."

"I remember," said Haley. "We talked about King Hezekiah in Sunday school last week."

"That's right!" said Mom. "King Hezekiah had become very ill. The prophet Isaiah came to Hezekiah and told him that the Lord said Hezekiah would die. Hezekiah prayed to God for healing. Through the prophet Isaiah the Lord told Hezekiah He had heard his prayers and that Hezekiah would recover and live another 15 years. We can trust God to do what is best in our lives. Grandma trusts Jesus for forgiveness. He has healed her sin. We pray she will be healed of this infection also. We can be sure God hears our prayers and will answer them as He sees best."

____Let's do: Begin a prayer list or notebook. Each day list the things to pray about. Also write how God answers your prayers.

____Let's pray: Loving God, help me to remember my love for You and others when I pray so many may learn to know You also. In Jesus' name. Amen.

D. N.

It's the Real Thing

John and his little cousin, Alex, decided to walk to the store for sodas. When they went to the register to pay for the drinks, Alex pulled play money from his pocket and said, "Let me pay for that." The clerk smiled.

"Thanks, Alex," said John. "Maybe you should save your money. I'll buy the sodas."

Why couldn't Alex use his money to pay for the sodas? Because it wasn't real. John had seen and used real money, so he recognized the real thing. He knew that what Alex had was fake.

Reading and learning about the real things in God's Word helps us to recognize false ideas. From the Bible we learn that God is perfect and expects us to be perfect. We also learn that we are born in sin and can never be perfect. In His great love and mercy, God sent Jesus to take our punishment for sin. By grace, God gives us the forgiveness Jesus earned.

Read from God's Word

Finally, brothers, whatever is true, whatever is noble, whatever is right, whatever is pure, whatever is lovely, whatever is admirable—if anything is excellent or praiseworthy—think about such things. Whatever you have learned or received or heard from Me, or seen in Me—put it into practice. And the God of peace will be with you. Philippians 4:8–9

God's Word also tells us the real story about how God wants us to live. It shows us that our sinful nature makes us want to put ourselves first, to get even, or to do what seems to feel right. Knowing the real things of God helps us want to share the real Good News with others.

_____Let's talk: What are the dangers of not knowing the truth about Jesus? Tell how the following things help you understand the real things of God: attending church and Sunday school, reading God's Word, praying, having Christian friends.

_____Let's pray: Help me know Your truth, dear God. Protect me from sin and danger. For Jesus' sake. Amen.

D. N.

Read from God's Word

He sent back this answer: "Do not think that because you are in the king's house you alone of all the Jews will escape. For if you remain silent at this time, relief and deliverance for the Jews will arise from another place, but you and your father's family will perish. And who knows but that you have come to royal position for such a time as this?" Esther 4:13–14

For Such a Time as This

Esther lived in Babylon, where God's people were slaves. When the king of Babylon married Esther, she became the queen.

An evil man named Haman tricked the king into passing a law that would mean death for God's people. Esther was the only one who could persuade the king to save them. Yet Esther was afraid to speak out.

Then her uncle, Mordecai, encouraged her with the words in today's Bible passage. He meant that perhaps God had made Esther queen so she could save her people.

The story has a happy ending. God gave Esther courage to talk to the king. He had mercy on God's people. In the end it was evil Haman who was put to death.

Like believers in Esther's time, we also have been given a death sentence. Because of our sin, we are guilty before God, our King, of breaking His laws. We deserve eternal punishment.

Praise God that our story has a happy ending too! In His great love, God sent His Son into the world "for such a time as this." Jesus lived a perfect life in our place. He took the punishment for our sins when He died on the cross. Because of Jesus we are forgiven and are now God's royal sons and daughters!

_____Let's talk: Consider how you are like Esther. Why do you think God placed you in your family? in your school? with certain friends? How might you serve Him and help save others?

_____Let's pray: Use me, O Lord, to help others in Your name. Show me Your plan for my life each day. I pray in Your Son's name. Amen.

D. N.

Strengthen What Remains

Read from God's Word

Wake up! Strengthen what remains and is about to die, for I have not found your deeds complete in the sight of my God. Remember, therefore, what you have received and heard; obey it, and repent. Revelation 3:2–3a

The funnel cloud formed without warning and within moments, everything in the tornado's path was reduced to piles of rubble. Then it was over.

Shocked families looked at the place that used to be their neighborhood. Finding even little things in the big mess—photographs, a favorite toy—brought joy. These little things helped people go on. They built new homes and lives, strengthened by these connections to the past.

Life is full of trouble. Trouble can be small, like homework that is hard or toys that break. Trouble can be overwhelming, like losing someone we love, an accident, or the loss of everything we own.

Trouble is in the world because of sin. Jesus came into the world to deal with sin. When He died on the cross, He led us out of trouble and into a right relationship with God. Someday we will live with Him forever.

Even in times of terrible trouble, Jesus gives us the strength to begin again. God tells us, "I am the Alpha and the Omega, the Beginning and the End" (Revelation 21:6). He is the connection that will take us from trouble to a brighter future.

No matter what, you can trust God to strengthen you with His neverfailing love and forgiveness. And by God's grace, go on!

_____ Let's do: Memorize this verse: "God is our refuge and strength, an ever-present help in trouble" (Psalm 46:1).

_____ Let's pray: You are my strength and help, O Lord. Help me remember to look to You when trouble comes. In Jesus' name. Amen.

D. N.

Read from God's Word

Show me Your ways, O LORD, teach me Your paths; guide me in Your truth and teach me, for You are God my Savior, and my hope is in You all day long. Psalm 25:4–5

Formed in His Ways

Abbie's Dad was putting a cement sidewalk next to their house. First he dug down into the soil, removing the grass and creating a hole where the sidewalk would be. Next he took long boards and fit them against the sides of the hole. Then he put shorter boards across the space between the longer boards. It looked like he had built a ladder on the ground.

When he poured the wet cement into the holes, the boards kept it in the shapes he wanted. Two days later the cement was hard and dry. Dad removed the boards. A perfect sidewalk now led to the side porch.

Sometimes learning to live in God-pleasing ways is like making a sidewalk. Our will is like the wet cement. We know what God wants, but we are not able to do it on our own. We need help to stay on the paths God wants us to be on.

God gives us that help! He sent His Son to be our Helper. Through Jesus, our heavenly Father forgives us for all the times we fail to obey His Law and do His will.

By the power of His Spirit, God helps us follow His commands. He will shape our will and lives.

_____Let's do: Think of someone you have difficulty liking or with whom you do not get along. Pray for God's help in dealing with this person.

_____Let's pray: Dear heavenly Father, I confess a sinful attitude about ________ . Thank You for sending Jesus to take away my sins. Forgive me for His sake. Create a clean heart and a new spirit in me. In Jesus' name. Amen.

D. N.

Journey with Jesus

The scouts were going on a hike. They had several meetings to plan the trip and gather supplies. A forest ranger gave them a guidebook that showed trails to follow and locations to find water and rest areas. It also showed them dangerous places to avoid. The ranger told them how to reach him if they needed help.

When they packed their backpacks, the scouts made sure they had everything they needed. They were careful not to take extra things that would add weight and tire them out. A big celebration was held at the place where the hike ended.

Lent is a 40-day season when we journey to the cross, remembering Jesus' suffering and death for us. Lent ends on Easter, when we celebrate His resurrection from the dead. During Lent we think about our own sins and confess them; sins weigh us down and make our journey difficult.

Read from God's Word

But thanks be to God, who always leads us in triumphal procession in Christ and through us spreads everywhere the fragrance of the knowledge of Him. 2 Corinthians 2:14

God is our guide on this life journey. He gives us the Bible to guide us along the right path. We have constant communication with Him through prayer. We are blessed by other believers who encourage and help us as we travel.

Our earthly journey will end when we die. Then we join an everlasting celebration in heaven with Jesus, our Savior!

_____Let's talk: What has been the best part of your faith journey so far? When have you lost your way or met a roadblock?

_____Let's pray: Father, thank You for being my constant guide and for all the wonderful blessings You have given me. I pray in Jesus' name. Amen.

D. N.

Read from God's Word

When John heard in prison what Christ was doing, he sent his disciples to ask Him, "Are You the One who was to come, or should we expect someone else?" Jesus replied, "Go back and report to John what you hear and see: The blind receive sight, the lame walk, those who have leprosy are cured, the deaf hear, the dead are raised, and the good news is preached to the poor. Blessed is the man who does not fall away on account of Me." Matthew 11:2–6

Doubts Answered

John the Baptist's whole life was linked to Jesus.

John and Jesus were cousins. God chose John to prepare people for the coming of the Messiah. He told people that Jesus was the Savior for whom they were waiting.

John was so fearless and determined that King Herod put him in prison to stop his preaching. Lonely and distressed, as John sat in prison he began to question his ministry. He needed encouragement.

John turned to Jesus. Jesus lovingly gave John the proof he needed: "the blind receive sight, the lame walk, those who have leprosy are cured, the deaf hear, the dead are raised, and the good news is preached to the poor." John was assured that Jesus was the Savior. His faith and belief were restored.

What are the "prisons" that cause you to doubt God's love? Does loneliness make you forget that the Savior who died for you will provide everything you need? Do troubles make you wonder if God is really there? Has someone tried to convince you that your faith in Jesus is foolish? Is it hard to trust that your sins are really forgiven?

Like John, you can go to Jesus. He hears all your prayers. He wants to strengthen your faith and show you His goodness. The Bible tells us so!

_____Let's talk: Have you ever doubted God's presence in your life? How does God show you that He is really there?

_____Let's pray: Dear Jesus, thank You for Your constant loving care, even when I doubt. Forgive me and strengthen me with Your Holy Spirit. I am trusting You for everything. Amen.

D. N.

Food for Your Thoughts

Read from God's Word

Finally, brothers, whatever is true, whatever is noble, whatever is right, whatever is pure, whatever is lovely, whatever is admirable—if anything is excellent or praiseworthy—think about such things. Whatever you have learned or received or heard from me, or seen in me—put it into practice. And the God of peace will be with you. Philippians 4:8–9

Have you heard the expression "you are what you eat"? What we eat affects our health. We know that foods low in fat, salt, and sugar are best for us.

We don't often hear about feeding our minds the right things. Yet this is very important to our spiritual health. You may have friends who use bad language or say unkind things about others. Perhaps you know someone who is disrespectful or who lies. Many TV programs, movies, videos, magazines, books, and songs are filled with language and ideas that dishonor God.

We might coin another accurate expression: "You are what you think." It is spiritually dangerous to watch, listen to, or read things that displease God. These things may change our attitudes and lead us into sin.

Our Bible reading mentions good things to feed our minds. The best food for our spirit is in God's Word. There we learn of God's great love for us. We read that our sins are forgiven because of Jesus' death on the cross. We learn that He is always with us and that someday we will live with Him in heaven. This wonderful "feast" for our minds strengthens us to live in ways that honor God.

_____Let's talk: Think of some things that are pure, lovely, or excellent. How do these things remind you of God's great love? Why are you grateful for them?

_____Let's pray: Heavenly Father, thank You for Your many good gifts. Help me keep my mind on things that are lovely in Your sight and wholesome for me.
In Jesus' name. Amen.

D. N.

Read from God's Word

But whatever was to my profit I now consider loss for the sake of Christ. What is more, I consider everything a loss compared to the surpassing greatness of knowing Christ Jesus my Lord, for whose sake I have lost all things. I consider them rubbish, that I may gain Christ and be found in Him, not having a righteousness of my own that comes from the law, but that which is through faith in Christ—the righteousness that comes from God and is by faith. I want to know Christ and the power of His resurrection and the fellowship of sharing in His sufferings, becoming like Him in His death, and so, somehow, to attain to the resurrection from the dead. Philippians 3:7–11

The Treasure Is Yours

Ruthie ties her shoes, drinks a glass of orange juice, and stuffs her books into her backpack. Suddenly she shouts, *"Where is it?* Dad! Mom! I can't find my book report!" And the frantic search begins.

Ruthie looks everywhere—under her bed, on the kitchen table, in her brother's room. Finally, it's time to leave for school. Ruthie sadly opens the refrigerator to get her lunch and shouts, *"I found it!* I stuck it in the refrigerator instead of putting away the juice."

Have you ever lost something? You were probably just as excited as Ruthie when you found it. It's like discovering a hidden treasure.

Jesus told about a man who did just that. When he found a hidden treasure in a field, the man sold everything he owned, took the money, and bought the field and the treasure.

What treasure is so important that someone would give up everything for it? The apostle Paul knew. Paul said everything in his past was like garbage. Being joined to Christ by faith in His death and resurrection and having the gift of eternal life was Paul's treasure.

You have received the same treasure through the power of God's Spirit. You can truthfully say, "Jesus is my Lord and my Savior."

_____Let's talk: Have you ever gone on a treasure hunt? What's it like to find the treasure? How do you feel when you know that Jesus has searched for you and found you and made you His own?

_____Let's pray: Lord Jesus, You are my greatest treasure. Help me rejoice in You each day of my life. Amen.

D. S.

Who's the Greatest?

Read from God's Word

The greatest among you will be your servant. For whoever exalts himself will be humbled, and whoever humbles himself will be exalted. Matthew 23:11–12

The biggest and the best. Do you worry about being the best athlete, the smartest student, or the most popular person in your group? It's easy to think others love us because of our high test scores, good looks, or special talents.

Those who lived during Jesus' time felt the same way. Surely the Master would love people who were powerful, rich, popular, or very religious. But Jesus reminds us that this is not how He judges greatness.

It's just the opposite. In today's Bible reading, our Lord says, "The greatest among you will be your servant. For whoever exalts himself will be humbled, and whoever humbles himself will be exalted."

Those who are humble will be great? This is definitely not what most people think! But the God who made all things in heaven and on earth isn't concerned about appearances. He wants only a childlike faith and a desire in your heart to serve Him. He gives you this by His Spirit, who works through the Gospel message—"For even the Son of Man did not come to be served, but to serve, and to give His life as a ransom for many" (Mark 10:45).

_____Let's talk: God has given each of us special abilities. What talents has He given you? How can you use your talents to help someone today?

_____Let's pray: Jesus, thank You for the talents You have given me. I'm glad You love me so much that You came to serve and save me. Help me be great for You by serving others. Amen.

D. S.

Read from God's Word

However, I consider my life worth nothing to me, if only I may finish the race and complete the task the Lord Jesus has given me—the task of testifying to the gospel of God's grace. Acts 20:24

Victory Guaranteed

Emilio," Nick asked after school, "what did you get on your English test? I got an A. Want to come over and play my new video game?" Nick continued. "Bet you can't get to the fourth level. Let's race to my house."

"Nick, all you care about is winning," Emilio said. "Can't we just have fun?"

Some people say that competition helps you be the best you can be. Others think competition is bad. Instead of concentrating only on winning, they think we should just have fun and strive to improve our skills.

There are ways to combine cooperation and competition. As part of a team, you have the opportunity to help your teammates and to work together. Cheering for both winners and losers encourages everyone to do their best.

How is it in our Christian life? Do we compete or cooperate? Thanks to our Savior, we've already won! Jesus defeated death, hell, and Satan for us. "Thanks be to God! He gives us the victory through our Lord Jesus Christ" (1 Corinthians 15:57).

Knowing this, we encourage others to take hold of the prize Jesus offers to all. We want everyone to be victorious because God wants everyone "to be saved and to come to a knowledge of the truth" (1 Timothy 2:4).

_____Let's talk: How do you feel when you're a winner? a loser? Which is more important—being first or enjoying what you're doing? How is your attitude toward life affected by the victory God gives you?

_____Let's pray: Father, because You love me, I want to live my life for You. Thank You for sending Jesus to win eternal life for me. Help me to share this wonderful victory with others. Amen.

D. S.

Days of Thunder

Many years ago the people of Europe believed a god named Thor created thunder by beating his hammer against an anvil. Eventually, Thor's Day became known as Thursday.

It's easy to imagine thunder sounding like a hammer, but does thunder sound like God's voice to you? One day a crowd heard Jesus explain that He would die soon. Jesus wanted to give glory to God by doing what the Father wanted, so He said, "Father, glorify Your name!" God spoke from heaven, "I have glorified it, and will glorify it again."

Many people in the crowd thought the voice from heaven was only thunder. They weren't willing to listen to God and understand His will.

Jesus heard God's voice. God wanted Him to die and rise again. And it's very good news for us that Jesus did this—He gained our salvation!

Do you ever hear God speaking? God speaks through Christian friends, parents, pastors, and teachers. But there's no better way to hear God's voice than to read the Bible. There we find the message of eternal life through faith in His Son, Jesus.

Read from God's Word

Jesus replied, "The hour has come for the Son of Man to be glorified. ... Now My heart is troubled, and what shall I say? 'Father, save Me from this hour'? No, it was for this very reason I came to this hour. Father, glorify Your name!" Then a voice came from heaven, "I have glorified it, and will glorify it again." ... Now is the time for judgment on this world; now the prince of this world will be driven out. But I, when I am lifted up from the earth, will draw all men to Myself." ... "You are going to have the Light just a little while longer. Walk while you have the Light, before darkness overtakes you. ... Put your trust in the Light while you have it, so that you may become sons of Light." When He had finished speaking, Jesus left and hid Himself from them. John 12:23–36

_____Let's talk: Can you think of an answer God gave you when you had an important decision to make? What did He use to help you decide?

_____Let's pray: Dear Jesus, give me ears to hear Your voice and a heart to understand and do Your will. Amen.

D. S.

Read from God's Word

As He went along, He saw a man blind from birth. His disciples asked Him, "Rabbi, who sinned, this man or his parents, that he was born blind?" "Neither this man nor his parents sinned," said Jesus, "but this happened so that the work of God might be displayed in his life. As long as it is day, we must do the work of Him who sent Me. Night is coming, when no one can work. While I am in the world, I am the light of the world." Having said this, He spit on the ground, made some mud with the saliva, and put it on the man's eyes. "Go," He told him, "wash in the Pool of Siloam" (this word means Sent). So the man went and washed, and came home seeing. John 9:1–7

Eyes That See

Do you wear glasses? If so, you're fortunate you didn't live 200 years ago. If you lived before glasses were invented, some strange methods were tried to correct vision problems. One remedy advised people to avoid eating meat and drink wormwood (a bitter drink). When glasses were finally invented, people didn't wear them, they held them in front of their eyes with their hand.

How about removing blindness with mud? This is what Jesus did. Jesus spit on the ground to make some mud and put it on the eyes of a man who was blind. Then Jesus instructed him to wash off the mud.

Immediately the man could see. He saw that Jesus was the Son of God, whom he could trust and follow.

The man told others about this miracle. When the religious leaders heard about it, they did not believe. They said the man hadn't really been blind. Even when it was proven that Jesus had given the man sight, they refused to believe that Jesus was true God.

Through His Spirit, God has opened our eyes so by faith we see our Savior. We believe that He is the Son of God and that by His sacrifice on the cross we have life unending.

_____Let's talk: You may not be able to see Jesus with your eyes like the man in the Bible story, but you can see Jesus with your heart. How can you see Jesus working in your life or in a friend's life today?

_____Let's pray: Dear Jesus, help me see You working in my life more and more each day. I'm excited to know that one day I will see Your face and know You far better. Amen.

D. S.

Listening for God's Voice

Read from God's Word

Then I heard the voice of the Lord saying, "Whom shall I send? And who will go for us?" And I said, "Here am I. Send me!" He said, "Go and tell this people: 'Be ever hearing, but never understanding; be ever seeing, but never perceiving.'" Isaiah 6:8–9

When he was a teenager, Patrick was captured and taken to be a slave in Ireland. For six years he took care of sheep and pigs until he finally escaped.

Patrick was glad to be home again. Then one night he dreamed of an angel and Irish people calling, "Come and walk among us once more." Patrick believed God was calling him to serve there. As a result, churches and schools were built, and many Irish people turned from the gods of the sun, wind, and sea and followed the true God.

It isn't easy to share our faith with others. We may be afraid and not know what to say. People may laugh at us or criticize our beliefs. Patrick and other Christians may have felt the same way when God called them. Yet they also knew that since God had called them, He would be with them.

God promises to give us the courage and the right words to say. We can let others know that we've been bought with the blood of Jesus, who paid for the sins of everybody in the world. Whenever God asks you to serve Him, trust His promises and say with confidence, "Here I am. Send me."

_____Let's do: Ask a parent, teacher, pastor, or other Christian adult how they felt when they were touched by a message from the Lord. What happened when they listened and followed God?

_____Let's pray: Dear Lord, help me always to listen for Your voice. Give me the courage and the words to say as I witness for You. Thank You for being with me wherever I go. Amen.

D. S.

Read from God's Word

But Christ has indeed been raised from the dead, the firstfruits of those who have fallen asleep. For since death came through a man, the resurrection of the dead comes also through a man. For as in Adam all die, so in Christ all will be made alive.
1 Corinthians 15:20–22

The End or the Beginning?

A legend says that Man and Woman were walking beside a river. "Let's decide on life after death," Man said. "If this buffalo chip floats, people will come back to life after they die." Man threw the buffalo chip into the water and it floated.

Woman said, "Let's use a stone instead. If it sinks, people will not come back to life after death." She threw the stone and it sank immediately.

Man and Woman had a child. The child became sick and died. Woman said, "Let's decide again about life and death." Sadly Man replied, "But don't you remember? We already decided."

Some people in Greece thought that when a person dies, the soul escapes but the body remains dead. To believe this meant Jesus didn't become alive again after His death and neither would we.

Paul wrote a letter to these people. He reminded them of all the people who saw Jesus after His resurrection. Paul explained how all the Scriptures came true when Jesus died and rose again.

It was not a lie or a trick or a legend—Christ was raised from the dead. Since Christ has power over death, we who believe in Him will also live again. Easter teaches that death is not the end—it's the beginning!

_____Let's talk: How do you think people who believe death is the end feel? How is your life different because you know by faith in Christ that you will live again?

_____Let's pray: Jesus, thank You for defeating death so I can live forever with You. Use me to share this good news with others. Amen.

D. S.

Full of Love

Read from God's Word

For this reason I kneel before the Father, from whom His whole family in heaven and on earth derives its name. I pray that out of His glorious riches He may strengthen you with power through His Spirit in your inner being, so that Christ may dwell in your hearts through faith. And I pray that you, being rooted and established in love, may have power, together with all the saints, to grasp how wide and long and high and deep is the love of Christ, and to know this love that surpasses knowledge—that you may be filled to the measure of all the fullness of God. Ephesians 3:14–19

"Fill 'er up," we say at the gas pump. "I'm full," we say after a big meal. There's another kind of fullness. You may say to someone, "I'm full up to here with you." This means you don't want anything more to do with him or her.

God wants to fill us with a different kind of fullness. His fullness is love—love exploding in kind words and actions; the kind of fullness Jesus had.

Pretend that you're "full up to here" with a guy named Mason. You might have every right to be mad at Mason. He's hard to deal with sometimes. But this time you decide not to let him have it. Instead, you want God's love to flow through you to Mason.

God's love can touch Mason in a way you never dreamed. Maybe you won't see it all at once. But God's love coming through you can change Mason from the inside out. It can also change your attitude toward Mason.

Next time you feel "full up to here" with someone, think these prayer thoughts: Fill me up, Jesus. Fill me with the fullness of Your love. Take away my thoughts of anger and hate that are about to explode. Let Your love overflow in me.

_____Let's do: Turn to someone you're angry with and think about this: Jesus lives in me. Jesus loves you. Even if I don't feel like loving you, Jesus in me loves you!

_____Let's pray: In today's Bible reading, Paul prays that we might be filled with all the fullness of God. This fullness comes from knowing God's love. Read the Bible passage again, praying Paul's prayer for yourself.

D. R.

Read from God's Word

Surely God is good to Israel, to those who are pure in heart. But as for me, my feet had almost slipped; I had nearly lost my foothold. ... Yet I am always with You; You hold me by my right hand. You guide me with Your counsel, and afterward You will take me into glory. Whom have I in heaven but You? And earth has nothing I desire besides You. My flesh and my heart may fail, but God is the strength of my heart and my portion forever. Psalm 73:1–2, 23–26

Jessica on the Balance Beam

Jessica was excited. She had qualified for her first state gymnastic meet. She had practiced and practiced, and now she was going to compete with the best gymnasts in the state.

The big day arrived. Before her routine, Jessica put her head down and closed her eyes as she pictured the action in her mind. She imagined performing each element gracefully, executing that split leap and hitting a solid cartwheel.

Jessica raised her head and opened her eyes. It was hard not to be nervous. Her muscles were quivering. *What if I fall?* she wondered. *I fell after my cartwheel at the last meet. Is the perfect routine just in my mind?*

On Sunday her pastor had talked about everybody falling short of the glory of God. "That's why God sent Jesus to die on the cross for us," said Pastor Phillips. "God loves us very much and when He looks at us, He sees the holiness and perfection Jesus has won for us on the cross. Because of His forgiveness our failures are erased from His mind."

The faith Jessica had in her heart gave her peace. Her nervousness went away. Jessica performed her routine without a single fall. She did her best and she was happy!

_____Let's talk: Do you aim for perfection in your activities, as Jessica did? How do you handle a fall? How does thinking about God's grace help you? Why is it good to thank God when you do well?

_____Let's pray: Heavenly Father, help me see myself as You see me—Your forgiven child. May I find peace in knowing that Jesus' death on the cross erases all my faults and failures. In His name I ask this. Amen.

C. T.

Dealing with a Troublemaker

Read from God's Word

"You have heard that it was said, 'Love your neighbor and hate your enemy.' But I tell you: Love your enemies and pray for those who persecute you, that you may be sons of your Father in heaven. He causes His sun to rise on the evil and the good, and sends rain on the righteous and the unrighteous. If you love those who love you, what reward will you get? Are not even the tax collectors doing that? And if you greet only your brothers, what are you doing more than others? Do not even pagans do that? Be perfect, therefore, as your heavenly Father is perfect." Matthew 5:43–48

James picked on his classmates in fourth-grade. He would say, "Did you really draw that stupid giraffe, Shannon?" On another day James bragged about the new bike he got for his birthday. Sometimes others would laugh, so James thought he was funny. But it wasn't funny to the person whose feelings he hurt. He was really getting on people's nerves.

Is there someone who hurts your feelings? God helps us deal with situations like this. He tells us what He did for us: "Even when we were God's enemies, He made peace with us, because His Son died for us. Yet something even greater than friendship is ours. Now that we are at peace with God, we will be saved by His Son's life" (Romans 5:10 CEV).

If you were James's classmate, how could you share God's kindness with him? The first thing you could do is pray for him. You might say, "Lord, love James and help him make friends."

God says to "Love your enemies" (Matthew 5:44). This isn't easy to do, especially if we continue having problems with someone. But we can trust the Lord to give us patience and a caring heart. As we pray for our enemies and love them, we realize that we don't have to solve the problem—God will!

_____Let's talk: Who are your enemies? Remember to pray for them. How might God change you so you're able to overcome bad feelings toward them?

_____Let's pray: Dear Father, help me remember that because of my sin I was Your enemy, but You still loved me and saved me. Thank You for Your mercy toward me, which helps me love my enemies also. In my Savior's name. Amen.

C. T.

Read from God's Word

Jesus replied, "If anyone loves Me, he will obey My teaching. My Father will love him, and We will come to him and make our home with him. He who does not love Me will not obey My teaching. These words you hear are not My own; they belong to the Father who sent Me." John 14:23–24

The Way Home

Sara was visiting her big brother Todd and her nephews, J. T. and Austin. Todd warned them, "Don't go into the woods," he said. "It's easy to get lost."

"And wander around until you die," J. T. said. Everybody giggled.

The next day, Sara and the boys weren't laughing. They had meant to stay at the edge of the woods, but they hadn't and now they were lost.

"Maybe we ought to pray," Sara said.

"Are you kidding?" J. T. said. "I've been praying."

"Me too," said Austin.

But they joined hands while Sara prayed aloud, "Dear Jesus, please help us find the way back. Amen."

They walked until it grew dark. Suddenly Austin shouted, "A car!" They scrambled toward the sound. Then they were out of the bushes, standing on a dirt road. "It's Todd!" Sara exclaimed as the car stopped. "Thank You, Lord. Thank You!"

In the Bible, God warns us against wandering off into sin, but it is easy to forget His warnings. Just a few steps in the wrong direction and we're in deep trouble! The good news is that Jesus died on the cross to rescue us from sin. We can't get so lost that He can't find us. He will always lead us back to the comfort of His forgiveness and love.

_____Let's talk: What does God want us to do about His warnings?

_____Let's pray: Lord, help me remember not to do the things You have warned me against. When I forget, forgive me and lead me back to You. Amen.

G. S.

More Than Just a Name

> **Read from God's Word**
>
> *For You created my inmost being; You knit me together in my mother's womb. I praise You because I am fearfully and wonderfully made; Your works are wonderful, I know that full well. My frame was not hidden from You when I was made in the secret place. When I was woven together in the depths of the earth, Your eyes saw my unformed body. All the days ordained for me were written in Your book before one of them came to be. How precious to me are Your thoughts, O God! How vast is the sum of them! Were I to count them, they would outnumber the grains of sand. When I awake, I am still with You. Psalm 139:13–18*

Caleb White's dad was making a family tree. His dad showed him a list of names on the Internet: "Anna Miller. Anna Miller. Anna A. Miller. Anna Alice Miller."

"Aunt Linda thought she had found your great-great-grandmother," Mr. White said, "but this Anna Miller probably isn't the right one. She lived in a different state."

"But there are a lot of Anna Millers! How can you tell which is which?"

"You can tell by birth dates, death dates, where they lived, who they married. We don't know these people. They're just names to us."

That night as he lay in bed, Caleb thought about names. He wondered how many other Caleb Whites there were. He wondered how many Caleb Whites were already dead. Pastor said that Christians' names are written in the book of life. What if several people had the same name?

Then he remembered Psalm 139. It didn't matter how many people shared his name. God knew him. God had known him even before he was born! God provided a way for him to be saved. He sent Jesus, His only Son, to die for the sins of all people in all times. Like you and me, Caleb was more than just a name to God. We are God's own children!

_____Let's do: Make a list of your cousins, aunts, uncles, and grandparents. Do any of them share a name? Do you share a name with a relative? Ask your parents to tell you some of your family history.

_____Let's pray: Lord God, how wonderful it is that You know me as Your own! You will never forget who I am. Forgive my sins, and help me to live always in You. Amen.

G. S.

Read from God's Word

"I have told you these things, so that in Me you may have peace. In this world you will have trouble. But take heart! I have overcome the world." John 16:33

Take Heart!

Isabel and her family were at a theme park. She and her brother Marco stopped in front of a tall building that looked as though it was made of bare old boards.

"Gravity House," Isabel read. "I wonder what this is?"

She soon found out. Inside, the floors and walls were set at crazy angles. Isabel seemed to be walking up a hill but the floor looked flat. When she sat in a rocking chair, it almost pitched her onto the floor. She nearly fell again in the next room. Her body told her she was going downhill but her eyes said the floor was level.

Some days nothing seems to go right; we may feel as if we're trapped in a gravity house.

Jesus told His disciples, "In this world you will have trouble." God created the world a perfect place. But when sin came in, it messed up God's perfect creation. Sin made the world topsy-turvy.

How glad we are that Jesus took us out of sin! With His death and resurrection, He earned for us forgiveness and new life in Him. We still live with the trouble that sin brings, but our souls rest in Jesus. He gives us safety, peace, and joy. He has overcome the world!

____Let's talk: Christians have a lot of different addresses. But every Christian actually lives in the same place. How can that be?

____Let's pray: Dear Jesus, You are stronger than any evil. You overcame the world, sin, and death. Thank You for letting me live in You! Amen.

G. S.

When God Visits Us

Chris looked forward to Sunday afternoons because it was the time for visiting. Sometimes he visited his grandparents who lived across town. Grandma always hugged him. Grandpa ruffled his hair and teased him about growing so much.

Sometimes he "visited" his grandparents in Texas. They had a new computer that sent pictures in their e-mail. It was almost like being right there with them!

Chris told his dad how much he liked Sunday afternoon visiting. "I like Sunday too," Dad said. "And not just Sunday afternoons. We visit on Sunday mornings too. At church we see our friends and we strengthen our faith by talking with them about God. We praise and worship God, and He visits with us there!"

"We don't have to go to church to be with God," Chris said. "He's with us all the time."

Dad agreed. "That's true. But there are special ways God comes to us in church. He comes to us through reading and studying the Bible. He comes through Baptism to forgive our sins and make us His own. He comes to us through Holy Communion. And He promises that when we meet in His name, He is with us. So church is a great place to go for a special visit with God!"

Read from God's Word

"For where two or three come together in My name, there am I with them." Matthew 18:20

Shout for joy to the LORD, all the earth. Worship the LORD with gladness; come before Him with joyful songs. Know that the LORD is God. It is He who made us, and we are His; we are His people, the sheep of His pasture. Enter His gates with thanksgiving and His courts with praise; give thanks to Him and praise His name. For the LORD is good and His love endures forever; His faithfulness continues through all generations. Psalm 100

_____Let's talk: What things are necessary to have a worship service? Could we have church on Tuesdays instead of Sundays? Could we have church without a church building?

_____Let's pray: Dear Lord, I can't see You when I meet with others to worship You. But I know You really are there. Thank You for all the wonderful ways You come to me! Amen.

G. S.

Read from God's Word

Do not merely listen to the word, and so deceive yourselves. Do what it says. Anyone who listens to the word but does not do what it says is like a man who looks at his face in a mirror and, after looking at himself, goes away and immediately forgets what he looks like. But the man who looks intently into the perfect law that gives freedom, and continues to do this, not forgetting what he has heard, but doing it—he will be blessed in what he does. James 1:22–25

Love One Another

Kelly could hardly believe her ears. Amanda and Sara were saying hateful things to Jessica as she stood there, tears in her eyes.

"Look at that hair," Amanda said. "It's dirty and full of bugs. Her mom ought to take a big pair of scissors and whack it off!"

"I bet she doesn't have a mom," Sara sneered. "Bet her mom left her 'cause she's ugly."

"Stop it!" Kelly said. "You shouldn't talk to anybody like that. A Christian respects other people!"

Amanda turned on her. "Shut up, Kelly. I go to church, just like you do. I say what I want to, when I want to." Then she and Sara turned and ran away. Kelly put her arm around Jessica and tried to help her dry her tears.

People can read the Bible and go to church, but that isn't enough. Jesus said, "As I have loved you, so you must love one another. By this all men will know that you are My disciples, if you love one another" (John 13:34–35).

God loved all of us so much that He gave His Son, Jesus, to die for our sins. Now we have joy and life in Him. God gives us His Spirit to help us live as His children.

_____Let's talk: Could a Christian say bad things to another person as Amanda and Sara did? Could other people tell whether Amanda was a Christian by the way she acted?

_____Let's pray: Lord, I don't always do what the Bible tells me to. Sometimes I may not even act like a Christian. Forgive me when I fail. Fill me with Your love so others will see Your love in me. Amen.

G. S.

Rejoice!

Kody pressed his nose to the window. He watched the trees bend as fierce winds blew. Rain struck the glass. Kody tried not to jump each time the thunder boomed.

"I'm scared," Kody's little sister, Keely, whimpered.

Mom hurried in and Keely ran to her. Kody didn't run, but he did sit by Mom on the couch. He squeezed Keely's hand. This was some storm!

"You know what?" Mom said to Kody. "I think this is a good time to rejoice."

"I think it's a good time to hide under the bed."

"No, really. It would be easy to rejoice if it were sunny outside, wouldn't it?"

"Sure, Mom, but we're in the middle of a storm!" Kody reminded her.

"Even in the middle of a storm," Mom said, "we have plenty to rejoice about. Help me think of all the reasons we have for being full of joy."

Read from God's Word

Rejoice in the Lord always. I will say it again: Rejoice! Let your gentleness be evident to all. The Lord is near. Do not be anxious about anything, but in everything, by prayer and petition, with thanksgiving, present your requests to God. And the peace of God, which transcends all understanding, will guard your hearts and your minds in Christ Jesus. Philippians 4:4–7

Anyone can be glad if there is happiness all around. But a Christian has reason to rejoice anytime, anyplace—even when others are sad. Because Christ died for our sins, we live as the forgiven children of God. We don't need to worry! Jesus is always near, and our loving Lord always hears our prayers. He gently comes to us to take away our fears.

_____Let's talk: In St. Paul's time, many Christians were killed because of their faith in Jesus. Some of God's people today also face death because they serve the Lord. Why would they rejoice?

_____Let's pray: Dear Lord, help me to be glad in You. When I am scared, hurt, or worried, help me remember that You are always near. Amen.

G. S.

Read from God's Word

But in your hearts set apart Christ as Lord. Always be prepared to give an answer to everyone who asks you to give the reason for the hope that you have. But do this with gentleness and respect, keeping a clear conscience, so that those who speak maliciously against your good behavior in Christ may be ashamed of their slander. It is better, if it is God's will, to suffer for doing good than for doing evil. For Christ died for sins once for all, the righteous for the unrighteous, to bring you to God. 1 Peter 3:15–18a

Remember His Love!

"What did you give up for Lent?" Matt asked David.

"Lint? You mean lint like in the dryer?"

Matt laughed. "No, Lent like the weeks before Easter. It's what we call the time when we remember Christ's suffering and death. That's when we get ready to celebrate His resurrection."

David seemed embarrassed. "Oh. I didn't know I was supposed to give anything up."

"You don't have to," Matt said. "But some people do. It's usually something they like a lot. I gave up candy."

"Why give up something you want just because Easter is coming?" David asked.

"Because every time I think about not eating candy, I remember what Jesus gave up for us. He gave up His life to pay for our sins. It doesn't make me extra good or anything," Matt said. "It doesn't make Him love me more. It's just a reminder of what Jesus did for me."

Lent is a season in the church year. The church year is built on important events in a Christian's life. During Advent we remember how people waited for the Savior and we prepare for His coming at Christmas. During Lent, we remember why Jesus died on the cross.

Jesus paid for our sins. Then He rose again, overcoming death itself for us!

____Let's talk: Jesus knew He would be in terrible pain as He died on the cross, but it was the only way we could be saved. He loved us so much He was willing to do it. How do we feel when we think of His great love for us?

____Let's pray: Dear Jesus, thank You for loving me. Thank You for dying for me. I am so glad that I am Yours! Amen.

G. S.

Something Important

Read from God's Word

Be joyful always; pray continually; give thanks in all circumstances, for this is God's will for you in Christ Jesus.
1 Thessalonians 5:16–18

Mika's mother woke her in plenty of time to get ready for school. Mika dressed, ate breakfast, made her bed, and carried her backpack to the door.

I'm forgetting something, she thought. Boomer, her gray cat, brushed her legs. "Oops, I forgot to feed you!" she said. She hurried to the laundry room and washed Boomer's tray. Then she gave him fresh food and water.

I'm still forgetting something, Mika thought. Then she remembered. She went back to her room and knelt by the bed.

"Dear Lord, forgive me for forgetting to pray. Thank You for this day and all other good things. Be with me and keep me safe. Help me share Your love with everyone I see. Amen." Now Mika knew she was completely ready.

Sometimes we pay so much attention to getting things done that we forget to give God time in our lives. How could we forget Jesus, the One who died for our sins? We may not like to admit it, but sometimes we push Him to the back of our minds and forget to pray.

Prayer is our chance to talk to God. We praise Him, thank Him, ask His forgiveness, and tell Him what we need. We don't have to kneel or fold our hands. But God wants us to pray often!

_____Let's do: Make a list of words that rhyme with pray. Can you use some of them to write a poem about praying?

_____Let's pray: Dear Father in heaven, let me always remember to honor You. Thank You for all You have given me, especially my Savior, Jesus. Forgive my sins. In the name of Jesus. Amen.

G. S.

Read from God's Word

This is the message we have heard from Him and declare to you: God is light; in Him there is no darkness at all. If we claim to have fellowship with Him yet walk in the darkness, we lie and do not live by the truth. But if we walk in the light, as He is in the light, we have fellowship with one another, and the blood of Jesus, His Son, purifies us from all sin. If we claim to be without sin, we deceive ourselves and the truth is not in us. If we confess our sins, He is faithful and just and will forgive us our sins and purify us from all unrighteousness. 1 John 1:5–9

Clean Hearts

Ali's desk certainly needed cleaning. When she took out a book, junk fell out. Sometimes she had to take out every book before she found what she needed.

Ali pulled out books, papers, notes, cough drops, and crumpled tissues. She found a valentine, a candy wrapper, broken crayons, and pencils. Finally she took out three notebooks and an old magazine.

Sometimes our lives are as full of junk as Ali's desk was. Our faith may be hard to find because sin is in the way. Love for Christ may be hidden by bad feelings.

We can clean out our desks, our closets, and our rooms. But we can't clean our own hearts and souls. We were born sinful and we sin every day. What we can do is ask God to make us clean again.

We can't be perfect on our own so Jesus was perfect in our place. He took all the punishment we deserve for our sin. When we confess our sins, we can be sure God forgives us. Each day He makes us clean and ready to serve Him in love.

_____Let's talk: Do we ever sin without being aware of it?
Who always knows when we sin?

_____Let's pray: Dear Father, You know my heart and soul.
Forgive me, make me new, and lead me in Your way.
In the name of Jesus, my Savior. Amen.

G. S.

The Right Response

He knows who we are," Josh said to his dad. He was so angry he could hardly talk. "He told you we could use the pond anytime we wanted to!"

Josh and his brother Jason had been fishing in Mr. Reed's pond when Mr. Reed had ordered them to leave. He said they were trespassing! Josh tried to tell Mr. Reed that they lived next door. He tried to remind Mr. Reed that he had offered to let them fish there.

Josh groaned. "We chased his cows and put them back in the pasture when they got out!"

"Three times!" said Jason. "And then he treats us like dirt. Dad, why did Mr. Reed forget what he promised you?"

What should these boys do? Punch something hard with their bare hands? Write Mr. Reed a nasty letter and tell him what a jerk he is? Cut Mr. Reed's fence so his cows will get out? Forgive Mr. Reed for what he did?

Read from God's Word

Therefore, as God's chosen people, holy and dearly loved, clothe yourselves with compassion, kindness, humility, gentleness and patience. Bear with each other and forgive whatever grievances you may have against one another. Forgive as the Lord forgave you. And over all these virtues put on love, which binds them all together in perfect unity. Colossians 3:12–14

Because we live in Christ, forgiveness is the only right answer. Jesus died to pay for our sins. When we believe in Him as our Savior, He freely forgives us. And, just as He forgives us, He wants us to forgive others.

_____Let's talk: God could have punished us for our sins instead of offering us forgiveness. What does His response to our sin tell us about Him?

_____Let's pray: Dear Lord, You have forgiven me, and I want to forgive others. Send Your Holy Spirit to strengthen me. Help me cheerfully to forgive those who wrong me. Amen.

G. S.

april

Contributors for this month:

Carolyn Sims

Jody Williams

Carol Albrecht

Eunice Graham

Kay L. Meyer

Christine Johnsten

April Fool

If you turn to page 25 of this book, you might find a five-dollar bill.

April fool! Although most April fools' jokes are harmless, feeling foolish is no fun. But the Bible says there is a time when it's okay to be called a fool.

People thought Jesus was foolish. He said not to hit back when someone hits you. In fact, He said it would be better to let that person hit you again. He said to forgive people who don't deserve it—not just once, but every time. Jesus had the power to destroy everyone who hurt Him, but He let Himself be put on a cross and die for you and me.

Does that sound wise? People who don't know Jesus call that foolish. But Jesus was not foolish. All He cared about was doing the will of His heavenly Father and showing how much He loves us.

Has anyone made fun of you because you're a Christian? When you are called a fool because you follow Jesus, remember it's the Holy Spirit working in your heart who causes you to act in ways the world would call foolish.

Trusting in Jesus as your Savior is the wisest thing you can ever do. No fooling!

Read from God's Word

Where is the wise man? Where is the scholar? Where is the philosopher of this age? Has not God made foolish the wisdom of the world? For since in the wisdom of God the world through its wisdom did not know Him, God was pleased through the foolishness of what was preached to save those who believe. Jews demand miraculous signs and Greeks look for wisdom, but we preach Christ crucified: a stumbling block to Jews and foolishness to Gentiles, but to those whom God has called, both Jews and Greeks, Christ the power of God and the wisdom of God. For the foolishness of God is wiser than man's wisdom, and the weakness of God is stronger than man's strength. 1 Corinthians 1:20–25

_____Let's talk: Why might people make fun of Christians who follow Jesus' ways? What can you remember at times when you're being made fun of because of your faith?

_____Let's pray: Dear Jesus, thank You for living and dying for me even though You were called foolish. Please send Your Holy Spirit into my heart so I can live in ways that please You. I am glad I can trust You to keep all Your promises to me. Amen.

C. S.

Read from God's Word

It is for freedom that Christ has set us free. Stand firm, then, and do not let yourselves be burdened again by a yoke of slavery. Galatians 5:1

Help!

Althea was stuck. Under her desk was a hole. She had poked her finger into the hole and it stuck! She tried to pull her finger out, but it just stuck tighter. Althea started to cry.

Mrs. Ramirez, the teacher's aid, sent for ice. The ice felt cool on Althea's finger, but it was still stuck.

Mr. Wolf, the janitor, said, "Try soap." Althea's finger stayed stuck.

Then Mrs. Sanchez, her teacher, gave Althea a hug. "Let me hold your hand," she said. As soon as Althea rested her hand in Mrs. Sanchez's, she relaxed. Her finger slipped out as easily as it had gone in.

Althea was unable to free herself. It took someone else to set her free.

No matter how hard we try to free ourselves from our sin, we can never do it. Jesus sets us free. Jesus died on the cross to take away our sins. He forgives us. Someday our Savior will take us to heaven. In the meantime, He holds us in His hand so we can live without feeling sad or scared or guilty or lonely.

Just as Althea rested in her teacher's hand and was set free, you and I are free too—because of Jesus.

_____Let's talk: Why couldn't Althea get free by herself? Why do we need Jesus to set us free from sin?

_____Let's pray: Dear Jesus, thank You for setting me free from sin. Send the Holy Spirit into my heart so I won't want to do what is wrong. Please keep me safe as I live my life for You. Amen.

C. S.

How Long Will You Live?

Read from God's Word

I have been crucified with Christ and I no longer live, but Christ lives in me. The life I live in the body, I live by faith in the Son of God, who loved me and gave Himself for me. Galatians 2:20

How old was Jesus when He died? The Bible doesn't tell us exactly. Jesus was about 30 years old when He started His work of teaching and preaching, and He was about 33 years old when He died and rose again.

At your age, 33 sounds old. Your parents may think that 33 is young. It doesn't really matter how old or young Jesus was. What matters is that He accomplished exactly what God intended Him to do.

He lived a perfect life for you and me. He died on the cross for our sins. He rose from the dead and proved that He has power over sin, death, and the devil. We who love Him will live forever in heaven.

You, too, are growing up to accomplish what God has in mind for you to do. In fact, Jesus is living in you! You are "Jesus" to others. That means you show Jesus' love and forgiveness in the way you act and in the words you speak.

It doesn't matter how old you will live to be or what kind of job you will have. What matters is that Jesus lives in you your whole life long and that, by the power of the Holy Spirit, you live your life for Him.

_____Let's talk: How could you show Jesus' love right now to someone in your family or class?

_____Let's pray: Dear Jesus, thank You for living and dying for me. Please live in me so I can love and help people just as You did. Help me tell others about You so they can live for You too. Amen.

C. S.

Read from God's Word

But the LORD said to Samuel, "Do not consider his appearance or his height, for I have rejected him. The LORD does not look at the things man looks at. Man looks at the outward appearance, but the LORD looks at the heart." 1 Samuel 16:7

The Inside Is What Counts

When three-year-old Alice looked at her dance recital costume, she noticed the tuxedo-style collar and tie. Alice asked, "Am I a boy?" She thought what she looked like on the outside made her what she was on the inside.

The Bible says what is on the inside is the most important. God looks at a person's heart. This is not the heart that pumps blood through the body. It's the heart that feels and loves.

On the outside you may smile at your mother, turn in your homework, and go to church. On the inside, you may feel angry at your mother's rules, copy someone else's homework, and daydream during church. What does God see when He looks at your heart?

Here's good news. God looks at your heart through His Son, Jesus. Instead of seeing anger or dishonesty, He sees a heart washed clean by Jesus' blood.

God puts faith into your heart so you believe in Him. The more you study God's Word and learn about His love, the stronger your faith grows and the more your faith shows in what you do on the outside.

You can be sure God is looking inside your heart where Jesus lives. He forgives you. And He knows who you really are—His child, inside and out!

_____Let's talk: How do you know Jesus is in your heart? What have you done today that shows on the outside the fact that Jesus lives inside you?

_____Let's pray: Dear Jesus, thank You for cleaning my heart from sin and for making Your home there. Please help me show Your love in all that I do. Amen.

C. S.

How Much Are You Worth?

Read from God's Word

"Therefore I tell you, do not worry about your life, what you will eat or drink; or about your body, what you will wear. Is not life more important than food, and the body more important than clothes? Look at the birds of the air; they do not sow or reap or store away in barns, and yet your heavenly Father feeds them. Are you not much more valuable than they?" Matthew 6:25–26

"What are you doing with that old hockey stick?" Logan asked. "It's cracked. You should throw it away."

Tyler held the stick even tighter. "No way. This was Wayne Gretzky's. He's the greatest hockey player ever!"

Logan couldn't believe it. "This was Wayne Gretzky's stick? How do you know?"

"My dad got it in New York. Gretzky even autographed it!"

Although it looked like junk, the stick was worth a lot. What made the difference? The hockey stick was valuable because of *whose* it was, not because of what it was.

The Bible reading today says God thinks you are of great value. Why? You aren't the world's greatest hockey player, student, or friend. Even when you try to do your best, you sometimes fail. It's easy to feel worthless in a world that makes being the greatest seem so important.

Yet Jesus has made you priceless. You are of great value because You belong to Him. He bought you from the power of sin by giving His life for you. You were expensive, but God paid the price because He loves you.

Like a hockey player uses a stick, God can use you to do wonderful things for Him—not because you're so great, but because *He* is.

_____Let's talk: What is your most valuable possession? What makes it valuable to you? How does God show that you are valuable to Him?

_____Let's pray: Dear Jesus, because You love me so much, You are the most valuable part of my life. Let everything I say and do show that I belong to You and how much I love You. Amen.

C. S.

An Opportunity to Do Good

Felicione was having second thoughts. When his family first talked about a foreign exchange student staying with them, he thought it was a good idea. But now he wasn't sure.

The more he thought about it, the more Felicione realized how many changes would take place. After his brother had left for college, he had a bathroom all to himself. Now he would have to share it. And it was nice having Mom and Dad all to himself too. That would certainly change when Andres arrived from Paraguay.

Felicione shared his concerns with his parents. Mom said she knew it would take time for the four of them to learn to live together. Dad reminded Felicione of the reason they had decided to open their house: "It's an opportunity to share the blessings God has given us with someone who doesn't have as many opportunities for a good education." Felicione had to agree with that.

"Besides," said Dad, "the information we received about Andres tells us he isn't a Christian. We'll be able to share the Good News of God's love in Jesus through our actions and words."

Felicione knew Dad was right. When they prayed together before supper, he thanked God for the chance to teach Andres that Jesus came to save everyone in the world.

_____Let's talk: Think of the many good things God has given you. What are some ways you can share these with others?

_____Let's pray: Dear God, thank You for the many blessings You have given us. We especially thank You for the blessing of forgiveness, earned for us by Your Son, Jesus, and the promise of eternal life with You. Please help us share __________ with others, especially with ________ . In Your Son's name we pray. Amen.

J. W.

What a Savior!

Martina liked the children's sermon at church. Her pastor did so many neat things. One day he told them this Bible story:

"All day long Jesus told people of God's love for them. He also healed many sick people. When evening came, Jesus and His disciples went for a boat ride." As he talked, Tina's pastor made a boat from a piece of paper.

"Jesus was tired and went to sleep. As He slept, a furious storm came up. The waves were high and water came into the boat. Jesus' friends were terrified." The pastor rocked the paper boat as if it were in a storm. He tore off the corners to show that the boat was battered.

"Jesus' friends shouted, 'Lord, save us! We're going to drown!' Jesus got up and talked to the wind and waves. He said, 'Quiet! Be still!' At once the storm was over. Jesus' friends were amazed. He had saved them from drowning. They realized how powerful He was."

Read from God's Word

Then He got into the boat and His disciples followed Him. Without warning, a furious storm came up on the lake, so that the waves swept over the boat. But Jesus was sleeping. The disciples went and woke Him, saying, "Lord, save us! We're going to drown!" He replied, "You of little faith, why are you so afraid?" Then He got up and rebuked the winds and the waves, and it was completely calm. The men were amazed and asked, "What kind of man is this? Even the winds and the waves obey Him!" Matthew 8:23–27

Then Tina's pastor said: "Later Jesus saved His friends from something else—their sins. He suffered and died on a cross to take the punishment for their sins and ours too."

Pastor unfolded the boat. The paper was in the shape of a cross.

What a wonderful, powerful Savior we have!

_____Let's talk: Why did Jesus save His friends from the storm? Why did Jesus save His disciples and us from our sins? (Read 2 Corinthians 5:15 for a clue.)

_____Let's pray: On the cross of Calvary, dearest Lord, You died for me. Help me, Lord; my sins forgive. Teach me, Lord, like You to live. (from *The Little Christian's Songbook,* © 1975 CPH.)

J. W.

Read from God's Word

Meanwhile Jesus stood before the governor, and the governor asked Him, "Are You the king of the Jews?" "Yes, it is as you say," Jesus replied. Matthew 27:11

"They will make war against the Lamb, but the Lamb will overcome them because He is Lord of lords and King of kings—and with Him will be His called, chosen and faithful followers." Revelation 17:14

What Kind of King?

Caleb held the palm branch tightly. His parents spoke often of the new king, Jesus. Now the king was coming and he would see Him for himself!

Soon a donkey came into view. A man rode on its back. This man didn't look like a king. He wore no royal robe, no crown. His mother and father must be wrong. Certainly this was not the king.

Caleb and many others in Jerusalem wanted an earthly king who would free them from their rulers, who would clothe and feed them. Someone to make their wishes come true.

But Jesus wasn't like other kings. He didn't come to earth to give us everything we want, but to give us something better—freedom from sin. He lived and died so we could be in His heavenly kingdom. He did more than any earthly king could do.

Sometimes we may want Jesus to grant our every wish. We are disappointed if He doesn't do things our way.

Jesus cares about our needs and wants, but He is more concerned about our souls. Jesus wants us to get excited about our real home, heaven, where He reigns forever as King of kings.

_____Let's talk: Write all the words you can think of that describe what a king is like. How does Jesus' kingship fit those words? How is it different?

_____Let's pray: Lord Jesus, I am glad You are the heavenly King who gave Your life for me. Amen.

C. A.

Real Beauty

I can't wait for you to visit," exclaimed Danae. "Marcy is coming too. She is so beautiful." Bridgett was nervous. If Marcy was so pretty, she might be stuck up.

When Bridgett walked in, she saw a girl in a wheelchair. Her legs were too small, and one arm hung limply. She wore thick glasses and a brace on her neck.

"Hi, I'm Marcy," said the girl. "I'm glad to meet you."

The girls played all afternoon. Marcy was smart and made them laugh. She was one of the nicest people Bridgett had ever met. Bridgett whispered to Danae, "Marcy really is beautiful!"

Bridgett learned something important that day: Beauty is on the inside. Samuel learned that too. God wouldn't let Samuel pick a king just because he was handsome. Instead, God told him, "the Lord looks at the heart."

Read from God's Word

The LORD said to Samuel, "How long will you mourn for Saul, since I have rejected him as king over Israel? Fill your horn with oil and be on your way; I am sending you to Jesse of Bethlehem. I have chosen one of his sons to be king." ... When they arrived, Samuel saw Eliab and thought, "Surely the LORD's anointed stands here before the LORD." But the LORD said to Samuel, "Do not consider his appearance or his height, for I have rejected him. The LORD does not look at the things man looks at. Man looks at the outward appearance, but the LORD looks at the heart." 1 Samuel 16:1, 6–7

When God looks at our hearts, He doesn't see the ugliness of our sin. Jesus died so our ugly sinful hearts could become beautiful. With faith in Jesus in our hearts, they are beautiful in God's eyes.

The king God chose was David. David loved the Lord. Through faith in the coming Savior, God made David's heart beautiful. He does the same for us so we are beautiful from the inside out.

_____Let's talk: What did Danae mean when she said Marcy was beautiful? Explain what makes someone beautiful. Are you beautiful in God's eyes? Why?

_____Let's pray: Thank You, Jesus, for dying for me. Thank You for forgiving my sins and coming to live in my heart. Thank You for making me beautiful on the inside. Amen.

C.A.

Read from God's Word

I know that after I leave, savage wolves will come in among you and will not spare the flock. Even from your own number men will arise and distort the truth in order to draw away disciples after them. So be on your guard! Remember that for three years I never stopped warning each of you night and day with tears. Acts 20:29–31

On Guard!

In ant colonies, guard ants keep out ants from other colonies that want to steal food. Guard ants can't tell by sight that robber ants don't belong—they tell by smell.

Robber ants are pretty smart. They wrestle with the guard ants, causing a scent from the guards to get on the robbers. The robbers leave, but they return and get past the guards because now they smell like guard ants. The robber ants march in and steal whatever they want.

The devil is like that. He tries to convince us that it is okay to sin. "It's okay to cheat on a test," he whispers. "After all, you did study."

"You don't have to listen to your parents," he sneers. "What do they know?"

"So what if you are mean to that new kid?" he says. "Everyone can tell he's a jerk!"

We are more fortunate than ants. We have Jesus on our side. While Satan may trick us into doing the wrong thing, he can't fool Jesus. The devil thought he won when Jesus died. But he didn't. After three days, Christ rose from the dead. The devil was defeated. Now our victorious Jesus fights for us and helps us say no to Satan. He stands guard with us against the devil's tricks.

_____Let's talk: Why do we always have to be on guard against the devil? What would have happened if Jesus had not defeated Satan? Why is the truth of Jesus always stronger than the lies of Satan?

_____Let's pray: Jesus, You know I cannot fight against Satan by myself. He is so tricky. Stand beside me and fill me with Your power and truth. Amen.

C. A.

Being Faithful

Read from God's Word

"His master replied, 'Well done, good and faithful servant! You have been faithful with a few things; I will put you in charge of many things. Come and share your master's happiness!'" Matthew 25:23

I'm glad you like Plumpkin so much. It's a big job to clean her cage," said Mrs. Lester to José.

José smiled. Cleaning Plumpkin's cage was a big job and not much fun. But his dad said anything worth doing was worth doing well.

"You've done such a good job of taking care of Plumpkin," Mrs. Lester said. "Would you keep her when I'm on vacation?"

Mrs. Lester let José take Plumpkin home because he was faithful in doing a good job. God calls us to be faithful too in whatever job we do. It might be homework, cleaning, or baby-sitting. God blesses faithfulness.

But that is not the end of it. God doesn't want us to be faithful just in our earthly work. He asks us to be faithful as we do His work. He wants us to use our talents for Him and to find joy in serving Him. He wants us to spread the Good News that Jesus died and rose for us.

It wasn't easy for José to be faithful in cleaning Plumpkin's cage. It won't always be easy for us to be faithful to God. But when we serve the Lord, we have the Holy Spirit to help us. The Spirit makes any job we do for God easier.

_____Let's talk: How do you feel when you do a job well? How can the Holy Spirit help us joyfully serve the Lord?

_____Let's pray: Lord, let the Holy Spirit help me be faithful in everything I do. Amen.

C. A.

Read from God's Word

"Simon, Simon, Satan has asked to sift you as wheat. But I have prayed for you, Simon, that your faith may not fail. And when you have turned back, strengthen your brothers." But he replied, "Lord, I am ready to go with You to prison and to death." Jesus answered, "I tell you, Peter, before the rooster crows today, you will deny three times that you know Me." Luke 22:31–34

Remember Peter

In the ninth century, church leaders required that every weathervane be shaped like a rooster to remind people not to deny their faith.

Maybe you remember the story. On the Thursday evening before He died on the cross, Jesus shared the first Lord's Supper with His disciples. Then Jesus told Peter He was praying for him. Peter didn't think he needed that prayer; he thought he was strong enough.

Later that night, Jesus was taken prisoner. Peter was scared. Maybe he would be taken prisoner too! People asked if Peter was a disciple of Jesus. Three times Peter said he didn't know Jesus. Then the rooster crowed. Suddenly Peter remembered what Jesus had said. He wept bitterly.

The rooster on the weathervane is a reminder: don't be like Peter! Don't think you're brave enough to stand up for Jesus all by yourself. There might be a time when it is hard to say you are a Christian.

Jesus knows we need His help to keep our faith strong. He gives us courage to confess that He died for us. He gives us forgiveness so we can know that He loves us, even when we are weak and deny Him. In prayer, ask Him to help you be faithful.

_____Let's talk: Why was it hard for Peter to say he loved Jesus? When might it be hard for you to say Jesus is your Savior? Did Jesus forgive Peter for denying Him? Would He forgive you?

_____Let's pray: Give me courage, Lord, to say I am Yours. As You forgave Peter, forgive me when I trust in my own strength or when I deny You. Amen.

C. A.

A Balm in Gilead

Gilead had one claim to fame—an ointment obtained from the resin of kind of a tree that grew there. The ointment soothed and healed when it was applied to a wound.

The children of Israel had a wound—a spiritual wound. Because they had forsaken God, He allowed them to be taken captive. Jeremiah, who was faithful to God, wept over the sins of his fellow Jews. How he longed for an ointment that could heal their souls the way Gilead's balm healed bodies!

Think about Good Friday. The word "good" seems all wrong. What is good about a holy, innocent man suffering so on the cross? What is good about a man who did nothing wrong but was put to death anyway?

The "good" in Good Friday is that Jesus became the greatest balm. Through His pain and death, the wound of sin was cured. The ointment of the forgiveness won by Jesus soothes our hurting hearts. Jesus took all our sins on Himself. He carried them to the cross so they would be covered by His blood. Jesus is both our spiritual doctor and our spiritual ointment. On Good Friday, we give thanks that Christ's blood was shed to heal us.

Read from God's Word

"The harvest is past, the summer has ended, and we are not saved." Since my people are crushed, I am crushed; I mourn, and horror grips me. Is there no balm in Gilead? Is there no physician there? Why then is there no healing for the wound of my people? … "But I will restore you to health and heal your wounds," declares the LORD, "because you are called an outcast, Zion for whom no one cares." Jeremiah 8:20–22; 30:17

_____Let's do: Write a prayer thanking Jesus for saving you from sin. Use your prayer in your family devotions or before you go to bed tonight.

_____Let's pray: My Savior, I thank You for dying for my sins. I am so happy that You gave Your life to heal me from sin. Please give me the balm of forgiveness every day. Amen.

C. A.

Read from God's Word

Wait for the LORD; be strong and take heart and wait for the LORD. Psalm 27:14

"Between" Time

Ravi put on his uniform and baseball cap. He grabbed his glove and baseball, and ran outside. Over and over Ravi tossed the ball in the air and caught it. After a while, he went into the house to look at the clock. Ravi groaned.

It was still more than an hour before the big game. How could he wait?

Ravi was having a "between" time. Maybe you have had a between time too. Time seemed to go so slowly. Maybe you were waiting for a piano recital to begin. Perhaps it was those final minutes before a big test.

You are in a between time right now. The day before Easter is between two of the church's holiest observances: The Good Friday remembrance of Christ's suffering and death and the Easter celebration of His resurrection.

We are waiting in another between time. Christ promised that, just as He was resurrected from the dead, we will be resurrected too and live with Him forever. That is the promise Easter gives. As we wait for that day, we know Jesus will be with us. After all, He loved us enough to die for us.

The next time you are in a between time, put your trust in the Lord. He will wait with you.

_____Let's talk: Do you remember having a between time? How did God help you through it?

_____Let's pray: Lord, be with me through all my between times. Especially teach me to wait for that day of resurrection when all sin and pain ends and only joy and love will live on in me. Amen.

C. A.

Empty!

Most things in this life are better when they are full. We like a full glass of lemonade and a full piggy bank.

There are some things, though, that are better when they are empty. An empty backpack at the end of the day means no homework. An empty trashcan means you won't have to take out the garbage for a while.

But do you know what the very best empty thing is? It is Jesus' tomb! The tomb was full on Good Friday. It held Jesus' lifeless body. And then what a surprise! On Easter Sunday the tomb was empty.

Why is that empty tomb such good news? It's good news because it means death couldn't hold Jesus. It means that everything He had said about how God was His Father was true.

But there is more good news about that empty tomb. Because Jesus' grave was empty, it means death isn't the winner anymore. Yes, we will die someday. But someday Jesus will return. He'll call us out of the grave. He will lift us up to heaven. Our tombs will be as empty as Jesus' grave was on Easter morning.

An empty tomb means eternal life. Jesus rose from the dead—and so will we. Hallelujah! Jesus is risen!

Read from God's Word

But Christ has indeed been raised from the dead, the firstfruits of those who have fallen asleep. For since death came through a man, the resurrection of the dead comes also through a man. For as in Adam all die, so in Christ all will be made alive. But each in his own turn: Christ, the firstfruits; then, when He comes, those who belong to Him. 1 Corinthians 15:20–23

_____Let's talk: What would have happened if Jesus' tomb had not been empty on Easter? Why is eternal life so wonderful?

_____Let's pray: I praise You, Lord, for having power over death. Thank You for leaving an empty tomb so I, too, can have eternal life. Amen.

C. A.

Read from God's Word

I pray also that the eyes of your heart may be enlightened in order that you may know the hope to which He has called you, the riches of His glorious inheritance in the saints, and His incomparably great power for us who believe. That power is like the working of His mighty strength, which He exerted in Christ when He raised Him from the dead and seated Him at His right hand in the heavenly realms, far above all rule and authority, power and dominion, and every title that can be given, not only in the present age but also in the one to come. Ephesians 1:18–21

Power and Strength

Lakeesha smiled. She was helping her friend Audrey Yin. Lakeesha held the back of a paper dragon while Audrey held the front.

"Dragons are make-believe," said Audrey, "but Chinese people like them. The dragon's head is like a lion, and a lion is brave. His body is like a snake, and a snake is smart. His feet are like a chicken's, and a chicken can run fast. His tail reminds us of a horse's tail, and a horse is powerful."

Lakeesha thought about the dragon. At recess she said to Audrey, "I know someone who is like the dragon, but He is real."

"Really?" asked Audrey. "Who?"

"Jesus!" exclaimed Lakeesha.

Lakeesha was right. Jesus was brave when He died on the cross. He's smart enough to know everything that is in our hearts. And He can be everywhere at once. That is pretty fast! Jesus is more powerful than anything, even death.

Because we have God's power through Jesus, we can resist Satan. We can do the things God wants us to do—like tell others about Him.

Maybe there is someone like Audrey in your life, someone who needs to know how wonderful Jesus is. Ask for God's power to share Him!

_____Let's talk: How can Lakeesha help Audrey learn more about Jesus? Think about one of your friends. How can you share Jesus with that friend?

_____Let's pray: Dear Jesus, all power is Yours. Please fill me with Your strength so I can live as Your child and share You with others. Amen.

C. A.

Just the Facts, Please!

Read from God's Word

For what I received I passed on to you as of first importance: that Christ died for our sins according to the Scriptures, that He was buried, that He was raised on the third day according to the Scriptures, and that He appeared to Peter, and then to the Twelve. After that, He appeared to more than five hundred of the brothers at the same time, most of whom are still living, though some have fallen asleep. 1 Corinthians 15:3–6

Did you know that one pound of mint oil can flavor 12,500 sticks of gum? Were you aware that the kiwi bird has a nostril at the end of its beak and is the only bird that finds food by smell? It is a fact that the earth gains 25 tons of weight a day, mostly from space dust.

Facts can be surprising, interesting, and even funny. But one thing we know about all of them: if they are facts, they are true.

Paul gives some interesting facts in today's Bible reading. He doesn't say, "I *think* Christ died for our sins" or "*Maybe* He was raised on Easter." What Paul says is fact: "Christ died for our sins. ... He was raised on the third day." Those things really happened. Those things are wonderful news.

It is a fact that Jesus gave His life for us. It is a fact that He rose again. And it is a fact that our sins are forgiven. It is a fact that Christians will spend eternity in heaven with their Savior.

This world is full of interesting facts. But only faith in the facts of Jesus' death and resurrection can save us. That makes them the most wonderful facts of all!

_____Let's talk: Why does it make a difference if something is true or made up? Why is it so important to know Jesus' death and resurrection are facts and not fiction?

_____Let's pray: How happy I am, Lord, that You really lived, died, and rose again. Thank You for the faith to believe the facts in the Bible. Help me share the facts of Your Word with others. Amen.

C. A.

Read from God's Word

"The kingdom of heaven is like treasure hidden in a field. When a man found it, he hid it again, and then in his joy went and sold all he had and bought that field. Again, the kingdom of heaven is like a merchant looking for fine pearls. When he found one of great value, he went away and sold everything he had and bought it." Matthew 13:44–46

A Treasure Worth Everything

Sara began taking gymnastics lessons when she was only five. Her class met twice a week, and she practiced an hour or two every day. Sara didn't mind, though. For her, gymnastics was more fun than anything.

Because of the time and energy she put into gymnastics, Sara didn't have time for school clubs or piano or soccer. She sometimes missed parties because of gymnastics meets. But none of that mattered to Sara. She loved gymnastics so much that she didn't mind missing other things that would interfere with her training.

Jesus said that being part of His kingdom is like this. He compared it to finding a treasure in a field or a very valuable jewel. He said that being in His kingdom was like finding something so wonderful that you were willing to give up everything else rather than miss out on it.

Jesus' love puts so much joy in our lives that we want to make Jesus our first priority. We get rid of things in our lives that interfere with our love for Him. His love, given freely, makes everything else less important. Best of all, it is ours forever!

____Let's talk: What things in life do you treasure? How much would you be willing to give up to keep those things? What was Jesus willing to give up to gain you as His treasure?

____Let's pray: Dear Jesus, thank You that You treasured us so much that You went all the way to the cross to make us Yours. Help us treasure You so much that we are willing to put You first in our lives. Amen.

E. G.

Missing One Baseball Card

Joe was flipping through his baseball card collection when he noticed that his card for Steve Jones of the Merrytown Mavericks was missing. This upset Joe. He looked through his cards and all over his room, getting more worried when it didn't turn up.

His brother, Tom, came in while Joe was looking. When Tom heard what the trouble was, he searched too. After a few minutes, Tom stopped looking. "You may as well give up," he told Joe. "Why do you care, anyway? It's not like that card is worth a lot of money!"

"Jones was important to the Mavericks last year. Without that card, my collection isn't complete!" Joe answered. He kept looking until he finally found the card under his bed.

Jesus' care for us is something like Joe's care for his baseball cards. He cares for each one of us individually. He wants each of us to be in His kingdom. You may feel that you are not worth all that much, but Jesus thinks you are.

Jesus compared His people to a flock of sheep. He said that if even one gets lost, He looks for it and is happy when He finds it. We can be thankful that Jesus has found us.

Read from God's Word

"What do you think? If a man owns a hundred sheep, and one of them wanders away, will he not leave the ninety-nine on the hills and go to look for the one that wandered off? And if he finds it, I tell you the truth, he is happier about that one sheep than about the ninety-nine that did not wander off. In the same way your Father in heaven is not willing that any of these little ones should be lost." Matthew 18:12–14

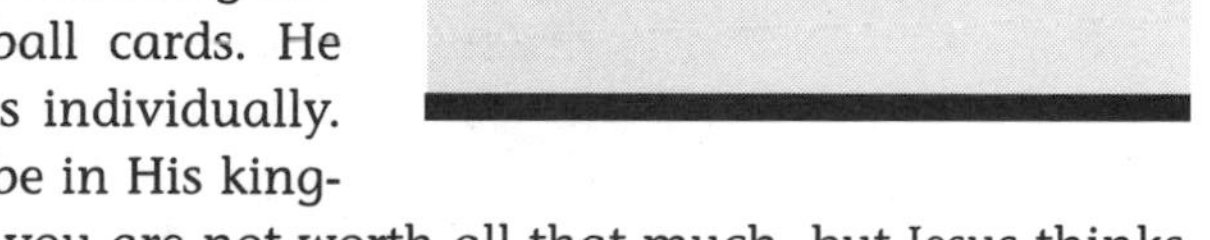

_____Let's talk: Were you ever sad because you lost something? Were you happy when you found it again? Do you think Jesus is happy when He finds those who have wandered away from Him?

_____Let's pray: Dear Jesus, thank You for finding us and bringing us into Your kingdom. Help us bring home those sheep still missing from Your flock. Amen.

E. G.

Read from God's Word

"Therefore, the kingdom of heaven is like a king who wanted to settle accounts with his servants. As he began the settlement, a man who owed him ten thousand talents was brought to him. ... The servant's master took pity on him, canceled the debt and let him go. But when that servant went out, he found one of his fellow servants who owed him a hundred denarii. ... [he] had the man thrown into prison until he could pay the debt. ... Then the master called the servant in. ... 'Shouldn't you have had mercy on your fellow servant just as I had on you?' In anger his master turned him over to the jailers to be tortured, until he should pay back all he owed. This is how My heavenly Father will treat each of you unless you forgive your brother from your heart." Matthew 18:23–35

The Forgetful Brother

One day Sam was playing ball in his front yard. Suddenly the ball got away and went through the huge picture window in the living room!

Sam felt sick to his stomach. He wanted to hide before his parents came home. But he knew he couldn't. His mom and dad were very unhappy about the window. Sam offered to pay for it by doing odd jobs in the neighborhood. But his dad said, "Sam, it would take you years to pay off a window like that. I'll pay for it." Was Sam ever relieved!

Two days later, Sam found out his little brother Bill had borrowed his favorite jacket without permission. And even worse, Bill had torn the jacket! Sam was so angry he yelled at Bill. Then his dad came in. "Sam," he said, "you seem to have forgotten how I let you off the hook about the window. If you can't let your brother off the hook for such a little thing, I shouldn't let you off the hook, either!" It took almost three years for Sam to pay for the window.

Jesus told a story like that. He wants us always to remember how much God has forgiven us and to forgive other people when they hurt us.

_____Let's talk: Can you think of a time when someone hurt you and you had a hard time forgiving that person? Where can we go for help when something like that happens?

_____Let's pray: Dear heavenly Father, thank You for sending Jesus to pay the full price for my forgiveness. Help me to forgive others as freely as You have forgiven me. In Jesus' name. Amen.

E. G.

The Big Party

Ciera was planning a big birthday party with a huge cake and even a juggler. Ciera invited the most popular kids in school to her party. But some of them played a really mean trick. They told her they didn't want to come.

Ciera was upset but she didn't let that get her down. She had also invited other kids: kids who weren't popular and kids she knew in the neighborhood. She had the party and everyone had a great time.

Jesus told a story about a party. The man giving the party had invited many people. But those people gave all kinds of excuses for not attending. So the man invited other people—those who were disadvantaged or who were strangers. He said that no one who was originally invited was welcome at his party.

But this isn't how God wants things to be. He wants everyone to be a part of His kingdom. Sometimes people who seem to be worthless are actually the ones for whom God has an extra special plan. He does not want us to miss out on His love. God's kingdom is a lot more exciting than a birthday party!

Read from God's Word

Jesus replied: "A certain man was preparing a great banquet and invited many guests. ... But they all alike began to make excuses. The first said, 'I have just bought a field, and I must go and see it. Please excuse me.' Another said, 'I have just bought five yoke of oxen, and I'm on my way to try them out. Please excuse me.' Still another said, 'I just got married, so I can't come.' ... Then the owner of the house became angry and ordered his servant, 'Go out quickly into the streets and alleys of the town and bring in the poor, the crippled, the blind and the lame.' 'Sir,' the servant said, 'what you ordered has been done, but there is still room.' Then the master told his servant, 'Go out to the roads and country lanes and make them come in, so that my house will be full. I tell you, not one of those men who were invited will get a taste of my banquet.'" Luke 14:16–24

_____Let's do: Think about the most exciting party you have ever attended. Who was there? Who wasn't? Invite someone to go with you to Sunday school and church.

_____Let's pray: Dear Jesus, thank You for loving everyone and wanting everyone to come to Your heavenly banquet. Thank You for including us. Help us invite others to come to Your heavenly feast. Amen.

E. G.

Read from God's Word

"No one sews a patch of unshrunk cloth on an old garment, for the patch will pull away from the garment, making the tear worse. Neither do men pour new wine into old wineskins. If they do, the skins will burst, the wine will run out and the wineskins will be ruined. No, they pour new wine into new wineskins, and both are preserved." Matthew 9:16–17

Time for a New Jacket

Marissa had worn the jean jacket for two years. She wore it everywhere. It was faded and torn and stained. But Marissa loved that jacket. It was very comfortable, and she wouldn't think of replacing it.

Then one day the jacket got caught on a nail. Now there was a jagged hole right in the middle of the back. Marissa knew she would need to patch the jacket if she wanted to keep on wearing it. So she got a patch, a needle, and some thread and began to sew.

Unfortunately, the material was so worn that with each stitch the coat tore even more. The new patch pulled at the old material until the hole was twice as big as before. Finally, Marissa realized that she could not keep wearing her old jacket. It was time for a new one.

Jesus wants us to realize that having His love in our lives changes our whole way of thinking and living. We can't keep doing things the old sinful way because the amazing love of Jesus keeps pulling at us like the new patch pulled at the old jacket. Our old hearts are worn out with sin, but Jesus gives us new hearts that can hold His love. What an incredible gift!

_____Let's talk: What are some ways that you sometimes try to hang onto your old heart? How does the love of Jesus tear at these old ways of thinking and living?

_____Let's pray: Dear Jesus, thank You for giving me a new heart, and thank You for filling it with Your wonderful love. Forgive me for the times I still try to use my old sinful heart. Show me Your love more and more each day! Amen.

E. G.

How Not to Learn Math

Ricardo was having trouble learning fractions. None of it made sense. He groaned just thinking about the two pages of problems he had for homework. His friend, Kevin, wanted to play some video games with him. When Ricardo said he needed to do his math first, Kevin offered to help. The boys did the assignment together.

The next day Ricardo's teacher, Mr. Oliviero, showed him his math paper. Every problem was wrong! "Ricardo," he said, "you don't seem to understand fractions. You need a little help so you can catch on."

"But Kevin helped me yesterday!" Ricardo said.

"Today I'll help you," Mr. Oliviero said. "It isn't much help when your helper doesn't understand fractions any better than you do!" Mr. Oliviero took some time to help Ricardo understand fractions and before long he did every problem correctly.

Read from God's Word

He also told them this parable: "Can a blind man lead a blind man? Will they not both fall into a pit? A student is not above his teacher, but everyone who is fully trained will be like his teacher." Luke 6:39–40

There are many things in life that we don't understand and there are times when we don't know what we should do. We need help, but we must be careful from whom we get help. Jesus is the best Teacher. He has made the trip to heaven, and He wants to show us the way there. He gives us His Word, parents, Christian teachers, and friends to guide us. We can trust Him to help!

_____Let's talk: Can you think of a time when a friend gave you bad advice? Why can you always trust the advice Jesus gives you?

_____Let's pray: Dear Jesus, thank You for making us Your brothers and sisters. Guide us safely to Your eternal home. Amen.

E. G.

Read from God's Word

"Why do you call Me, 'Lord, Lord,' and do not do what I say? I will show you what he is like who comes to Me and hears My words and puts them into practice. He is like a man building a house, who dug down deep and laid the foundation on rock. When a flood came, the torrent struck that house but could not shake it, because it was well built. But the one who hears My words and does not put them into practice is like a man who built a house on the ground without a foundation. The moment the torrent struck that house, it collapsed and its destruction was complete." Luke 6:46–49

Wise and Foolish Builders

Ted and Jon decided to build a fort. However, they couldn't agree where to build it, so they each built their own fort. Ted built his on the sandy banks of the stream. Jon built his on a steady, large rock at the top of a hill. Both boys enjoyed playing in their forts.

But one week there was a lot of rain and the stream washed over its banks. Ted's fort was swept away. Jon's fort, far from the rushing water, remained standing.

Jesus told a story a lot like this. But He was talking about something much more important than play forts or real houses. He was talking about people's lives.

We can choose to build our lives on Jesus' teachings or on something else: money, power, sports, or popularity. These other things may seem great for a while, but they are temporary. A life built on Jesus is the only kind of life that will last forever. One day Christ will come again to prove His power over all those other things.

We can be sure that building our life on Jesus' teachings is a good plan. He showed us how certain His love is by dying for us and rising again. That is a rock-solid foundation we can count on!

_____Let's talk: What kinds of things do we sometimes try to build our lives on instead of on Jesus and His teachings?

_____Let's pray: Dear Jesus, thank You for being the rock-solid foundation of our lives. Help us trust in You always. Amen.

E. G.

Keep on Asking!

Read from God's Word

Then Jesus told His disciples a parable to show them that they should always pray and not give up. He said: "In a certain town there was a judge who neither feared God nor cared about men. And there was a widow in that town who kept coming to him with the plea, 'Grant me justice against my adversary.' For some time he refused. But finally he said to himself, 'Even though I don't fear God or care about men, yet because this widow keeps bothering me, I will see that she gets justice, so that she won't eventually wear me out with her coming!'" Luke 18:1–5

Ms. Simchak didn't seem to care much about the kids in her class. When Doug figured this out, he owned recess. If he wanted to play on the swings, the other kids had better let him. If he wanted a ball, it was his. He ordered other kids off the basketball court, the climbing bars, or anyplace he wanted to be.

The other kids realized this wasn't fair. One of them, Jill, decided to talk to Ms. Simchak about it. The teacher wouldn't listen, but Jill didn't give up. She kept talking and talking. Ms. Simchak ignored Jill at first. Then she yelled at Jill for bothering her. But finally Ms. Simchak made Doug stop bullying the other kids just so Jill would stop bothering her.

Jesus told a story like this to help us understand that we can always ask God for help. We might worry that God doesn't want to hear about our problems—but He does. And if He doesn't seem to answer right away, you can keep on asking. It doesn't bother Him. He will help you in the way that is best because He loves you so much. And if you have any doubts about that, just remember that He loves you so much that He sent Jesus to die for you.

_____Let's talk: Do you think God likes you to pray to Him? What are some things you would like to pray about right now? Do it!

_____Let's pray: Dear heavenly Father, thank You for showing Your love by sending Your only Son to die for me. Help me always know that I can come to You in prayer with all my needs and problems. In Jesus' name. Amen.

E. G.

Read from God's Word

And He told them this parable: "The ground of a certain rich man produced a good crop. He thought to himself, 'What shall I do? I have no place to store my crops.' Then he said, 'This is what I'll do. I will tear down my barns and build bigger ones, and there I will store all my grain and my goods. And I'll say to myself, "You have plenty of good things laid up for many years. Take life easy; eat, drink and be merry."' But God said to him, 'You fool! This very night your life will be demanded from you. Then who will get what you have prepared for yourself?' This is how it will be with anyone who stores up things for himself but is not rich toward God." Luke 12:16–21

What a Fool!

Bo wanted some exercise equipment he'd seen on TV. Bo saved his allowance, got a paper route, and did odd jobs in the neighborhood. It seemed he spent almost every spare minute working for that equipment.

Bo was too busy to see his friends. His grades slipped. He quit soccer and baseball so he could devote all his time to earning money for the exercise equipment.

Finally, the day came when the equipment was delivered to his house. But it wasn't as great in real life as it had appeared on TV. It broke within two weeks. Worse, Bo hurt his leg using it and wasn't able to play sports that summer. When his friends talked about him, they said, "What a fool!"

Jesus told a story about a man that God called a fool. This man was so caught up in getting more and more things that he didn't have time for God. In the end, he didn't even enjoy all that he had piled up for himself and he missed out on eternal life with God in heaven.

Jesus doesn't want us to miss out on His blessings here on earth. But most of all, Jesus doesn't want us to miss out on living forever with Him in heaven.

_____Let's talk: What are some things God wants you to care about? What should we think about money and the things money can buy?

_____Let's pray: Dear Jesus, thank You for winning eternal life for us in heaven. Please guard us from letting anything get in the way of being with You forever. Amen.

E. G.

Look Around; Don't Worry!

Read from God's Word

"Therefore I tell you, do not worry about your life, what you will eat or drink; or about your body, what you will wear. Is not life more important than food, and the body more important than clothes? ... O you of little faith? So do not worry, saying, 'What shall we eat?' or 'What shall we drink?' or 'What shall we wear?' For the pagans run after all these things, and your heavenly Father knows that you need them. But seek first His kingdom and His righteousness, and all these things will be given to you as well. Therefore do not worry about tomorrow, for tomorrow will worry about itself. Each day has enough trouble of its own." Matthew 6:25–34

Siu Wan had lived in the street and never had enough to eat or wear. She couldn't remember her mother.

Someone took Siu Wan to an orphanage. Now she was going to be adopted by a family. She already knew that there were two other daughters in the family. She wondered if her new parents would have enough food and clothes for her. She wondered if there would be room for her in their house. That made Siu Wan worry.

When she met her new family, she saw that her sisters were wearing nice clothes. They looked like they had plenty to eat. They showed her a picture of their house. It looked like there was plenty of room for her too. She could see that her new parents took good care of her new sisters and that they would take care of her too. In time, Siu Wan learned not to worry.

Jesus tells us to look at some of God's other creations—the birds and flowers—to see how God takes care of them. When we do, we'll remember that God takes care of us too. We are far more important to God than birds or flowers. He shows His love for us in Jesus. That is why we never need to worry.

_____Let's talk: What do you sometimes worry about? How can you be sure God cares about you?

_____Let's pray: Dear heavenly Father, help us not to worry about things. Keep reminding us of Your love for us, and help us trust in You. In Jesus' name. Amen.

E. G.

Read from God's Word

Finally, be strong in the Lord and in His mighty power. Put on the full armor of God so that you can take your stand against the devil's schemes. For our struggle is not against flesh and blood, but against the rulers, against the authorities, against the powers of this dark world and against the spiritual forces of evil in the heavenly realms. Therefore put on the full armor of God, so that when the day of evil comes, you may be able to stand your ground, and after you have done everything, to stand. Ephesians 6:10–13

The Gutter Balls of Life

Bowling is going to be fun!" Lillian laughed as she and her friend Shannon looked for an eight-pound bowling ball.

"I've never bowled before," said Sharon. "Do you think I'll get any strikes or spares?"

"It'll be easy. All you have to do is throw the ball down the lane and hit the pins. Anybody can do it."

The girls may find that bowling isn't as easy as it looks. They may roll many gutter balls and few strikes or spares.

Just as bowling looks easy, being a Christian looks easy to many people. But we find as we go through life that "gutter balls" often happen. We fail to trust in the Lord when troubles threaten us. We may turn away from someone who needs our help.

St. Paul tells us, "Put on the full armor of God so that you can take your stand against the devil's schemes." God's armor is His Word and the power of His Spirit.

The greatest armor God has given us is the victory of His Son, Jesus Christ. He died for our sins and lives eternally at the right hand of the Father. He won't let those gutter balls in life destroy our faith. Instead, He will strengthen our faith and trust in Him.

_____Let's talk: When have gutter balls occurred in your life? How did you deal with them? How can remembering God's promises sustain you through life's problems?

_____Let's pray: Heavenly Father, keep me looking to You and Your Son when problems come up in my life. Hold me securely in Your loving, forgiving arms and sustain my faith through Your Word. In Jesus' name. Amen.

K. L. M.

God Supplies Our Needs

"Put the worm on the hook!" said Mickey. "Hurry, Grandpa. I see a big fish!"

"Hold your horses, Mickey. I'm doing it as quickly as I can."

"Not horses, Grandpa—fish!"

"All right, now cast your line and keep still. The fish won't bite if you're constantly making noises."

Grandpa softly began telling Mickey a story as they waited to catch a fish. "The disciples worried a lot. 'Where will we get the money to pay our taxes?' they may have wondered. Jesus told them to go fishing! He said they would find a coin in the mouth of the first fish they caught. It would be enough to pay the taxes they owed."

"Did they really find money inside a fish, Grandpa?"

"Yes, Mickey, they did. Sometimes we worry like Jesus' disciples. I worry about getting older and you worry about catching fish.

"We can remember that Jesus loved us so much that He died for us. He promises that God the Father will supply all our needs. Jesus rose again to assure us of eternal life with Him and to give us His peace. We don't need to worry. God is in control."

Mickey had one more question: "Grandpa, do you think Jesus will give us a fish?"

Read from God's Word

After Jesus and His disciples arrived in Capernaum, the collectors of the two-drachma tax came to Peter and asked, "Doesn't your Teacher pay the temple tax?" "Yes, He does," he replied. When Peter came into the house, Jesus was the first to speak. "What do you think, Simon?" He asked. "From whom do the kings of the earth collect duty and taxes—from their own sons or from others?" "From others," Peter answered. "Then the sons are exempt," Jesus said to him. "But so that we may not offend them, go to the lake and throw out your line. Take the first fish you catch; open its mouth and you will find a four-drachma coin. Take it and give it to them for My tax and yours." Matthew 17:24–27

_____Let's talk: How did Jesus stop His disciples from worrying about money? Has God ever supplied your needs in an unusual way? Share with your family or classmates how He did this. Why can we have peace?

_____Let's pray: Lord Jesus, when I worry, comfort me. Give me peace and assurance in knowing that You're in control. Amen.

K. L. M.

The Perfect Image

Hello, El Lardo!" "Want to play basketball, Four Eyes?" "Where ya going, Tinsel Teeth?"

Are any of these sayings familiar to you? They may be funny if they refer to someone else's appearance, but what happens when one of these sayings is directed at you? Then it's not so funny. Why? Because most people are very touchy about how they look. A survey of young people showed that most of them don't like themselves or their appearance. They have a poor self-image.

What is a good self-image? Commercials and some people would like you to believe that in order to be accepted, in order to have a good image, you need perfect hair, perfect teeth, a perfect smile, perfect skin, a perfect personality. No wonder you feel like a failure when it comes to your self-image. After all, nobody's perfect.

However, one person *was* perfect: Jesus. Unlike movies or TV, Jesus doesn't look at our imperfect features. He sees us as His children made perfect by His forgiving love. Whew, what a relief!

God sent His Son to save everyone—not just people with clear skin or nice clothes. That's wonderful to know. Jesus loves us, imperfect as we are. His love gives us the power to love ourselves too. Now that's a good self-image.

_____Let's talk: What do you think about yourself? What does God think about you?

_____Let's pray: Dear Jesus, forgive me when I think I must look and be perfect. Help me realize I am loved by You so I can share that warm love with others who don't have a good self-image. Amen.

C. J.

m a y

Contributors for this month:

Gloria Lessman

Carol Albrecht

Julie Dietrich

Malinda Walz

Read from God's Word

Finally, be strong in the Lord and in His mighty power. Put on the full armor of God so that you can take your stand against the devil's schemes. For our struggle is not against flesh and blood, but against the rulers, against the authorities, against the powers of this dark world and against the spiritual forces of evil in the heavenly realms. ... And pray in the Spirit on all occasions with all kinds of prayers and requests. With this in mind, be alert and always keep on praying for all the saints. Ephesians 6:10–18

Strong in the Lord

There you are, three rows up from the third base line, ready to watch the play-off game that will determine the baseball champions.

Then the home team runs onto the field without their uniforms—no batting helmets, no gloves, no shoes. They have shown up to play the toughest game of the season in T-shirts, shorts, and sandals!

We have received the gift of forgiveness and eternal life won by Jesus. Now we are to "live a life of love, just as Christ loved us and gave Himself up for us" (Ephesians 5:2).

This is not easy. The only way we can live in love is to "be strong in the Lord and in His mighty power"—by wearing "the full armor of God." That armor is God's uniform.

Trying to live our life without God and the strength He provides would be as foolish as a baseball player playing without a uniform, glove, and bat. God would not send us out unprotected and unprepared. Putting on this uniform of armor will enable us to be strong, no matter whom or what we face.

_____Let's do: Open your Bible and read the passage. List all the pieces in God's uniform of armor (six in all). If you'd like, draw a picture of one of God's children in full uniform, labeling the pieces.

_____Let's pray: Dear God, You are my strength and power. Thank You for giving me the protection I need. Make me strong in You. Amen.

G. L.

Our Scouting Report

Read from God's Word

Put on the full armor of God so that you can take your stand against the devil's schemes. For our struggle is not against flesh and blood, but against the rulers, against the authorities, against the powers of this dark world and against the spiritual forces of evil in the heavenly realms. Therefore put on the full armor of God, so that when the day of evil comes, you may be able to stand your ground, and after you have done everything, to stand. Ephesians 6:11–13

Sports teams often send scouts, people who watch the opponent play, to help them prepare for upcoming games. Being ready for the opponent enables teams to prepare a strong defense.

These verses tell who our opponent is in the game of life. Our opponent is the devil with all his schemes, rather than flesh and blood people.

Paul has a full scouting report on the opponent. Verse 12 explains that we're not playing in the minor leagues, we're up against the "rulers," the "authorities," the "powers of this dark world." We have the toughest opponent, one who can take over the playing field.

And what an accurate description of the devil and his team! They're tough, powerful, and tricky. They're constantly scheming to get a foothold in our lives by tempting us to sin: "So what if you cheat just this once?" "Go ahead, take it—the store will never miss one thing." "Everyone else smokes; why don't you?"

How wonderful that God gives us a defense against the devil and his evil forces. Jesus died on the cross and rose again, winning the victory over sin, death, and the devil. Yes, sometimes we sin and let the devil gain a little ground, but Jesus has won our forgiveness.

_____Let's do: Think of a time when you resisted the temptation to sin. How did Jesus help you stand up to temptation? What could you tell a friend who is facing temptation?

_____Let's pray: Lord Jesus, You are my Victor. Thank You for winning the battle against the devil once and for all. Be my defense in my daily battles. Amen.

G. L.

3 may

Read from God's Word

Put on the full armor of God so that you can take your stand against the devil's schemes. ... Therefore put on the full armor of God, so that when the day of evil comes, you may be able to stand your ground. Ephesians 6:11a, 13a

Fully Protected

In Greek mythology, Achilles was a great warrior. According to the story, when Achilles was small his mother dipped him in a magical river. The water from this river protected Achilles so enemy arrows would not hurt him. But Achilles died when an arrow hit his heel—the place where his mother had held him as she dipped him in the river.

In today's Bible verses, we read that we need the "full armor" of God to withstand the devil.

Like Achilles, we are under attack. Our attacker is Satan. We cannot stand strong against him unless we have God's full armor of power and might. Our protective covering is the righteousness Jesus won for us when He died and rose again. Our protection is complete; there are no places left unprotected by our Savior's mercy and grace.

Sometimes we try to get by without God's armor. We forget His promises and believe what the world says. We don't make time to read His Word. We do what we know is wrong. We aren't certain about God's forgiveness.

But Jesus does forgive us—completely and fully. Be assured that He has protected us totally and forever. We are winners because God's strength covers us from head to toe.

_____Let's talk: Think about a time when you were afraid. What did you do about it? What ways does God use to remind us that He is always with us?

_____Let's pray: Dear Jesus, You are my Savior. Thank You for covering my sins completely when You died on the cross. Help me use Your armor each day to stay fully covered by Your protective grace and mercy. Amen.

G. L.

Buckle Up!

Read from God's Word

Stand firm then, with the belt of truth buckled around your waist, with the breastplate of righteousness in place. Ephesians 6:14

Do you wear a seat belt when riding in a car? Seat belts give extra protection and hold us in place as we travel. Seat belts save lives.

Today's Scripture passage identifies the first piece of God's armor that we are to put on—the belt of truth. With the belt of truth, we're able to stand firm against the devil.

But what is truth? What can we buckle on to secure us, to protect us? In John 14:6, Jesus says He is the truth. Jesus is real—someone we can count on.

The devil and the world around us try to convince us that truth is found someplace else. The devil tells us that the right way to go is to pursue things like money, sports, or popularity. Although they're tempting, these things don't last, and they don't save us from our sin or take us to heaven. Trying to find security in the devil's lies means eternal death!

When we have accidents, troubles, hurts, or simply a bad day, Jesus and His love hold us up—not money or popularity. Jesus, our "belt of truth," gives us eternal life in heaven, which He won for us on the cross.

So let's buckle up—with Jesus. He protects us and keeps us securely in place.

_____Let's do: The next time you get in a car, buckle up and remember that Jesus is your true protection against sin, death, and the devil.

_____Let's pray: Dear God, You are everything I need. Thank You for providing me with so many blessings. Remind me to always depend on You to take care of me. In Jesus' name. Amen.

G. L.

Read from God's Word

Stand firm then, with the belt of truth buckled around your waist, with the breastplate of righteousness in place. Ephesians 6:14

Is Your Heart Covered?

The second part of Ephesians 6:14 tells us that without the "breastplate of righteousness in place," we're out of uniform.

Soldiers in days past wore a breastplate, a protective covering, to cover the heart. Protecting the heart was a matter of life and death.

As God's soldiers, we also keep our hearts covered to stay alive. Since the time of Adam and Eve, the hearts of all people have been sinful. We all sin every day. Although we try to be good and do what is right, we aren't able to be perfect; sin fills our hearts.

But God covers our sinful hearts. 2 Corinthians 5:21 tells us that God made Jesus, His perfect Son, to be our sin. Jesus died to pay for everything we do wrong, and then He arose from the dead to make us "righteous" (all right). Jesus covers our naturally sinful hearts with His perfect right-ness, and the Holy Spirit gives us power to live in harmony with God.

But the fact that we're covered by God's right-ness doesn't mean we can sin all we want. The way we behave identifies us to the rest of the world. Others can tell by our actions who we are. Our "right living" says thanks to Jesus for His perfect breastplate of righteousness.

_____Let's do: Look up "armor" in an encyclopedia. See how the chest is covered with a breastplate? Remember that your heart is protected by Jesus' righteousness.

_____Let's pray: Lord God, You are my Redeemer. Thank You for sending Your perfect Son to live the righteous life that I cannot live. Help me show my thanks by praising and honoring You with my life. Amen.

G. L.

Fast Feet

There are shoes for running, walking, and hiking; shoes for soccer, basketball, tennis, football, and baseball. Wearing the proper shoes requires that you know the purpose for which the shoes will be worn.

God's armor includes shoes. Today's Bible verse tells us that our feet are to be ready. Ready for what? Isaiah 52:7 tells us to be ready to "bring good news" and "proclaim peace." In Bible times, information didn't arrive by TV, e-mail, or newspaper. News came on foot from messengers who often ran miles to do so.

We also deliver news—it is the message of God's salvation and peace. Jesus came to save everyone. He did it by being executed in our place. Because we know the love and mercy of our Savior, we want to tell others about it.

Read from God's Word

Stand firm then, with the belt of truth buckled around your waist, with the breastplate of righteousness in place, and with your feet fitted with the readiness that comes from the gospel of peace. Ephesians 6:14–15

But often when it comes to sharing the good news of Jesus, we drag our feet. We are afraid of being laughed at or ridiculed. Or maybe we have good intentions but aren't really prepared to share the Gospel. We stumble and fall because we don't know what to say or how to say it.

Soccer, football, basketball—whatever our sport, we practice and train for it. So it is with sharing God's Good News. We get better when we practice.

_____Let's do: Practice telling someone about the Good News of salvation in Jesus. Then go do it! Share your faith with someone who needs to know about God.

_____Let's pray: Dear God, You are the best news I know. Thank You for choosing me to tell others of Your love. Train me to always be ready to proclaim the Gospel of peace. Amen.

G. L.

A Shield to Stop Satan

Jump!" "Move to the right!" "Duck!" "Look out!"

Her teammates on the sidelines warned Erin of the shots to come. She was the last team member remaining in dodge ball. The balls were coming fast and Erin was getting tired. Eventually, she just couldn't keep out of the way any longer.

Today's passage says that the devil ("the evil one") is shooting flaming arrows at us. Have you ever been hit by one of Satan's arrows? His arrows are sadness, pain, disappointments, anger, sickness. None of us escapes those.

But read verse 16 again. Paul tells us we can put out these flaming arrows with a shield of faith. The shields carried by soldiers in Bible times were covered with leather. Before battle, the soldiers soaked their shields in water. When the opponents' burning arrows hit the shields, the fire would go out.

God's shield of faith does the same for us. By the power of the Holy Spirit, we have strong faith that Jesus loves us, stays with us, and cares for us—enough to die for us and take us to heaven to live with Him forever. This shield of faith can snuff out anything Satan throws at us.

_____Let's talk: Have you ever been hit by one of Satan's arrows? How did God help you then? How does He help you for the future?

_____Let's pray: Dear Lord, You are my shield. Thank You for staying close to me in times of trouble. Give me Your strength when Satan strikes. Amen.

G. L.

God's Helmet for Your Head

What's on your mind? What did you think about as you fell asleep last night? as you went to school today?

As God's children, our head is covered with the helmet of salvation. Our salvation is a gift (Ephesians 2:8). We know for certain that our sins are forgiven, that we'll live forever with Jesus because He gave His life for us.

That helmet means that the gift of salvation (and the Giver of salvation) should be uppermost in our minds. Our thoughts should be filled with praise and thanksgiving, with ways to serve and please the Lord.

But that isn't always the case. We worry about grades, not fitting in, about quarrels, things we've done wrong. We think about getting even with the bully at school, how unfair a teacher is, how different that new kid acts.

Read from God's Word

Take the helmet of salvation and the sword of the Spirit, which is the word of God. Ephesians 6:17

Since, then, you have been raised with Christ, set your hearts on things above, where Christ is seated at the right hand of God. Set your minds on things above, and not on earthly things. Colossians 3:1–2

Now read Colossians 3:1–2.

Salvation through Jesus has removed our sins and guilt. His death paid for those. We think differently because our minds are focused on Christ. We think about all the blessings He gives us in our daily lives. We thank Him by giving Him glory in our thoughts, words, and actions.

That's the outward appearance of the helmet of salvation. That's where our head belongs—in thoughts of thanking and serving our Lord!

_____Let's do: Try this: for the next week, keep track of the first thing you think about as you wake each morning. Then, remember that all the blessings in our lives come because of God's love for us in Jesus.

_____Let's pray: Dear Father in heaven, You are the focus of my life. Thank You for Your gift of salvation. Help me keep my thoughts and priorities centered on You and Your will. In Jesus' name. Amen.

G. L.

Read from God's Word

Take the helmet of salvation and the sword of the Spirit, which is the word of God. Ephesians 6:17

For the word of God is living and active. Sharper than any double-edged sword, it penetrates even to dividing soul and spirit, joints and marrow; it judges the thoughts and attitudes of the heart. Hebrews 4:12

A Sword of Words

Missiles, long-range weapons, tanks, jets, submarines, and more exist for waging war.

Battle was much different in Bible times. The most effective weapon was a sharp sword. Soldiers depended on it in combat. It was important for each soldier to be familiar with his sword and be skilled in using it.

Read the verse again and look at what "the sword of the Spirit" is—the Word of God. God's Word is the only weapon we have in our battle with Satan. Whatever we're up against, God's Word comforts, defends, forgives, strengthens, and encourages. We depend on it for survival.

When Jesus was tempted in the wilderness, He answered all Satan's temptations with quotes from the Holy Scriptures. The Word of God was the only weapon Jesus needed. That is why we spend time in Bible study, Sunday school, vacation Bible school, and daily devotions. These things help us become skilled in using God's Word to resist Satan whenever he strikes.

The Holy Spirit keeps God's Word alive and active in our lives. He lives in our heart through Baptism and helps us recall His promises when we need them most. This "sword of the Spirit, which is the word of God," is ours to use every day.

_____Let's do: Memorize Ephesians 6:13. The next time you are frightened or tempted to sin, say this verse to yourself. You are protected!

_____Let's pray: Dear Lord, You are the living Word. Thank You for the precious gift of the Holy Scriptures. Open my heart as I read and study Your message of salvation. Amen.

G. L.

Count on the Coach

Read from God's Word

And pray in the Spirit on all occasions with all kinds of prayers and requests. With this in mind, be alert and always keep on praying for all the saints. Ephesians 6:18

Teams are more likely to win when the coach knows the game well and has a game plan. The team counts on the coach to guide them.

We constantly turn to God, our Coach in life. He knows the game, for He created it and everything in it. He knows the game plan, for He is in control of everything. And He's always there when we need Him, always ready to listen and act.

Sometimes we think we don't have time to pray. Sometimes we think God doesn't care about our concerns. Sometimes we think God is away somewhere, too busy and too far away to help us. And that's just what the devil wants us to think.

The truth is that God wants us to talk to Him. He wants us to pray on all occasions (happy and sad), with all kinds of prayers (in thanks, in need) and all kinds of requests (big and small). We come to God in Jesus' name because His death on the cross made us children of our heavenly Father.

Just as time-outs with the coach are important for rest and guidance, time-outs with the Lord are vital for us. He is the Coach who knows the game and leads us to certain victory forever!

_____Let's do: Put a rock near your bed where you are sure to see it. Let the rock be a reminder to go to God in prayer.

_____Let's pray: Holy Spirit, You are my leader and guide. Thank You for always being available. Keep me in touch with You and help me rely on Your strength throughout each day. I pray because of Jesus. Amen.

G. L.

Read from God's Word

Then Noah built an altar to the LORD and, taking some of all the clean animals and clean birds, he sacrificed burnt offerings on it. The LORD smelled the pleasing aroma and said in His heart: "Never again will I curse the ground because of man, even though every inclination of his heart is evil from childhood. And never again will I destroy all living creatures, as I have done. As long as the earth endures, seedtime and harvest, cold and heat, summer and winter, day and night will never cease." Genesis 8:20–22

Spring's Promise

Kelsey dropped the seeds into the hole her father had dug. Carefully she smoothed the moist dirt over her seeds. "This is fun, Daddy!" she exclaimed.

Her big sister Kim laughed. "You say that every year, Kelsey!"

"Well, it's fun every year," declared Kelsey. "Daddy," she asked, "how does spring know it's supposed to come back? And how does winter know it's time to go away?"

"It happens because of the way the earth revolves around the sun. The sun's rays are more direct," Dad explained.

"I don't get it," Kelsey said.

"It is pretty hard to understand," admitted Dad.

"No, it's not," chimed in Kim. "Spring comes because God said it would. We learned that in Sunday school. God said winter and spring would always come back until the world ends."

"Kim's right," said Dad. "God made a promise. And we know God always keeps His promises."

Do you know some of those promises? God promised Adam and Eve that He would send a Savior, and He did. God promises to forgive our sins, to take care of us and love us. He promises us eternal life in heaven. And the best part of all is that God always keeps His promises!

_____Let's talk: What do you think is the best promise God made? How do you know He will keep that promise?

_____Let's pray: Dear God, You have kept all Your promises to me, and I thank You. I especially thank You for keeping Your promise to send a Savior. Because of that, I know I will spend eternity in heaven. Amen.

C. A.

Our Strong and Mighty God

Read from God's Word

O LORD God Almighty, who is like You? You are mighty, O LORD, and Your faithfulness surrounds You. Psalm 89:8

The tree was grand. Standing big and tall, its limbs seemed to stretch across the entire yard. Branches, perfectly placed for climbing, held summer-green leaves, which supplied plenty of shade for a nap on a lazy afternoon.

One bolt of lightning during a storm changed everything. In a matter of seconds, the tree collapsed to the ground.

No tree on earth can be compared to our strong and mighty God. His loving arms can hold every single person on this earth. His arms are perfect for falling into when we need comfort and strength from our heavenly Father.

Think about it. There is no one who can compare to Him. When we are weak, He is strong. When we are unfaithful, He is the same faithful God He has always promised to be. God showed just how faithful He is when He sent His only Son to die on the cross. God's faithful promise of eternal life through His Son, Jesus, will never be broken. No other person can keep a promise like that.

God will remain strong and mighty forever. No bolt of lightning will change that! Satan would like to tear down and defeat God, but Christ has defeated Satan. God promises to be faithful through eternity. What a strong and mighty God we have!

_____Let's talk: Is there someone in your life who stands taller in your eyes than God? What things get in the way of your faith growing strong and mighty?

_____Let's pray: Dear strong and mighty God, continue to show us Your faithful love. Work in us a strong and mighty faith. In Your mighty name. Amen.

J. D.

Read from God's Word

It was He who gave some to be apostles, some to be prophets, some to be evangelists, and some to be pastors and teachers, to prepare God's people for works of service, so that the body of Christ may be built up until we all reach unity in the faith and in the knowledge of the Son of God and become mature, attaining to the whole measure of the fullness of Christ. Ephesians 4:11–13

How Will You Serve?

Jacob's dad is famous for mixing together any and all leftovers. Some of the combinations are strange. Which combination will go down in history as the most disgusting? The winner has to be chili on pancakes—with syrup!

The Holy Spirit gives each of us special gifts and talents to be used in building up the body of believers in Christ. However, no two believers share the same exact gifts from the Spirit. Today's Bible reading tells us how Christ gave people different gifts. Each person who serves God has a different "flavor." Christ combines these "flavors," or gifts of His people, to be used for the same purpose—to share His love with all people and to build up the body of believers.

What "flavor" are you? How will you serve Christ? Perhaps you're already serving Him in one way or another.

Each of us, created differently, is blessed with such special gifts. Christ knows exactly how you can serve Him. If you're unsure how Christ wants you to serve, pray. Ask Him to lead you and be your guide. Christ will show you where and how you can serve Him—no matter what flavor you are!

_____Let's talk: What makes you different from the other people you know? How can you use your differences to serve Christ?

_____Let's pray: Heavenly Father, thank You for sending Your Son to be the true example of a servant. Show us where and how You want us to serve You. Strengthen us to be Your faithful servants. Amen.

J. D.

Inside and Out

Would your mom know how to make "one egg with a bump of cheese in the middle"? For a first-grader named Allie, the golden yolk of an egg looks exactly like a bump of cheese. It's the only way she knows how to describe it.

The yolk of an egg does look like cheese. Outward appearances can sometimes be deceiving. Take Samuel and Eliab, for example. Samuel was chosen by God to anoint a new king to replace Saul. God sent Samuel to Jesse's house. One look at Jesse's son Eliab, and Samuel thought he had surely found the new king God had chosen. God's Word in 1 Samuel 16:7 tells us God didn't care how the king looked on the outside. Rather, God looked at the heart. God did not choose Eliab; He chose David. David loved God with his whole heart.

What does God see when He looks at us? God looks right past our outward appearance. God looks *inside*. There's no doubt He sees sin inside every one of us. But because He loves us, God didn't want us to live with the guilt of our sins. He sent Jesus Christ to be the sacrifice for our sin. God takes away our sin, letting His Holy Spirit fill our hearts with joy and love for Him.

Read from God's Word

But the LORD said to Samuel, "Do not consider his appearance or his height, for I have rejected him. The LORD does not look at the things man looks at. Man looks at the outward appearance, but the LORD looks at the heart." 1 Samuel 16:7

_____Let's do: Stand in front of a mirror. Remind yourself that God doesn't see what you're looking at. Ask God to fill your heart with love for Him.

_____Let's pray: Dear Father, thank You for loving us enough to send Your Son to die for our sins. May Your love fill our hearts and be known to others around us. Amen.

J. D.

Read from God's Word

"All this I have spoken while still with you. But the Counselor, the Holy Spirit, whom the Father will send in My name, will teach you all things and will remind you of everything I have said to you. Peace I leave with you; My peace I give you. I do not give to you as the world gives." John 14:25–27a

Attention, Please!

How would you get someone's attention at a noisy shopping mall? Perhaps you might wave your hands in the air. Maybe you would shout or whistle. What about in a quiet movie theater? Would a shout or whistle be appropriate? Definitely not! Waving your hands in the air might work, unless someone behind you was watching the movie.

Do you think God ever has a problem getting our attention? Definitely, yes! We won't see any waving arms or hear a shout or whistle from God. God uses the Holy Spirit through His Word to get our attention.

Before His death on the cross, Jesus told His disciples they could be assured of the Holy Spirit's presence in their lives after He was gone. God would send the Holy Spirit, in Jesus' name, to remind them of the things Jesus had said while on earth. After Jesus' ascension into heaven, the disciples were filled with the Holy Spirit at Pentecost.

We received God's Holy Spirit the day we were baptized. Because of our sinful nature, it's easy for us to try to ignore the Spirit's call to be disciples of Christ. God forgives us for failing to see the Spirit's presence in our lives. God continues to love us, forgive us, and renew us each day.

____Let's talk: What are some ways God gets our attention? How can you answer His call to follow Him?

____Let's pray: God, help me focus on You. Use Your Word to get my attention and be a witness to those around me. Amen.

J. D.

Give Thanks to God

Read from God's Word

Give thanks to the LORD, for He is good; His love endures forever. Psalm 107:1

Grandma and Grandpa had just come home from vacation and brought a small gift for their granddaughter, Maggie. After she opened the gift, her mother said, "What do you say, Maggie?" Maggie asked, "What is it?" Maggie's mother wasn't expecting that reply. She had thought Maggie would say "thank you"!

What if God allowed us to have only the things we thanked Him for? What would you have? It's easy to take for granted all the things we've been given. God blesses us, usually without a "thank You" from us.

Today's Bible verse might be familiar to you. Perhaps you've used these words as a table prayer. But giving thanks to God isn't just a mealtime thing. God gives us more than just food and drink. He blesses us with family, friends, food, and shelter. God gives us churches, schools, teachers, and pastors. The list goes on and on. God's blessings are immeasurable. Without His blessings, we'd have nothing.

Along with His blessings, God also gives forgiveness. God's promise of forgiveness is forever because He sent Jesus to die on the cross in payment for our sins. When we forget to thank God for each blessing He gives us, we can tell Him we're sorry. God is there with open arms, ready to forgive us.

_____Let's do: Write today's Bible verse on several index cards. Place the cards where you are most likely to see them throughout the day. Thank God for the many blessings in your life.

_____Let's pray: Dear good and glorious God, thank You for so richly blessing my life. Help me be more aware of these blessings and daily thank You for each and every one. Amen.

J. D.

Read from God's Word

What good is it, my brothers, if a man claims to have faith but has no deeds? Can such faith save him? Suppose a brother or sister is without clothes and daily food. If one of you says to him, "Go, I wish you well; keep warm and well fed," but does nothing about his physical needs, what good is it? In the same way, faith by itself, if it is not accompanied by action, is dead. James 2:14–17

Let Your Faith Show

Hold a rubber band between a finger on each hand. Ask a friend to pluck the rubber band. What happened? Now stretch the rubber band as far as you can without letting it snap. Ask your friend to pluck the band. What did you see? What did you hear? You probably saw the rubber band vibrating. At the same time, you should have heard a high-pitched sound.

Sound is made when the air around a vibrating object is moved. Without vibrations, no sound can be heard. The rubber band needed to be stretched tight to produce vibrations to make a sound.

Picture your faith in Jesus as a rubber band. Are you producing "faith vibrations"? Do your friends and family, classmates, and even strangers hear the "sounds of your faith"? James 2:17 says "faith by itself, if it is not accompanied by action, is dead." Is your faith active or is it in need of a little stretching?

Faith is a gift from God. Look for ways to show others your faith in Jesus. Be encouraged by those people God has put in your life to help your faith be active and alive. Let your "faith vibrations" be seen and the "sounds of your faith" be heard! The Holy Spirit will help you.

_____Let's do: Carry a rubber band in your pocket. Let it be a daily reminder to you of how your faith can be shown to others.

_____Let's pray: Jesus, help me show others my faith in You. Amen.

J. D.

Something to Smile About

If you could use only one word to describe what others see when they look at your expression, what would it be? Happy? Sad? Angry?

A simple look at someone's face can often tell a lot about that person's mood. Tears running past a quivering chin means something upsetting, frightening, or sad has probably happened. A wrinkled forehead might mean confusion, worry, or disappointment.

Sometimes, it isn't easy to tell people's mood just by looking at their face. But one facial expression is unmistakable—a huge smile!

God gave us something to smile about! He sent His Son, Jesus, to take all of our sins to the cross. His death means victory over death, sin, and the devil. God wants us to share that message with those around us. We can start by showing others how much this gift of grace means to us. We can start with a smile! Let others around you know you've got a happy heart, filled with God's love.

Read from God's Word

A happy heart makes the face cheerful, but heartache crushes the spirit. Proverbs 15:13

_____Let's do: Make a special effort to show others how happy your heart is. Share a smile with as many people as you can. It will make your heart even happier!

_____Let's pray: Jesus, because of Your death on the cross, we have reason to be happy. May Your Holy Spirit remind us to share our happiness with everyone we meet. Amen.

J. D.

Read from God's Word

"Can a mother forget the baby at her breast and have no compassion on the child she has borne? Though she may forget, I will not forget you! See, I have engraved you on the palms of My hands; your walls are ever before Me." Isaiah 49:15–16

God Remembers You

Keisha and her family were on vacation and decided to visit a gift shop for souvenirs. Keisha's parents were ready to leave, but Keisha could not decide what to buy.

Finally, she spotted a charm bracelet. She didn't really want a bracelet, but she wanted to buy something. And although it cost more than she had planned to spend, she bought it anyway.

When they were only halfway home, two charms fell off. When she got home, the clasp wasn't working. Keisha knew she had made a mistake in buying the bracelet. She threw it in her jewelry box and forgot about it.

God never has moments like that! When God chose us to be part of His family, it was no mistake. He showed us His love by paying a much bigger price than Keisha paid. God paid with His Son, Jesus. Because of Jesus' death on the cross, the payment for our sins is forever paid.

What if we make the wrong choice and forget God like Keisha forgot her bracelet? God's never-ending grace and forgiveness will still be there for us. As today's Bible reading says, we are "engraved" on the palms of His hands. Be assured of God's promise—He will always remember us!

_____Let's do: Write this on your hand: "Jesus loves me." Every time you see it, thank God for loving you so much that He sent Jesus to be your Savior.

_____Let's pray: Thank You, God, for making me a part of Your family. Help me daily to remember Your love for me. Amen.

J. D.

Wait for the Lord

Only one word could describe Mrs. Caruthers's morning—terrible! Her alarm clock did not go off. A button fell off her skirt. Her toast burned. Mrs. Caruthers knew her day couldn't get any worse! Or could it?

A train had blocked the crossing. Mrs. Caruthers thought of how much had happened to her that morning and wanted to cry.

Waiting can sometimes be unbearable, especially when we're in a hurry. There's no way to make a train go faster. Getting around one is impossible too. We just have to wait for it.

Waiting for the Lord to act in our lives sometimes feels the same way. We want His answer *immediately*. Days, weeks, even months or years can seem an eternity to wait for an answer to prayer. The Lord wants us to wait for His perfect timing. Our selfishness can get in the way, making us think our timing is better than His. Through God's perfect plan of salvation, His forgiveness is ours. Even on our worst days, He's right there with His merciful love and forgiveness.

The next time you're stopped at a train crossing, think about the Lord. Thank Him for the unexpected opportunity to talk to Him in prayer. Ask Him for patience in waiting for His answer to your prayers.

Read from God's Word

I wait for the LORD, my soul waits, and in His word I put my hope. My soul waits for the LORD more than watchmen wait for the morning, more than watchmen wait for the morning. Psalm 130:5–6

_____Let's do: The next time you see a train, count the number of train cars. Think of one blessing for each car.

_____Let's pray: Dear Lord, help me be patient as I wait for You. Show me how to appreciate each moment You've given me and to wait for Your perfect timing. Amen.

J. D.

Held in God's Hand

Nighttime thunderstorms scare Claire. She heads to her parents' room at the first sign of a storm. Snuggling under the warm blankets, with a parent on each side, gives Claire a sense of protection.

What scares you? Is it making friends in a new situation? playing sports in front of a crowd? taking a big test? Having someone nearby through the scary times sure can help. There are times, however, when we are alone. Or are we? There's always Someone nearby—our heavenly Father.

God's Word tells about the protection He gives us. God tells us, "I will uphold you with My righteous right hand." What an awesome promise that is! God's mighty right hand is holding us, not only in times of trouble, but always!

Had God not sent His Son to pay for our sins on the cross, our lives would be filled with fear. Without Jesus' death and resurrection, we would have to pay for our own sins. Thanks to God's loving plan of salvation, Jesus made payment for our sin. The promise of eternal life in heaven is ours!

When frightening times come your way, remember whose hand protects you. There will never be a moment when you are alone. God's there, and He always will be!

____Let's do: Trace your hand on a piece of paper. Ask someone with a larger hand to trace his or her hand over your tracing. The larger hand represents God's hand. Write today's Bible verse on the page. Know that you always fit perfectly in God's hand.

____Let's pray: Heavenly Father, remind me of Your presence when I feel scared and alone. Thank You for promising to keep me in Your hand. Amen.

J. D.

The Least of These

Lauren was sitting at the same lunch table where she always sat, surrounded by her friends. She was watching Sara, sitting where she always sat—alone. Lauren noticed that Sara kept her head down while she ate.

"Maybe we should ask Sara to eat with us," Lauren said.

No one answered. It was clear that Lauren's friends did not agree with her.

But Lauren couldn't stop thinking about Sara. That night she told her mom about it.

"It sounds like you have a tough decision to make," her mom said. "Jesus knew what it was like to be in your situation. He made a lot of people uncomfortable when He chose to spend time with tax collectors, lepers, and other people who were considered not very nice. Let's pray about this." Lauren and her mom prayed that God would give Lauren the wisdom to deal with the situation in love.

The next day, as she walked over to Sara, Lauren could feel the looks and hear the whispers from her usual table. It was hard, but she tried to keep thinking about the people Jesus used to hang out with. Although she had a lot of fears, she felt peace in her heart when her question "May I sit with you?" was met with a great big smile!

Read from God's Word

"Then the King will say to those on His right, 'Come, you who are blessed by My Father; take your inheritance, the kingdom prepared for you since the creation of the world. For I was hungry and you gave Me something to eat, I was thirsty and you gave Me something to drink, I was a stranger and you invited Me in, I needed clothes and you clothed Me, I was sick and you looked after Me, I was in prison and you came to visit Me.' Then the righteous will answer Him, 'Lord, when did we see You hungry and feed You, or thirsty and give You something to drink? When did we see You a stranger and invite You in, or needing clothes and clothe You? When did we see You sick or in prison and go to visit You?' The King will reply, 'I tell you the truth, whatever you did for one of the least of these brothers of Mine, you did for Me.'" Matthew 25:34–40

_____Let's talk: Do you know someone who could use a friend? How can you reach out to her or him?

_____Let's pray: Dear Jesus, thank You so much for the love You have shown to me. Help me to know the best ways to share Your love with others. Amen.

M. W.

Read from God's Word

Then Jesus came to them and said, "All authority in heaven and on earth has been given to Me. Therefore go and make disciples of all nations, baptizing them in the name of the Father and of the Son and of the Holy Spirit, and teaching them to obey everything I have commanded you. And surely I am with you always, to the very end of the age." Matthew 28:18–20

The Time Is Now!

A missionary from Guatemala was telling Kayla's Sunday school class about the interesting and adventurous things she had done. Kayla sighed and said, "Maybe someday I can do the Lord's work too."

Kayla's heart was in the right place, but she thought she had to wait until she was an adult to do the Lord's work. However, God calls all Christians—including children—to do His work every day! Many times the things He calls us to do are not exciting or adventurous. Sometimes they seem boring or unpleasant. But they are the Lord's work just the same.

Telling others about Christ or showing them your faith is the Lord's work. Thinking of your neighborhood and classroom as a "mission field" can show some of His work to be done.

We are all given gifts from God: The gift of forgiveness through Jesus. The gift of faith in Him as Savior by the power of the Holy Spirit. Most important, we have the gift of eternal life through that faith in Christ. And we have a responsibility, given to us by God, to share those gifts.

Maybe someday God will call Kayla to be a missionary in a foreign country. Until then, she can spread God's Word and do His work right now—and so can you!

_____Let's talk: How can you do the Lord's work right now in your life?

_____Let's pray: Dear Jesus, help me to see the important work You want me to do for You today. Amen.

M. W.

Important Parts

Try scratching your nose without using
your fingers,
Or kicking a ball without using your feet.
Smell a rose without a nose, and the
scent never lingers.
With no tongue you can't taste your
favorite treat.
Without ears you can't hear your favorite
tune.
Without legs you can't jump or run
when you play.
Without eyes you can't see the stars or
the moon.
Without hands you can't write to friends
far away.
The body hurts when it's missing even
one little part.
Each one is important, not just the brain
or the heart.
So it's the same with Christ's body, you see.
It's not whole without you, your best
friend, or me.
So don't think you don't matter as much
as the others,
When you look at your friends or your sisters or brothers.
When it seems like the others are better than you—
Remember you're special—God said it, it's true!

Read from God's Word

Just as each of us has one body with many members, and these members do not all have the same function, so in Christ we who are many form one body, and each member belongs to all the others. We have different gifts, according to the grace given us. If a man's gift is prophesying, let him use it in proportion to his faith. If it is serving, let him serve; if it is teaching, let him teach; if it is encouraging, let him encourage; if it is contributing to the needs of others, let him give generously; if it is leadership, let him govern diligently; if it is showing mercy, let him do it cheerfully. Romans 12:4–8

Praise the Lord that He has made us all different! He did it for a reason. Each of us is blessed with gifts that fit God's plan for us. Just because you don't have the same gifts as others doesn't mean you don't have gifts or that they aren't important. God loves you and has given you an important job—to be you! Using the special gifts God has given you will always be pleasing to Him and a blessing to you and others. Praise God that He made us the way He did!

_____Let's talk: What special gifts do you have? How are they different from the gifts of your close friends or family members?

_____Let's pray: Dear Lord, thank You for giving everyone different gifts. Help me always to use and appreciate those gifts in myself and others. Amen.

M. W.

Can I Get a Little Respect?

Read from God's Word

Everyone must submit himself to the governing authorities, for there is no authority except that which God has established. The authorities that exist have been established by God. ... Therefore, it is necessary to submit to the authorities, not only because of possible punishment but also because of conscience. This is also why you pay taxes, for the authorities are God's servants, who give their full time to governing. Give everyone what you owe him: If you owe taxes, pay taxes; if revenue, then revenue; if respect, then respect; if honor, then honor. Romans 13:1–7

Jason, for the umpteenth time, sit down and be quiet!" Mrs. Schneider said in her I-mean-business teacher voice. "Why can't you show a little more maturity and self-control?"

"Why can't you just lighten up?" Jason shot back.

Later, after Jason returned from the principal's office, Nathan said, "I can't believe you said that to Mrs. Schneider. It was so disrespectful."

Jason growled, "When she starts showing me some respect, I might start showing her some."

It may be natural for us, in our sinfulness, to think this way. The question is, though, whether such attitudes are pleasing to God.

Scripture addresses issues of respect and obedience. Ephesians 6:1 says, "Children, obey your parents in the Lord, for this is right." Hebrews 13:17 says, "Obey your leaders and submit to their authority." Parents, teachers, policemen, and others are in positions of authority. God makes it clear that they are to be respected and obeyed.

You may ask why God put so many people in your life to tell you what to do. God loves you. He has blessed you with people to guide you and help you to grow into the person He wants you to be. After all, when you consider that those in authority have been placed there by God, maybe they do deserve respect.

_____Let's talk: Who are the people God has placed in authority over you? How can you show more respect toward them?

_____Let's pray: Dear Jesus, please forgive me when I'm not respectful. Please help me show respect to those placed in positions of authority. Give me a heart willing to accept the guidance of those You have given me to help me grow. In Jesus' name. Amen.

M. W.

Don't Deny It

"Isn't that where you go to church?" Matt asked.

Billy felt his face get hot. Matt was not a "church friend." In fact, he had heard Matt laugh about "church-going goody-goodies."

"Yeah, I go there—when my parents make me," Billy stammered. The truth was that Billy went to church and Sunday school every week with his family.

"Dude. I'm glad my parents don't make me go," Matt laughed.

Billy thought he handled the situation pretty well. After all, he didn't exactly lie—he just stretched the truth. Later, though, Billy felt guilty. He realized that instead of taking the opportunity to witness, he had denied his faith and, in doing so, denied Christ. That night Billy prayed that God would forgive him and give him courage to stand up for his faith.

The Bible tells about another person who denied Christ. After Jesus was arrested, Peter denied even knowing Jesus three times in one night. Then Peter felt so bad that he cried.

The good news is that Jesus doesn't deny us. He loves us and forgives us time after time. It is because of His love that we can find the courage to take a stand for Him. After all, He took the ultimate stand for us on the cross.

Read from God's Word

For God did not give us a spirit of timidity, but a spirit of power, of love and of self-discipline. So do not be ashamed to testify about our Lord, or ashamed of me his prisoner. But join with me in suffering for the gospel, by the power of God, who has saved us and called us to a holy life—not because of anything we have done but because of His own purpose and grace. This grace was given us in Christ Jesus before the beginning of time. 2 Timothy 1:7–9

_____Let's talk: Have you ever denied Christ when you were trying to fit in with others? How can you become more courageous about standing up for what you believe?

_____Let's pray: Dear Jesus, please forgive me when I deny You. Help me and give me courage to stand up for You, even when it's hard to do. Thank You for always loving me. Amen.

M. W.

Read from God's Word

And we, who with unveiled faces all reflect the Lord's glory, are being transformed into His likeness with ever-increasing glory, which comes from the Lord, who is the Spirit.
2 Corinthians 3:18

A Beautiful Transformation

In spring the world seems to transform. Things that appeared to be dead come to life. It starts with crocuses, which sometimes bloom while there is snow on the ground. Next come daffodils, then tulips, and flowering trees. Soon everything is alive. Birds sing. Grass gets green. The world is changed.

There was a time when our hearts were as dark as winter. Sin caused a separation from God that kept us away from His light and life. Then, with Christ's death and resurrection, He brought spring to our lives. When Christ died, He took our sins to the grave with Him. When He rose on Easter, we were brought back to life. We were transformed.

And just like the changing of the seasons, our transformation is ongoing. Every day we sin and are lost in darkness. But because of Jesus, we have forgiveness. Our relationship with God is restored. We are no longer separated from His light and life.

Every time you look at the flowers and trees around you, let them remind you of the change that has taken place. The world has been transformed from death to life, and so have you. Let Christ's love grow in you and bloom for everyone to see!

_____Let's do: Plant a few grass seeds in a cup filled with soil. Water them gently. After a few days, the grass will sprout and grow. How is God's love growing in you?

_____Let's pray: Dear Jesus, thank You for Your transformation from death to life so I may also be transformed from death to eternal life. Help me to let my transformation be seen by everyone. In Jesus' name. Amen.

M. W.

See You Later!

Read from God's Word

But our citizenship is in heaven. And we eagerly await a Savior from there, the Lord Jesus Christ, who, by the power that enables Him to bring everything under His control, will transform our lowly bodies so that they will be like His glorious body. Philippians 3:20–21

My grandfather died when he was 81 years old. He had always been in good health, but when he had knee surgery, he developed some complications. He just got sicker and sicker, and the doctors discovered more and more problems.

I loved my grandpa very much, and I prayed and prayed that God would make him better. However, this time my prayers were being answered with a no. It was God's will that Grandpa would go to heaven. As much as I loved him and wanted him to live on earth, how could I not be happy for him? He was going to heaven to be with Jesus.

When my grandpa died, I was very sad. It still makes me sad sometimes because I miss him. I am comforted though, because he is in heaven and because I will see him again someday.

Memorial Day is when we remember those who have served our country in the military. We also remember those who have died and the blessings we received through their lives. For Christians, though, it doesn't have to be a sad day. Because of Jesus' death and resurrection, it is a day to remember that someday all Christians will be in heaven, singing and celebrating with the Lord.

_____Let's talk: Have you ever been to a funeral? What was it like? Although we are sad when someone dies, we can be glad that Jesus came to earth so everyone can live with Him in heaven some day.

_____Let's pray: Dear Jesus, thank You for giving me the gift of eternal life through Your death and resurrection. Comfort me when I have to deal with earthly death. Help me remember that I will see You and all Christians in heaven someday. Amen.

M. W.

Seeing the Open Doors

Megan prayed that she would make the volleyball team. All the cool people were on the team, and they had a lot of fun.

"Megan, I'm sorry," Coach Wallace said after tryouts. "I know you really wanted to be a part of the team. Maybe the Lord has something else in mind for you."

The next day Megan saw a sign on the bulletin board at school that auditions for the annual musical would be held the following week.

"You should try out," Megan's friend, Annie, said.

"Well, maybe—but only if you try out too," Megan responded.

Three weeks later the girls were caught up in rehearsals, getting costumes together, and practicing their lines with other cast members. Megan couldn't remember when she'd had so much fun.

When Megan saw Coach Wallace after school, she said, "Remember what you said about the Lord having something else in mind for me? Well, He did!"

"I'm so happy for you, Megan," the coach said. "I hope you always remember that the Lord loves you and has a plan for your life."

"Thanks, Coach, I'll remember. Will you come see the musical?"

"I wouldn't miss it," Coach Wallace said, then offered up a silent prayer of thanks of her own.

_____Let's talk: When has a disappointment in your life turned out to be a blessing? What disappointment are you facing now that you can place in the Lord's hands?

_____Let's pray: Dear Lord, thank You for knowing what's best for me. Help me trust You and place my disappointments and hurts in Your hands. In Jesus' name. Amen.

M. W.

Who's Going on Vacation?

No more pencils, no more books, no more teacher's dirty looks.

Many students chant this rhyme on the last day of school. Although you value your education, you are probably looking forward to summer vacation. It is often a time to do different things.

Unfortunately, many people think that as summer comes, it's time to take a vacation from God too. In many churches, attendance at worship and offerings decrease during the summer months. Sometimes Sunday school classes even stop because so many people quit coming.

Fortunately, God, in His grace and mercy, never takes a vacation from us. He never leaves us, and He never stops loving us. Wherever we are, He is right there with us. He never decides that He has more important things to do than pay attention to our needs and care for us—even during vacation.

This summer, think of the time away from school and homework as an opportunity to improve your relationship with God. Take a Bible with you on vacation. Talk to your parents about having daily family devotions if you don't already do so. Try to spend at least 10 minutes a day reading the Bible and praying on your own. Remember—God wants to go on vacation with you. Don't leave Him behind.

Read from God's Word

I lift up my eyes to the hills—where does my help come from? My help comes from the LORD, the Maker of heaven and earth. He will not let your foot slip—He who watches over you will not slumber; indeed, He who watches over Israel will neither slumber nor sleep. The LORD watches over you—the LORD is your shade at your right hand; the sun will not harm you by day, nor the moon by night. The LORD will keep you from all harm—He will watch over your life; the LORD will watch over your coming and going both now and forevermore. Psalm 121

_____Let's talk: What specific things will you do to help you stay close to God this summer?

_____Let's pray: Dear Jesus, please forgive me when I try to put You aside. Thank You for never taking a vacation from me. Help me never take a vacation from You. In Jesus' name. Amen.

M. W.

Read from God's Word

Be joyful always; pray continually; give thanks in all circumstances, for this is God's will for you in Christ Jesus. 1 Thessalonians 5:16–18

Can We TALK?

You probably hear a lot about the importance of prayer. Have you ever wondered how you are supposed to pray? Don't worry, even the disciples asked Jesus to teach them to pray. That's when Jesus taught them the Lord's Prayer.

The truth is that God isn't picky about how we pray. It is helpful, though, to have a guideline to follow. It can help you stay focused during your prayers.

There are many prayer guidelines you can follow. Here's one:

When you pray, just T-A-L-K to God.

T— Thanksgiving. Give thanks and praise to God for His greatness and for all of the ways He blesses you and takes care of you.

A— Ask for forgiveness. Confess your sins to the Lord and ask for His help in resisting temptation.

L— Lift. Lift up your requests to God and allow Him to lift the burden of worry from you.

K— Know. Know that the Lord hears your prayers and will answer in His time and in His way.

Whether you use this guideline, another one, or simply pray in your own way, the important thing is that you do pray. Prayer is one of our main ways of communicating with God. It is a privilege we can use daily.

_____Let's talk: Do you have a special time set aside each day for prayer? What things do you need to pray about right now?

_____Let's pray: Thank You, Lord, for the privilege of prayer. Forgive me when I don't use it the way You want me to. Help me remember to talk with You daily. In Jesus' name. Amen.

M. W.

june

Contributors for this month:

Julieanne Thompson

Robin J. Williams

Pat List

Julie Stiegemeyer

Read from God's Word

Therefore God exalted Him to the highest place and gave Him the name that is above every name, that at the name of Jesus every knee should bow, in heaven and on earth and under the earth, and every tongue confess that Jesus Christ is Lord, to the glory of God the Father. Philippians 2:9–11

To Know Him by Name

What would it be like if no one had names? This might be interesting for a while, especially when a teacher called on a student who didn't want to answer. But it would be difficult to tell when someone was talking to you.

Names are special. Our name separates us from everyone else. It is personal; it gives us identity. When people hear our name, they think of us—what we look like, how we act, what we say and do, who we are. Jesus knows you by your name.

The Bible says that God gave Jesus a name that is greater than any other name. The Bible is full of the names of God. One book lists over 365 names for Jesus alone! Just as our name reminds others of who we are, Jesus' names remind us of Him.

For example, Jesus is our Savior (one who saves). Just as a lifeguard rescues someone from drowning, Jesus has rescued and saved us by dying on the cross in our place. There are many people in our world who need to be saved. We have the good news of a rescuer, our Savior, to share with them.

Jesus' names, such as Savior, can remind us how much God has already done, as well as how much He can do.

_____Let's do: Ask your parents to show you what your name means in a Christian name book.

_____Let's pray: Dear Jesus, I'm so glad You know me by name! I am special in Your eyes and You love me. Thank You for being my Savior, my rescuer from sin. I know that when I call You by name, You hear me. Amen.

J. T.

Jesus, Our Example

Julie and Susie were in Russia to tell people there about Jesus.

One day, they visited an outdoor market where they saw a cart of oranges. They each bought a bagful.

Julie thought of the treasure she had found. At home in California she often ate oranges. But in Russia this fruit was scarce.

As they walked home, Susie kept stopping to share her oranges. Finally she sat next to a tired-looking woman. Susie offered her last orange then gave the woman a Bible. The woman hugged Susie.

Julie stared at Susie's face. She had given away all her oranges but she was radiant!

Julie felt empty inside. She had thought only of herself. Then she saw the joy that comes from a generous heart. She asked God to forgive her. And the next week, she shared oranges as she told people how God freely gave the best gift—Jesus!

Read from God's Word

To this you were called, because Christ suffered for you, leaving you an example, that you should follow in His steps. ... He himself bore our sins in His body on the tree, so that we might die to sins and live for righteousness; by His wounds you have been healed. 1 Peter 2:21, 24

God is the perfect example of selflessness and generous love. He loved us so much He sent His only Son to die for us. Jesus' resurrection proves that He has power over sin. He knows we fail sometimes, but He forgives us and helps us do what is right.

_____Let's do: Surprise someone with a special treat. How did they respond? How did it make you feel?

_____Let's pray: Thank You for being my best example in everything, dear Jesus. Please rule in my heart and life that I may point others to You by what I say and do. Thank You for Your generous love and mercy toward me and for Your forgiveness when I forget You and focus on myself. Amen.

J. T.

Read from God's Word

Jesus Christ is the same yesterday and today and forever. Hebrews 13:8

Immune to Change

"Do we have to move?" Ben was sad to think of moving away. He had great friends, and his soccer team had done so well this year! "Why do things have to change?" Ben wanted to know.

What changes have happened in your life? Has someone you loved died or left you? Have you moved to a new home, new school, new city, or another church? It seems that as soon as life is "just right," things around us change. It is normal to want the good things in our life to stay the same.

Everyone deals with change in different ways. How do you deal with change?

In the middle of millions of changes happening every day, there is One we can depend on never to change! "I the Lord do not change," God says in Malachi 3:6.

Our Scripture reading for today tells us that Jesus is the always the same. All the promises we find in the Bible that were true yesterday are true today and will be true forever. Jesus always keeps His promises, never leaves us, always loves us, forgives us, and helps us live in a way that pleases and brings honor to Him.

Change does not change Him—our God is immune to change!

_____Let's do: Read Romans 8:28. On a blank piece of paper or in a journal, write at least five reasons why God might let change happen in order to benefit your life.

_____Let's pray: Thank You for bringing change into my life, Lord Jesus. It reminds me that You are changeless. Help me see how change can help me. In Jesus' name I pray. Amen.

J. T.

Jesus—The Real Treasure

Read from God's Word

I became a servant of this gospel by the gift of God's grace given me through the working of His power. Although I am less than the least of all God's people, this grace was given me: to preach to the Gentiles the unsearchable riches of Christ. ... His intent was that now, through the church, the manifold wisdom of God should be made known to the rulers and authorities in the heavenly realms, according to His eternal purpose which He accomplished in Christ Jesus our Lord. In Him and through faith in Him we may approach God with freedom and confidence. I ask you, therefore, not to be discouraged because of my sufferings for you, which are your glory. Ephesians 3:7–12

Have you ever asked your mom or dad to buy a box of cereal because of something (other than cereal) inside the box?

When I was young I went shopping with my mom one day. I noticed a box of cereal that had three toy cars inside. I pleaded with her to buy it. As I sat eating my first bowl, I saw on the back of the box a picture of three real cars. As I read, I learned that if I would mail in a form, I might win the "real thing"!

After I mailed my entry, I began to think a lot about what the car would look like, where I would keep it, and who would drive it. I waited months for the news that I had won a car. I never heard. All my grand plans of winning the "treasure" disintegrated.

The Bible refers to Jesus as our "treasure." Have you ever thought of Jesus this way? What are His death, resurrection, love, and salvation worth to you? Psalm 19 refers to God's Word as a treasure to be sought after more than gold. It points to the greatest Treasure—Jesus Himself—in whom we have salvation from sin, death, and the devil.

_____Let's talk: What is the most important treasure you have? Would you ever give it away? How can you share the treasure of God's love for you with others?

_____Let's pray: Dear Jesus, You are of greater value than any earthly thing. You are my most valuable possession. Help me see through the treasures valued by the world and seek first Your kingdom and Your righteousness. Amen.

J. T.

Read from God's Word

For You created my inmost being; You knit me together in my mother's womb. I praise You because I am fearfully and wonderfully made; Your works are wonderful, I know that full well. My frame was not hidden from You when I was made in the secret place. When I was woven together in the depths of the earth, Your eyes saw my unformed body. All the days ordained for me were written in Your book before one of them came to be. How precious to me are Your thoughts, O God! How vast is the sum of them! Were I to count them, they would outnumber the grains of sand. When I awake, I am still with You. Psalm 139:13–18

In the Creator's Image

A little girl stood in front of a mirror, looking into her brown eyes. She shut her eyes and prayed in faith that God would please, please, please make her eyes blue. She opened her eyes, and to her amazement they were still brown! She could not understand why God did not answer her prayer.

That little girl, Amy Carmichael, grew up to reach many people for Christ as a missionary in India. Amy later said that if God had answered her prayer and given her blue eyes, she would not have been as well accepted into the culture of India (where usually all but the eyes are covered). God's original design had been best, although Amy did not realize it at the time.

As God's children, we recognize that we are created in the image of a holy God. We thank Him for making us just the way He did.

Accepting the way God made our physical features is acknowledging Him as our perfect Creator, who lovingly knows best in every area of our lives. Just as He designed a perfect way of salvation and forgiveness of our sins through Jesus' death and resurrection, we can know without doubt that He did not make a mistake as He formed us in our mother's womb. We are His workmanship!

_____Let's do: Look at your reflection in a mirror. Who do you look like? your mom? your dad? your brother or sister? Smile at yourself and know that God made you as His special creation.

_____Let's pray: Dear Lord Jesus, thank You for the way You made me. Please help me see my features as Your marks of ownership and part of Your plan for my life. Use them in my life to prepare me to further Your kingdom. In Jesus' name I pray. Amen.

J. T.

Obedience

One of my earliest and most painful lessons came when I decided to look at the family pictures on the top of the piano.

My parents had told me that the piano was "off-limits." However, when they were out of the room, my curiosity got the better of me. I climbed on the bench and leaned over. I got a good look at a wedding picture just before I fell. As I fell, I knocked my shins against the keyboard and my mouth hit the top of the piano. There was a terrible racket and I began to cry.

The consequences of my disobedience were immediate and painful—my teeth had chipped. But I'll always remember the love and tenderness of my parents as they rushed in to scoop me up in their arms.

Although Jesus didn't disobey like I did, He learned obedience to the will of God. Being perfect, as God, He is the source of salvation for all who obey and put their trust and faith in Him.

Read from God's Word

During the days of Jesus' life on earth, He offered up prayers and petitions with loud cries and tears to the One who could save Him from death, and He was heard because of His reverent submission. Although He was a son, He learned obedience from what He suffered and, once made perfect, He became the source of eternal salvation for all who obey Him. Hebrews 5:7–9

I have learned that, as a child of God, His grace and forgiveness cover all my sins. However, it still is best to obey the Lord and honor my parents. These are privileges I will never outgrow!

_____Let's talk: Have you ever gotten hurt doing something you weren't supposed to be doing? How did your parents respond? What did you learn from your injury?

_____Let's pray: Lord Jesus, You were perfect yet You learned obedience through suffering. Thank You for being obedient unto death—even death on the cross! Thank You for doing the will of Your Father in heaven for my sake. Your obedience makes it possible for me to have eternal life. Amen.

J. T.

Read from God's Word

"Then you will know the truth, and the truth will set you free." John 8:32

Jesus answered, "I am the way and the truth and the life. No one comes to the Father except through Me." John 14:6

Truth Untangles

The driver of a car accidentally hit a man riding a bike. The bicyclist was badly hurt, but the driver of the car didn't stop. As the driver tried to ignore the guilt he felt in his heart, he became tangled in a web of lies.

Years ago, when he was a boy, this same man's father had a special gold watch. One day, as a boy, this man accidentally broke it but he denied ever having touched it.

This lie led to telling more lies to cover up what he had done. Pretty soon he was in the habit of lying. In fact, he lied so much that he often convinced himself that a lie was actually the truth.

Jesus is called the Truth. The opposite of truth is lying. Did you know that Satan is called the "father of lies"?

If we have told a lie, the Lord will forgive us and help us to tell the truth. Just as lying creates a web of deceit, confessing and telling the truth untangles that web. Eventually, the man confessed that he hit the bicyclist. Although there were severe consequences, he was free on the inside.

Because Jesus is Truth, those who love Him love truth. God is so good to us!

_____Let's talk: What does freedom mean to you? What does it mean to be free in Christ?

_____Let's pray: Thank You, Lord, that You are Truth. Thank You for dying on Calvary for my sins so I might be free from the power of sin and lying. Help me in all I say and do. Please forgive the lies I have told and help me ask forgiveness of those I have lied to. In Jesus' name I pray. Amen.

J. T.

The Battle and the War!

Wars and battles have been fought over many things, such as land, people, wealth, and power. In a battle it is important to have the right weapons, know the enemy's weak points, and have a battle plan.

Did you know that the Bible refers to life as a battle? If we are in a battle, who is our enemy? Today's Bible reading tells us that the enemy of every Christian is Satan. Satan wants to keep us from trusting Jesus. His goal is to distract us and keep us busy so we don't have time for Jesus.

As God's baptized and redeemed children, we have a special armor to wear in the battle of life. The armor God gives us is truth, righteousness, readiness to tell the Gospel, faith, salvation, the Word of God, and prayer.

In this battle, the good news is that the war has already been won—Jesus has won the war! Jesus overcame death, and through His resurrection we have the assurance that our faith is in a living God. Even the name of Jesus scares the enemy (Satan) because he knows his time is limited on earth.

As God's children, we can joyfully tell others about the battle and how they can be on the winning side—Jesus' side!

Read from God's Word

Therefore put on the full armor of God, so that when the day of evil comes, you may be able to stand your ground, and after you have done everything, to stand. Stand firm then, with the belt of truth buckled around your waist, with the breastplate of righteousness in place, and with your feet fitted with the readiness that comes from the gospel of peace. In addition to all this, take up the shield of faith, with which you can extinguish all the flaming arrows of the evil one. Take the helmet of salvation and the sword of the Spirit, which is the word of God. And pray in the Spirit on all occasions with all kinds of prayers and requests. With this in mind, be alert and always keep on praying for all the saints. Ephesians 6:13–18

_____Let's talk: What are some of the devil's tricks? How does God help us watch out for the devil and his evil ways?

_____Let's pray: Dearest Father in heaven, thank You for sending Your Son, Jesus, to earth to die for my sin. Thank You for the forgiveness I have in His name. Thank You for loving me so much that You provided a way for me to know You—through Jesus. Amen.

J. T.

Read from God's Word

"You have heard that it was said, 'Love your neighbor and hate your enemy.' But I tell you: Love your enemies and pray for those who persecute you, that you may be sons of your Father in heaven. He causes His sun to rise on the evil and the good, and sends rain on the righteous and the unrighteous. If you love those who love you, what reward will you get? Are not even the tax collectors doing that? And if you greet only your brothers, what are you doing more than others? Do not even pagans do that? Be perfect, therefore, as your heavenly Father is perfect." Matthew 5:43–48

Liking and Loving

What's the difference between liking and loving someone?

For now, let's say liking is feeling close to a person or having a friend. Loving a person is being polite and friendly, as in "brotherly love." It is treating others with kindness, even those who are not our friends.

Jesus said, "Love your enemies." Love people who are rude or mean? That's what Jesus tells us to do. It isn't easy, but God wants us to love people who do not love us. We don't have to like everyone, but He wants us to love them.

It's okay to be closer to some people than to others. Jesus was closer to Peter, James, and John than to the other disciples. But Jesus loved all His disciples, even Judas.

Being kind to our friends is easy. Even people who do not believe in God love their friends. But we are to love all people, just as God does. In this way we show that we are His children. Others will see us being kind to all people. Then they will know that God's love is in us.

_____Let's talk: What is hard about being kind to other people? Why are we to love others? How did Jesus demonstrate His love for you?

_____Let's pray: Dear Lord, help us show Your love by being kind to others. Give us the strength we need when loving others is hard to do. We ask this through Jesus, who loved us all the way to His death on Calvary. Amen.

R. J. W.

Where's Your Trust?

Read from God's Word

The LORD is my strength and my shield; my heart trusts in Him, and I am helped. My heart leaps for joy and I will give thanks to Him in song. The LORD is the strength of His people, a fortress of salvation for His anointed one. Save your people and bless your inheritance; be their shepherd and carry them forever. Psalm 28:7–9

The Cannden family enjoyed their vacation at the lake, swimming and splashing in the water. One day they decided to make toy boats and let them drift on the lake.

Nick used a plastic container. Jake used a small cardboard box. At first both boats floated, but soon, Jake's boat sank.

"Why didn't my boat float?" Jake asked.

"Because you made it out of something that didn't last," said Nick.

Some people put their trust in things that don't last. Some feel that with enough money, they'll have everything they need. Others feel that their friends will always stand by them and never let them down.

Sometimes people trust only themselves. When they are in control, they think, nothing can go wrong.

Earthly things can break or fall apart. Friends may not be able to help us. Even we ourselves may not be able to control everything.

What can we always depend on? The answer is God. We know He will never let us down. We know He is always with us and cares for us. Most important, we know God took care of our salvation. Because He sent Jesus as our Savior, we'll live with Him in heaven. We can trust God above everyone and everything!

_____Let's do: Put a small plastic container or a small box by your bed. Every day, when you get up and when you go to bed, remember that you can always depend on God's grace and mercy.

_____Let's pray: Dear Lord, help me trust in You above everything else. Thank You for promising to never let me down. Forgive me for those times when I fail to trust in You completely. Amen.

P. L.

Read from God's Word

Let the word of Christ dwell in you richly as you teach and admonish one another with all wisdom, and as you sing psalms, hymns and spiritual songs with gratitude in your hearts to God. And whatever you do, whether in word or deed, do it all in the name of the Lord Jesus, giving thanks to God the Father through Him. Colossians 3:16–17

Which Is More Valuable?

Alaina could hardly wait to open her birthday gift from Aunt Dorothy.

As the last of the wrappings fell to the floor, Alaina fought to hide her disappointment. "It's a Bible," said Alaina.

"You can read a chapter or two each day," suggested Mom.

Weeks went by before Alaina opened her new Bible. Imagine her surprise when she discovered an envelope inside it. The envelope held $10 and a note from Aunt Dorothy.

"Dear Alaina," the note said, "I hope you enjoy your two gifts. Let me know which you think is more valuable."

Alaina thought about the gifts. It would be fun to buy something with the money. And to think, she had almost missed it!

But Alaina almost missed a much more important gift. The Bible contains wonderful messages from God especially for us. It tells about God's work of creation. It tells how Jesus rescued us by His death and resurrection. It tells how the Holy Spirit puts faith in our hearts and makes that faith grow stronger.

The next day Alaina wrote a letter. "Dear Aunt Dorothy, Thank you for the wonderful gifts. I spent my money on a game and I've started reading my Bible every day. You asked me to tell you which gift is more valuable. Here's what I think: __________."

_____Let's talk: Why wasn't Alaina excited about Aunt Dorothy's gift at first? What can be exciting about the Bible? How do you think Alaina finished her letter?

_____Let's pray: Dear God, thank You for the Bible. Help me understand how wonderful it is. Help me realize that Your words are for me and that they will lead me closer to Jesus, my Savior. Amen.

P. L.

Hearing but Not Listening

Read from God's Word

"Announce this to the house of Jacob and proclaim it in Judah: Hear this, you foolish and senseless people, who have eyes but do not see, who have ears but do not hear: Should you not fear Me?" declares the LORD. "Should you not tremble in My presence? I made the sand a boundary for the sea, an everlasting barrier it cannot cross. The waves may roll, but they cannot prevail; they may roar, but they cannot cross it. But these people have stubborn and rebellious hearts; they have turned aside and gone away." Jeremiah 5:20–23

As Isabella left for school, her mom reminded her to wear a jacket. But Isabella said she was warm enough. When they went outside for recess, she was cold.

At lunch the cafeteria was serving pizza, Isabella's favorite. But she had not listened when the teacher announced it the day before and she brought her lunch from home.

Isabella hadn't listened when the teacher had announced a geography quiz either, so she didn't study.

Isabella had heard the warnings but she didn't listen.

Sometimes people ignore messages. Their hearing is fine but they don't pay attention.

The prophet Jeremiah announced the same thing to people in Bible days. These people knew what God wanted them to do, but they didn't follow His directions. They ignored Him. When God punished them, they grumbled, "Why didn't God tell us?" The truth is, He did.

We have pastors, teachers, and parents to tell us what God desires for us. We have Sunday school lessons and devotions. Most important, we have the Bible, where we can read God's message.

All these people and things can give us the exciting news of God's love. They are there to tell us that Jesus suffered and died for us. Let's pray that the Holy Spirit will give us power to listen!

_____Let's talk: How does God talk to you today?
Who can you tell about your faith in Jesus?

_____Let's pray: Lord God, I'm sorry that I don't always pay attention to You and Your Word.
Help me do better. In Jesus' name I pray. Amen.

P. L.

Read from God's Word

Blessed is the man who finds wisdom, the man who gains understanding, for she is more profitable than silver and yields better returns than gold. She is more precious than rubies; nothing you desire can compare with her. Long life is in her right hand; in her left hand are riches and honor. Her ways are pleasant ways, and all her paths are peace. She is a tree of life to those who embrace her; those who lay hold of her will be blessed. By wisdom the LORD laid the earth's foundations, by understanding He set the heavens in place; by His knowledge the deeps were divided, and the clouds let drop the dew. Proverbs 3:13–20

Is Graduation the End?

The Lewis family was invited to three graduation parties. Cousin Jim was graduating from grade school, their friend Marla was finishing high school, and Uncle Tony was getting his degree from college.

"Boy, they're lucky to be graduating," said Moyna. "Now they won't have to study and learn things!"

Dad laughed. "Not really. Jim will be learning in high school, Marla will continue to learn in college, and Uncle Tony will learn a lot in his new job."

"We never stop learning, honey," Mom said. "God gave us powerful brains to use to the best of our ability. He wants us to grow mentally, physically, and spiritually."

"What does that mean?" Moyna asked.

"Think of all the things God put in this world. Do you know everything about all of them?" replied Mom.

"I know more than I did last year, but I don't know everything," laughed Moyna.

"And when we read the Bible, go to church and Sunday school, and have devotions," Mom answered, "we learn what God wants us to do and not do. We learn that He loves us and sent Jesus to die for us and take us to heaven. That's what growing spiritually means."

"So graduation isn't the end, especially when it comes to learning about God's love," added Moyna.

____Let's do: Look up the word "graduate" in a dictionary. What does it mean?

____Let's pray: Heavenly Father, we are thankful that You have given us the ability to learn. We know there are many things You want us to know, especially about Your love in Jesus. Help us gladly take time to learn more about You. In Jesus' name. Amen.

P. L.

New City, Same God

Patrick and his family were moving to a new city. When the moving the van drove away, his mom said "everything we own is in that truck." It was a scary thought. What if something happened to the truck?

Even scarier was the thought that they knew no one in the new city. Their house would be new to them. The streets would be unfamiliar. There would be a new school.

There was one thing that would be the same, though. God would be the same! He would love them and take care of them just as He always had. And of course they could still pray to Him anytime and anywhere. Knowing that God was with them made all the difference!

Patrick soon made new friends. His parents learned which streets to take. Patrick visited his new school. They prayed to God in their new house just as they had in the old one. And they found a new church where they worshiped and praised God.

Perhaps you are moving to a new home. Remember that God is always with you. He never changes and His love for you never changes. He always has mercy on you because of Jesus. In Him you are secure.

Read from God's Word

The LORD had said to Abram, "Leave your country, your people and your father's household and go to the land I will show you. I will make you into a great nation and I will bless you; ... So Abram left, as the LORD had told him; and Lot went with him. Abram was seventy-five years old when he set out from Haran. He took his wife Sarai, his nephew Lot, all the possessions they had accumulated and the people they had acquired in Haran, and they set out for the land of Canaan, and they arrived there. ... The LORD appeared to Abram and said, "To your offspring I will give this land." So he built an altar there to the LORD, who had appeared to him. From there he went on toward the hills east of Bethel and pitched his tent, with Bethel on the west and Ai on the east. There he built an altar to the LORD and called on the name of the LORD. Genesis 12:1–8

_____Let's talk: What are some things that can be scary about moving? How can a new home be different? How can it be the same? What never changes about God?

_____Let's pray: Unchanging God, we thank and praise You for remaining the same, even when things all around us are changing. Stay close to us and guide and direct us when we're scared. Thank You for loving us. In Jesus' name we pray. Amen.

P. L.

Read from God's Word

Then Jesus declared, "I am the bread of life. He who comes to Me will never go hungry, and he who believes in Me will never be thirsty. But as I told you, you have seen Me and still you do not believe. All that the Father gives Me will come to Me, and whoever comes to Me I will never drive away. For I have come down from heaven not to do My will but to do the will of Him who sent Me. And this is the will of Him who sent Me, that I shall lose none of all that He has given Me, but raise them up at the last day. For My Father's will is that everyone who looks to the Son and believes in Him shall have eternal life, and I will raise him up at the last day." John 6:35–40

The Food of Life

As Alex and her dad finished hanging their new bird feeder she asked, "What happens if the birds don't come to our feeder?"

"Just wait," Dad said. "They will."

Dad was right. By the end of the week, the birds had discovered the feeder. Soon they had to fill it almost every day.

"What would happen if we didn't put any more seeds into the feeder?" asked Alex.

"The birds depend on us for their food," Dad replied. "If we didn't give them food, they might die."

We depend on God to feed us. It's true that He provides us with vegetables, meat, and other food. But God also gives us spiritual food. In our Bible reading Jesus said, "I am the bread of life. He who comes to Me will never go hungry, and he who believes in Me will never be thirsty."

Some people thought Jesus was talking about earthly food. But He was talking about heavenly life. He wants us to live with Him forever, and He provides the only way to get there.

When the end of the world comes, the people who have believed that Jesus died for their sins and rose again will go to live in heaven with Him. What a wonderful, exciting day that will be!

_____Let's talk: Why do we need the food of life that God gives us? What would happen if someone didn't eat the heavenly food that God offers?

_____Let's pray: Dear Jesus, You are truly the bread of life. You came to earth to suffer and die for us so we can live with You forever. Help us share this Good News with everyone we know, so they can also enjoy heaven with You. In Your name we pray. Amen.

P. L.

Are You Successful?

The fourth graders at St. John's were given the following assignment: Tell what being successful means. Here are some of their answers:

Timmy said, "Being successful means having enough money to buy anything you want."

Janelle wrote, "Being successful means having a job where I can help people."

Quianna answered, "Being successful means being good at whatever I do."

Different people have different ideas of what success means. For some it means being famous or rich. For others it means helping people. And still others think being successful means doing a good job all the time.

Do you think Jesus was successful? He didn't have a big house—He didn't even own a house. He didn't have lots of money—money wasn't important to Him. Jesus traveled from place to place teaching, healing, and preaching about God's love. Many people listened to Jesus but others rejected Him. Does that mean He wasn't successful?

Success for Jesus meant coming to earth to suffer and die for us and then to rise from the dead. When we think about it that way, Jesus was certainly successful.

When we are baptized, the Holy Spirit puts faith into our hearts so we can believe in Jesus as our Savior. And that's what success for Christians is all about!

Read from God's Word

Jesus replied, "The hour has come for the Son of Man to be glorified. I tell you the truth, unless a kernel of wheat falls to the ground and dies, it remains only a single seed. But if it dies, it produces many seeds. The man who loves his life will lose it, while the man who hates his life in this world will keep it for eternal life. Whoever serves Me must follow Me; and where I am, My servant also will be. My Father will honor the one who serves Me. Now my heart is troubled, and what shall I say? 'Father, save Me from this hour'? No, it was for this very reason I came to this hour. Father, glorify Your name!" John 12:23–28

_____Let's talk: How would you define success? Are you successful? How does success differ for Christians and non-Christians?

_____Let's pray: Holy Spirit, thank You for making me a Christian. Work in me so all my thoughts, words, and deeds show my love for You. Amen.

P. L.

Read from God's Word

Surely He took up our infirmities and carried our sorrows, yet we considered Him stricken by God, smitten by Him, and afflicted. But He was pierced for our transgressions, He was crushed for our iniquities; the punishment that brought us peace was upon Him, and by His wounds we are healed. We all, like sheep, have gone astray, each of us has turned to his own way; and the LORD has laid on Him the iniquity of us all. Isaiah 53:4–6

The Best Doctor

Dr. Byrum's office. How may I help you?" said the voice on the other end of the phone.

"I'd like to make an appointment to see the doctor," Mrs. Lu replied.

"Can you come at 10 o'clock tomorrow?" the receptionist said.

The next day, the doctor checked Mrs. Lu's temperature and looked in her ears and throat. He said she had an infection and gave her a prescription for medicine to help her get well. As she drove home, Mrs. Lu thought, *it is very comforting to have a good doctor.*

Christians have an even better doctor. That doctor is God. God cured the world of the most awful disease—the disease of sin. He didn't cure sin by giving medicine. No one had to get a shot to be cured of sin.

God looked at the sinful world and knew how to take care of everything. God sent Jesus to take the punishment for our sins and to die in our place.

Now when God looks at us, He sees His perfect children. He sees persons who no longer have the sin they were born with or the sins they have done. He sees persons who have been washed clean by Jesus' blood. He sees children of God who are healed!

_____Let's do: Think about the last time you went to the doctor to get medicine or shots. We go to doctors to help us stay healthy and strong. We go to church and Sunday school to learn more about the best doctor ever—God—to help us stay strong in our faith in Him.

_____Let's pray: Dear God, You are the best doctor in the world. You took care of our disease of sin by sending Your Son, Jesus. He took the punishment for us, and now we are healed. Thank You for making us perfect in Your sight. Amen.

P. L.

The Most Important Thing

What is most important in the following situations:

Situation 1: A person has car trouble and is stranded in a desert. Which is the most important: A closet full of expensive clothes. Diamonds. A good mechanic.

Situation 2: A person is in the middle of a lake and can't get her boat started. Which is the most important thing: $1,000. Her favorite CD. Oars for rowing to shore.

Situation 3: A person is standing before God at the end of time. Which is most important? Video games. A big house. Faith in Jesus as Savior.

In our Bible reading, Mary listened to Jesus. Martha cooked and cleaned. When Martha complained that Mary wasn't doing any work, Jesus taught the sisters and His disciples what is really important. He said that Mary had chosen the most important thing. She was being strengthened in her relationship with Jesus, who came to seek and save all people.

How about us? Have we received from God the most important thing? Or are we missing it because we're busy with sports, school, and computer games?

At the end of the world, there is only one important thing—faith in Jesus Christ as our Savior. With that faith in our hearts, we will go to heaven and live with God forever.

Read from God's Word

As Jesus and His disciples were on their way, He came to a village where a woman named Martha opened her home to Him. She had a sister called Mary, who sat at the Lord's feet listening to what He said. But Martha was distracted by all the preparations that had to be made. She came to Him and asked, "Lord, don't you care that my sister has left me to do the work by myself? Tell her to help me!" "Martha, Martha," the Lord answered, "you are worried and upset about many things, but only one thing is needed. Mary has chosen what is better, and it will not be taken away from her." Luke 10:38–42

_____Let's do: Do you spend time with Jesus every day? Remember to start and end your day by talking to Him in prayer. And take time to read God's Word too!

_____Let's pray: Dear Jesus, our lives are very busy. Sometimes we don't take time to be with You. Forgive us for those times. Give us Your Holy Spirit so no matter how busy we are, we can make time for You in our lives. Help us want to know You as our Savior and Friend. In Your name we pray. Amen.

P. L.

Read from God's Word

"But a time is coming, and has come, when you will be scattered, each to his own home. You will leave Me all alone. Yet I am not alone, for My Father is with Me. I have told you these things, so that in Me you may have peace. In this world you will have trouble. But take heart! I have overcome the world." John 16:32–33

Powers for POWs

When countries are at war, soldiers may be held captive. They are called prisoners of war, or POWs.

POWs cannot write to their families. The food isn't good. When they are finally released, some POWs tell stories that make us uncomfortable.

But sometimes a former POW will tell a different kind of story. One man was allowed to have one book in his prison cell. He chose a Bible. During the time he was a prisoner, he read the Bible over and over. He read how God created the world, how God sent Jesus to be our Savior, and how God is with us all the time. God's Word gave him comfort and hope.

No other book could have given him the peace that the Bible did. It points people to Jesus, who said, "In Me you may have peace. In this world you will have trouble. But take heart! I have overcome the world."

Most of us probably have many books at our house. Can any other book be as helpful or as valuable as our Bible? Can any other book give us the peace that the Bible does? As we read and study it, let's remember to thank God for giving us such a wonderful book, filled with His great messages and written especially for us.

_____Let's talk: What is your favorite book? If you could have only one book, what would you choose? Do you have your very own Bible?

_____Let's pray: Lord, there are many people in the world who need You today. Be with the prisoners of war who may be held in countries far away. Help them remember that You love and care for them. Remind them that You haven't forgotten them. If it is Your will, bring them home safely. In Jesus' name we pray. Amen.

P. L.

Is My Sin Too Big?

Read from God's Word

Praise the LORD, O my soul; all my inmost being, praise His holy name. Praise the LORD, O my soul, and forget not all His benefits—who forgives all your sins and heals all your diseases, who redeems your life from the pit and crowns you with love and compassion, who satisfies your desires with good things so that your youth is renewed like the eagle's. Psalm 103:1–5

Tina was 16 years old and unmarried when she found out she was pregnant. Tim cheated on his math test and was suspended from school for a week. Billy was caught running from a convenience store with stolen candy in his pocket.

Like these people, we fall into temptation, and we sin against God. Sometimes we wonder, "Is my sin too big for God to forgive?"

Close to the time of Jesus' crucifixion, two of His disciples committed serious sins. Judas betrayed Jesus by handing Him over to His enemies. Peter denied that he knew Jesus, thus failing to stand up for his Lord. Satan attempted to destroy both disciples' faith as they wrestled with their sins. Each one responded differently.

Judas allowed himself to be convinced that Jesus could never forgive him. So he despaired and took his own life. Peter remembered that no matter how bad his sin was, Jesus would have mercy on a repentant heart. Jesus forgave Peter and restored him to the group of disciples, even making him their leader.

We sing in church, "Lamb of God, who takes away the sin of the world, have mercy on us." The Lamb of God, who took away all sins through His death and resurrection, wipes out even the "big" sins of our repentant hearts.

_____Let's talk: Have you ever felt that you could not be forgiven? What happened? How can you be sure that God will always forgive you?

_____Let's pray: Dear Jesus, I need Your love and forgiveness every day. Help me be sorry for my sins and remember that You can forgive any sin. Amen.

J. S.

Awake at Night

Chrissy couldn't sleep. She was worried about what had happened that afternoon. Her mom and dad told her they weren't going to live together anymore. Chrissy couldn't stop thinking about all the things that were happening to her.

Sometimes our worries keep us up at night. What do you worry about? Maybe you worry about something someone said or someone who is sick. Perhaps you worry about a big test at school.

Worrying is easy to do, especially at night when we can hear nothing but our thoughts. Worry is caused by a lack of trust in God and is a result of sin.

The future belongs to God; He'll take care of it. When you can't stop worrying, remember that God loves you. Think about a Scripture verse you have memorized or read your Bible. Write your concern on a piece of paper. Pray about your worry. And finally, trust that it is in God's hands.

Chrissy's troubles would not end right away by praying, but she knew God loved her family and would be with them. "Cast all your anxiety on Him because He cares for you" (1 Peter 5:7). Your life is safe in God's love and mercy. He will always take care of you.

_____Let's talk: Read Psalms 42; 62; and 91. Are there other verses in the Bible that can help you leave your worries in God's hands?

_____Let's pray: You are powerful and loving, Lord, and I know You are strong enough to take care of me, even in bad situations. Please help me with ________________ (fill in a situation you're worried about). Thank You for Your love. Amen.

J. S.

Summer Vacation

What are you doing this summer? You might be involved in sports or vacation Bible school. Maybe your family will go on a vacation or you'll visit your grandparents. Have you included a service project in your schedule?

God gives us many good gifts. Best of all are forgiveness and salvation in Christ. When you think of God's kindness to you, how do you respond? The story of the widow's offering gives us a wonderful picture of a generous response to God's love. The poor woman in the story gives "all she had to live on" because God first gave to her.

In response to God's kindness to you, what could you give? Perhaps you could organize a group to pick up litter around your church property. Maybe your vacation Bible school could use your help with the preschool class. You could make and send cards to people in your congregation who can't get out much. You could volunteer to do something extra at home, like cooking a simple dinner for your family. There is a service project to fit everyone's talents.

Enjoy the time this summer with your friends and family and doing things you like to do, but also think about ways you can serve others. "We love because He first loved us" (1 John 4:19).

Read from God's Word

As He looked up, Jesus saw the rich putting their gifts into the temple treasury. He also saw a poor widow put in two very small copper coins. "I tell you the truth," He said, "this poor widow has put in more than all the others. All these people gave their gifts out of their wealth; but she out of her poverty put in all she had to live on." Luke 21:1–4

_____Let's talk: List some of your talents. How can you use these talents not only to enjoy yourself but also to help others?

_____Let's pray: Dearest Jesus, thank You for Your gifts of salvation and mercy. Thank You also for the talents and time You have given me. Please help me to find ways to use Your gifts to help others. Amen.

J. S.

Read from God's Word

At one time we too were foolish, disobedient, deceived and enslaved by all kinds of passions and pleasures. We lived in malice and envy, being hated and hating one another. But when the kindness and love of God our Savior appeared, He saved us, not because of righteous things we had done, but because of His mercy. He saved us through the washing of rebirth and renewal by the Holy Spirit, whom He poured out on us generously through Jesus Christ our Savior, so that, having been justified by His grace, we might become heirs having the hope of eternal life. This is a trustworthy saying. And I want you to stress these things, so that those who have trusted in God may be careful to devote themselves to doing what is good. These things are excellent and profitable for everyone. Titus 3:3–8

The Treasure Chest

Jeremy searched the playroom, under the couch, the back porch, and even inside the refrigerator. But his treasure chest was gone!

Jeremy cried himself to sleep that night. Shortly after he'd fallen asleep, his dad found the treasure chest behind the basement door. Dad set it on Jeremy's dresser and the next morning Jeremy had quite a surprise! He carefully looked at everything in the box, making sure nothing was missing. Jeremy promised himself he would never misplace it again.

You are treasured by God, though not like a treasure box. He treasures you with a sacrificial and forgiving love. "But when the kindness and love of God our Savior appeared, He saved us, not because of righteous things we had done, but because of His mercy." To understand this verse, we must first recognize that our sin separates us from God. Because God is good and righteous, He cannot "put up" with sin.

Yet God solved our problem with sin by showing us mercy. Jesus gave up His life to take away our sin. In Baptism, our sins are washed away and we receive God's forgiveness and mercy. God has lovingly taken away your sin and changed you into the most valuable treasure of all!

____Let's do: Ask your parents to tell you about your Baptism. Do you have items that remind you of that day, a candle or white cloth perhaps? Make a sign for your room that says "I am Baptized. I am God's child."

____Let's pray: When I am feeling unwanted, Lord, help me to remember that I am treasured by You. In Jesus' name. Amen.

J. S.

Is God Too Busy for Me?

Read from God's Word

In those days Hezekiah became ill and was at the point of death. The prophet Isaiah son of Amoz went to him and said, "This is what the LORD says: Put your house in order, because you are going to die; you will not recover." Hezekiah ... prayed to the LORD, "Remember, O LORD, how I have walked before You faithfully and with wholehearted devotion." ... And Hezekiah wept bitterly. Before Isaiah had left the middle court, the word of the LORD came to him: "Go back and tell Hezekiah, the leader of My people: ... 'I have heard your prayer and seen your tears; I will heal you. ... I will add fifteen years to your life. And I will deliver you and this city from the hand of the king of Assyria. I will defend this city for My sake and for the sake of My servant David.'" 2 Kings 20:1–6

Jason pulled on his father's shirt. His father was busy working on a project he had been trying to finish. "Daddy," Jason said, his voice becoming loud "look at my picture!"

"Jason, I'm busy right now," replied his father.

Jason quietly left the room.

Have you ever felt like Jason while waiting for someone's attention? As a Christian, you can trust in God's promised gifts. The most important gift of God is forgiveness in Jesus. Because of Christ's death on the cross, your sins are forgiven, canceled, erased. God also promises to hear us when we pray.

Hezekiah was near death. He did not know how God would answer his prayer, but he begged for God's help as he lay dying. God heard his prayer and granted Hezekiah restored health and 15 more years of life.

This is also how God cares for you. We don't know how God will answer our prayers. Sometimes the answer is yes, sometimes no, sometimes wait, but God always hears us and knows what is best for us. He always has time for us. God listens and answers prayer, and we trust that even when an answer is not what we want, He knows what's best for us.

_____Let's talk: Has God ever said "wait" or "no" in answer to one of your prayers? How did that make you feel? Tell about a time when God said "yes" to a prayer.

_____Let's pray: Father in heaven, thank You for Your promise to forgive my sins. Thank You also for hearing me when I pray. Please help me to trust You when I don't understand things that are happening around me. Amen.

J. S.

Read from God's Word

"You shall not misuse the name of the LORD your God, for the LORD will not hold anyone guiltless who misuses His name." Exodus 20:7

God's Name Is Special

Which is the correct way to use God's name?

"O my God, I seek Your kindness in the morning. In the evening, I am not disappointed because Your love is always with me."

"O my God! I can't believe she said that!"

We get used to hearing "O my God!" as an expression, but we don't think about the fact that it is God's name that is being misused.

The name of God is special. We are given the name of God in our Baptism. Like a child receives the family name at birth, so God's name identifies us when we are baptized into His family. We are "Christians."

We read in the *Small Catechism:* "God's name is kept holy when the Word of God is taught in its truth and purity, and we, as the children of God, also lead holy lives according to it. Help us to do this, dear Father in heaven!"

Our God through Jesus has shown us great kindness. Even when we do not honor God's name, we can be assured of forgiveness because of Jesus' death on the cross. Because we know Jesus loves us enough to give everything—even His own life—we, in turn, want to love and honor Him and His name.

_____Let's talk: How can you keep God's name holy today? What motivates you to do so?

_____Let's pray: Dear Lord, thank You for giving me Your name in Baptism. I pray that You would help my words reflect Your love and kindness. Amen.

J. S.

Wanting Too Much?

Jenny's birthday was tomorrow. She was excited about the party, cake, and big dinner, but all those presents—that's what she couldn't stop thinking about.

Do we really need everything we want or wish for? How often is your attitude similar to Jenny's?

Today's Bible reading reminds us: "Godliness with contentment is great gain." Contentment is being satisfied with what God has given us. This can apply to all areas of our lives, but in light of these verses, we are to be satisfied with what we have, with what God has given us.

This passage reminds us that the important thing is not what we have or don't have, but how much we want things.

Jesus said, "But seek first [God's] kingdom and His righteousness, and all these things will be given to you as well" (Matthew 6:33). Our God has given us riches in Jesus: love beyond understanding, faith, life, hope, forgiveness. We can count ourselves truly rich as our lives are shaped by Jesus, who gave up everything for us. He died on the cross to take away our sins of greed and discontent. He, who loves us beyond measure, has graciously given us all we need to support our bodies, lives, and all that we are.

Read from God's Word

But godliness with contentment is great gain. For we brought nothing into the world, and we can take nothing out of it. But if we have food and clothing, we will be content with that. People who want to get rich fall into temptation and a trap and into many foolish and harmful desires that plunge men into ruin and destruction. For the love of money is a root of all kinds of evil. ... But you, man of God, flee from all this, and pursue righteousness, godliness, faith, love, endurance and gentleness. Fight the good fight of the faith. Take hold of the eternal life to which you were called when you made your good confession in the presence of many witnesses.

1 Timothy 6:6–12

_____Let's do: Write the words of Matthew 6:33 on a piece of paper and put it where you will see it every day. Rejoice that you are God's own child.

_____Let's pray: Dear Jesus, thank You for giving up everything so I can be forgiven. Please help me trust You to provide everything I need and to be content with that. Amen.

J. S.

The Mind of Christ

Read from God's Word

Since, then, you have been raised with Christ, set your hearts on things above, where Christ is seated at the right hand of God. Set your minds on things above, not on earthly things. For you died, and your life is now hidden with Christ in God. When Christ, who is your life, appears, then you also will appear with Him in glory. Colossians 3:1–4

Have you heard someone say, "Evolution is a fact. Creation is a myth."

As Christians, we believe that when God's Word tells us that God created the world, it actually happened that way. Science may contradict that. But "by faith we understand that the universe was formed at God's command, so that what is seen was not made out of what was visible" (Hebrews 11:3).

We do not need to hide or be afraid that someone, a teacher perhaps, might believe differently than we do. We can learn about different understandings of the world and still believe that God's Word is true. While you should not disrespect your teacher, it may be possible to present your beliefs about how the world started to your classmates in some way.

Our faith and life in Jesus as our Savior shape how we think, speak, and live. Your faith is nurtured and strengthened in worship, Sunday school, and family or personal devotions. Hearing God's Word and understanding who we are as His people shapes us into the thinkers God wants us to be.

Are you giving yourself opportunities to learn about Jesus and His love for you? Is your faith in Jesus shaping how you think about the world? Let your mind dwell on the life-changing message of the overflowing love of God.

_____Let's talk: What is a theory? Why do you think people believe that evolution is truth and creation is just a story?

_____Let's pray: Thank You, Lord, for creating me and saving me. Please give me understanding and wisdom so Your Word may shape my thinking, speaking, and living. Amen.

J. S.

Bullies

Read from God's Word

Therefore, as God's chosen people, holy and dearly loved, clothe yourselves with compassion, kindness, humility, gentleness and patience. Bear with each other and forgive whatever grievances you may have against one another. Forgive as the Lord forgave you. And over all these virtues put on love, which binds them all together in perfect unity. Colossians 3:12–14

What is a bully? Someone who makes mean comments just to show she can? Someone who pushes other kids around? Do these descriptions sound like someone you know—perhaps even yourself at times?

God's Word tells us to "clothe yourselves with humility toward one another, because, 'God opposes the proud but gives grace to the humble'" (1 Peter 5:5). Jesus showed us what it means to be humble. It does not mean thinking you are worthless. That is not how God thinks of you or how you should think of yourself. Jesus showed us true humility by suffering and dying for our sins. He didn't have to do it—He chose to do it in obedience to His Father's will and out of love for us.

So what do you do about a bully? It's important that you do not respond to a bully in a threatening way because then you may get into trouble. Tell your parents or teacher, not to "tattle" but to make sure the situation doesn't get any worse.

Bullies—ourselves included—need the love of Jesus and forgiveness of sin. Pray that God would help you to show love through your words and actions and to respond in a loving but wise manner to those who try to bully you.

_____Let's talk: Can you think of a positive way to talk to someone who seems to have problems making friends?

_____Let's pray: Thank You, Jesus, for dying for me and the whole world. Please help me to show Your love to others in humility and kindness. Amen.

J. S.

Read from God's Word

"As the Father has loved Me, so have I loved you. Now remain in My love. ... I have told you this so that My joy may be in you and that your joy may be complete. My command is this: Love each other as I have loved you. Greater love has no one than this, that he lay down his life for his friends. You are My friends if you do what I command. I no longer call you servants, because a servant does not know his master's business. Instead, I have called you friends, for everything that I learned from My Father I have made known to you. You did not choose Me, but I chose you and appointed you to go and bear fruit—fruit that will last. Then the Father will give you whatever you ask in My name. This is My command: Love each other." John 15:9–17

Who Is Your Best Friend?

Tara found it difficult to make friends. She couldn't relate to the kids at school. She was alone at recess, at lunch, waiting for her bus.

Jesus understands what it is to be friendless. He suffered a terrible, lonely death. Why? By dying for our sins, Jesus re-created friendship between God and humankind. His death takes away our sin so we are no longer enemies of God but are His dearly loved friends.

Your best friend is Jesus. He loves you with an unconditional, sacrificial love. We are all sinners, and all of us have problems with our relationships at one time or another. Yet your best Friend, Jesus, will never let you down. He is always ready to help you, listen to you, rescue you, save you. If you are feeling lonely, remember that God is always your friend.

God created us to be in relationship with Him, but also with other people. If you have a hard time making friends, consider your attitudes or behavior. Sometimes you don't have friends because you are not a good friend to others.

Maybe there is someone on your soccer team or a neighbor that you've wanted to talk to, but haven't had the courage. Try to talk to that person. Your kindness to them might begin a wonderful friendship.

_____Let's talk: Who is your best Friend? How can God's kindness to you spill over onto your other friendships?

_____Let's pray: Dear Lord, thank You for being my best Friend. Thank You for making friendship with God possible because of Your death on the cross. Please help me reach out in kindness to others because of Your great love for me. Amen.

J. S.

Complaining

Read from God's Word

Do everything without complaining or arguing, so that you may become blameless and pure, children of God without fault in a crooked and depraved generation, in which you shine like stars in the universe. Philippians 2:14–15

I don't like pork chops! Why did you make pork chops, Mom?"

"I hate chores. Why do I have to do them?"

"Aw, Dad, I'm tired. Let me sleep."

Does this sound familiar?

A man named Daniel was a righteous and upright man who believed in God, did his job faithfully, and was highly favored by King Darius. But some of the other leaders were jealous of Daniel so they convinced King Darius to punish those who prayed to anyone but him.

Daniel was faithful in prayer. "Three times a day he got down on his knees and prayed, giving thanks to his God" (Daniel 6:10). Daniel was thrown into a lions' den because he didn't pray to the king, but God protected him and "shut the mouths of the lions" (Daniel 6:22).

Does this story shed new light on complaining? We have much to thank God for. He daily gives us everything we need—food, clothing, shelter, people to care for us. Luther wrote in the *Small Catechism,* "God certainly gives daily bread to everyone without our prayers, even to all evil people, but we pray in this petition that God would lead us to realize this and to receive our daily bread with thanksgiving." Thank God today for His many gifts to you!

_____Let's do: Try this: the next time you are tempted to complain, say a prayer instead. Thank God for the thing that you don't like or don't want to do and ask Him to let you see His goodness in everything.

_____Let's pray: Dear Father in heaven, You give all good gifts. Please make me truly thankful for all the kindness You show me. Amen.

J. S.

july

Contributors for this month:

Annette Schumacher

Kay L. Meyer

Jeannette A. Dall

Mary Jane Gruett

Janet Robson

Brian Dill

The Perfect All-Star

I made the all-star team!" Eric shouted as he burst into the house.

The ballots were in. The results were complete. Eric had finally made the team—a dream come true.

Eric loves baseball. He got his first little bat, ball, and glove when he was only two years old. He started with T-ball and then went on to Little League Rookies and Minors. Now, at age 10, he plays in the Majors.

For his birthday, Eric's grandma gave him a picture of a boy at bat, ready to swing. Behind him is Jesus, with His hands on the bat too. The picture reminds Eric (and each of us) that Jesus is with him.

Although he made the all-star team, Eric doesn't hit a home run every time he bats. He strikes out sometimes. In fact, every player on the all-star team makes an error now and then. Nobody's perfect except God. Our perfect God sent His perfect Son to be our Savior so we might join Him in heaven, where all things will be perfect. Our errors are forgiven. Our sins are taken care of by our All-Star, Jesus.

Read from God's Word

For you know that it was not with perishable things such as silver or gold that you were redeemed from the empty way of life handed down to you from your forefathers, but with the precious blood of Christ, a lamb without blemish or defect. 1 Peter 1:18–19

_____Let's talk: What gifts has God given you? How are you a helper at home, a loving son or daughter, or a friend to someone who really needs a friend?

_____Let's pray: Dear Giver of all gifts, we thank You for our special gifts and for our All-Star, Jesus. Amen.

A. S.

Read from God's Word

Sing to the LORD a new song, for He has done marvelous things; His right hand and His holy arm have worked salvation for Him. Psalm 98:1

The Whale's Song

The humpback whale is the fifth-largest animal on the planet, growing to a size of 45 tons. Just one weighs the same as 11 elephants or 600 humans! Maybe you've never seen 11 elephants together, but you can probably think of a time when you were with 600 people. Maybe you were at a Christmas service or in a sports arena. Imagine all of those people together. Now you have some idea of the weight of the humpback.

Some humpbacks migrate from Alaska in the summer to Hawaii in the winter. Tourists can take whale-watch cruises that allow them to see these whales. Some get to see see a whale "breaching" (leaping out of the water). And some see baby whales (calves) swimming with their mothers.

Maybe you have learned that humpback whales "sing" a different song every year. They were designed this way by God, their Creator. We, too, can sing different songs. We can praise God, for He has done marvelous things.

God worked out a wonderful plan of salvation. His only Son, Jesus, took our place on the cross. He died for our sins. Then He rose again on Easter. One day we will rise again too. Like the whales, we can sing a new song—a song of praise to God!

_____Let's do: Look up and read about whales in an encyclopedia or on the Internet. Write your own song of praise.

_____Let's pray: Dear Creator, thank You for whales. We praise You for everything and everyone in Your creation. We especially thank You for our Savior. In His name we pray. Amen.

A. S.

Ducks in Raincoats

I once saw a card with a picture of a duck wearing a raincoat. Above the duck were these words: "Into each life some rain will fall." The inside of the card said, "It's the sudden storms we can do without!"

Has it ever rained on a special event in your life? Maybe it was a ball game, a picnic, or your birthday. Did you feel like a duck needing a raincoat?

The duck on that card was not just standing in a gentle rain. That duck was in a storm. In our lives there are "sudden storms." Those storms could be losing a friend, moving to a new school, serious illness, or death. Sometimes we even feel like we are in a storm when we think nobody understands our problems.

But God always understands our troubles. God has even helped us with our greatest problem—sin. He promised us a Savior, and Jesus kept that promise by suffering and dying to save us from eternal punishment for sin. Because God always keeps His promises, we look forward to spending eternity with Him in heaven. It doesn't matter what rainy days or stormy problems come our way.

Read from God's Word

"And surely I am with you always, to the very end of the age." Matthew 28:20b

_____Let's do: Make a list of some "sudden storms" in your life. Then put the list in your Bible or in your pocket to look at throughout the day. This will remind you to give all your problems to God in prayer and to trust in His promises.

_____Let's pray: Dear caring God, we know You are always in control of everything. Give us peace for Jesus' sake. Amen.

A. S.

Read from God's Word

When the day of Pentecost came, they were all together in one place. Suddenly a sound like the blowing of a violent wind came from heaven and filled the whole house where they were sitting. They saw what seemed to be tongues of fire that separated and came to rest on each of them. All of them were filled with the Holy Spirit and began to speak in other tongues as the Spirit enabled them. Now there were staying in Jerusalem God-fearing Jews from every nation under heaven. When they heard this sound, a crowd came together in bewilderment, because each one heard them speaking in his own language. Acts 2:1–6

Fireworks!

In the United States today, people celebrate the birthday of our country in a variety of ways. Flags are proudly displayed on many homes. Parades are held. In big cities thousands watch huge fireworks shows, like the one Milwaukee holds on the beach of Lake Michigan. In smaller communities, only a few hundred people gather to see fireworks.

Christians are like fireworks in God's kingdom on earth. Some are moved by the Holy Spirit to tell the Gospel story to large groups of people. The disciples of Jesus were moved like that on Pentecost, when tongues of fire appeared on their heads. They became like the big fireworks displays as they preached to thousands of people.

Most of us are like small displays of fireworks. We tell the story of Good Friday and Easter to small groups of people or to just one person at a time. That's okay too. God helps each of us to sparkle where He puts us.

Maybe you will have both kinds of opportunities. You might talk about your faith to thousands or to a few! God leads each of us in the direction He wants us to go as we work for Him in His kingdom.

_____Let's talk: How do you plan to celebrate the birthday of our country? Whether big or small, know that you're important and loved by God!

_____Let's pray: Dear loving God, lead each of us to work in Your kingdom according to Your plan for us. In Jesus' name. Amen.

A. S.

Christmas in July

Read from God's Word

"She will give birth to a son, and you are to give Him the name Jesus, because He will save His people from their sins." Matthew 1:21

"Happy birthday, dear Maggie. Happy birthday to you," sang her family. Maggie celebrates her birthday the day after the United States celebrates its birthday. Sometimes her mom decorates a cake to look like the US flag.

Is your birthday on or near a holiday? Brian's birthday is near Christmas, so his family has many pictures of him opening birthday presents by the Christmas tree. Joshua sometimes celebrates his birthday on Easter Sunday because he was born in April. He and his cousins had an Easter egg hunt on his birthday one year.

At a Christian children's camp, the campers and staff celebrate Jesus' birthday in July with a Christmas service and party. The campers sing Christmas carols and decorate a Christmas tree. After a special service, they sing happy birthday to Jesus and share a huge birthday cake. That evening around the campfire, the camp director leads everyone in prayer. He thanks Jesus for coming to us at Christmas, dying for us on Good Friday, and rising for us on Easter.

Jesus came into the world to save His people from their sins. Christmas and Easter are festival days we can celebrate no matter what day of the year it is. The gift of salvation can be shared every day.

_____Let's do: Talk to your family about celebrating Christmas in July. (Forget the presents!) Make it simple with Christmas songs and prayers.

_____Let's pray: Dear Jesus, thank You for Christmas, Good Friday, and Easter. Move us to share that good news with people we meet any time of the year. Amen.

A. S.

Read from God's Word

When He had finished speaking, He said to Simon, "Put out into deep water, and let down the nets for a catch." Simon answered, "Master, we've worked hard all night and haven't caught anything. But because You say so, I will let down the nets." When they had done so, they caught such a large number of fish that their nets began to break. So they signaled their partners in the other boat to come and help them, and they came and filled both boats so full that they began to sink. When Simon Peter saw this, he fell at Jesus' knees and said, "Go away from me, Lord; I am a sinful man!" For he and all his companions were astonished at the catch of fish they had taken, and so were James and John, the sons of Zebedee, Simon's partners. Then Jesus said to Simon, "Don't be afraid; from now on you will catch men." So they pulled their boats up on shore, left everything and followed Him. Luke 5:4–11

Two Kinds of Fishing

"The fish got my worm, Grandpa. I need another one, please," said Gail.

"Hurry, Grandpa," said David. "I see a lot of fish down there waiting for me to catch them!"

Gail, David, and Grandpa enjoyed a good day of fishing. First they stopped at the Bait Shack to buy Grandpa's fishing license and a container of worms. Then on to the lake they went. At the end of the day, they had caught many fish.

The disciples in today's Bible story weren't so successful. They had fished all night and had caught nothing. Then Jesus told them to try one more time. They did as Jesus said and caught so many fish that their boats began to sink! What a miracle!

The disciples were astonished. Peter said, "Go away from me, Lord; I am a sinful man!" Peter felt humbled in Jesus' presence.

Jesus answered, "From now on you will catch men." Jesus meant that the disciples would preach to thousands of people (men, women, and children) who would become believers in Him. They would tell the Good News of salvation. People would be "caught for Christ."

When you, like the disciples, share the Good News about Jesus, you too are "catching" people for Christ. Have fun fishing!

_____Let's talk: Do you enjoy fishing? Are you fishing for people like Jesus explained in the story? What are some ways to do that kind of fishing? Make a list of those ways.

_____Let's pray: Dear Jesus, guide us and show us opportunities to catch people for You. Amen.

A. S.

Lava Lessons

Read from God's Word

How great is the love the Father has lavished on us, that we should be called children of God! And that is what we are! The reason the world does not know us is that it did not know Him. ... Dear children, do not let anyone lead you astray. He who does what is right is righteous, just as He is righteous. 1 John 3:1, 7

Have you ever seen an active volcano? Not a picture, but a real erupting volcano? Tourists in Hawaii can take a helicopter flight over a volcanic mountain. They can see the red-hot molten lava flowing from the mountain. What a real "mountaintop experience!"

The Bible says, "How great is the love the Father has lavished on us, that we should be called children of God!" The word *lavish* gets its meaning from the word *lava*. Lava means a great downpour, like the lava pouring down the side of the mountain. So much lava flows out of a volcano that it makes a mountain. Think of the downpour of God's love at Christmas, Holy Week, and Easter, when we celebrate the Savior's birth, death, and resurrection. We have a mountain of love.

Another mountaintop experience happens when we look back in our lives, remembering God's love flowing down to us when we were baptized. How thankful we are to be children of God! Praise God for the downpouring of His love!

_____Let's do: The next time there is a Baptism in your church, watch how the water and the Word are poured out onto the person who is being baptized. Think of how lavish God's love is for you.

_____Let's pray: Dear loving God, we thank You for the downpouring of Your love, which comes to us every day! In our Savior's name we pray. Amen.

A. S.

Read from God's Word

"Fear not, for I have redeemed you; I have summoned you by name; you are Mine." Isaiah 43:1b

First Steps

Children have many "firsts": first word, first tooth, first birthday, first haircut. It is fun to remember these special days. Ask your mom or dad about your "firsts." Maybe they have a baby book or pictures you can look at.

Baptism is an important "first" in our lives as Christians. It is the first day a child enters the family of God. In Baptism we receive forgiveness of sins and faith in Jesus. Baptism is the first step in our life of service to our Savior.

When babies and young children are baptized at church, the pastor reminds the godparents to pray for their godchildren. He may also suggest that they celebrate the Baptism birthdays of their godchildren.

Many Christian schools celebrate Baptism birthdays. The class may sing a Baptism song. The Baptism birthday child may be given a special bookmark or banner picturing a shell with water dripping from it and the words, "I have called you by name. You are Mine."

Our heavenly Father needs no reminder of our Baptism day. He knows it. He knows each one of us by name because we are His children. He made us His on our Baptism day.

Remember what God has done for you. Celebrate your Baptism, your first day in God's family.

_____Let's do: Make a Baptism bookmark. Keep the bookmark in your Bible, Bible storybook, or devotion book.

_____Let's pray: Dear heavenly Father, I'm so happy to be Your child. Thank You for calling me by name at my Baptism and always. Amen.

A. S.

God's Energy Snack

Read from God's Word

I can do everything through Him who gives me strength. Philippians 4:13

"You can do it, Mom," said Paul as his mom biked up a steep hill. Paul and his mom were among more than 1,500 bikers in a 150-mile, two-day ride for the National Multiple Sclerosis Society.

Bikers start early on a Saturday morning. Rest stops for the bikers are every 10 to 12 miles. Volunteers run the rest stops. They serve high-energy snacks and drinks. Some people have fun cooling the bikers by squirting them with water (they ask for permission first). Participants stay overnight along the route. And at the end of the second day, everybody cheers as they cross the finish line!

Do your family and friends participate in fund-raisers for charities or your church? It's a great way to share God's caring love with others.

God gives us the strength we need to help others in many ways. He will give us many opportunities to work for Him in His kingdom. He will even help us say the right words when we are sharing the Good News of Jesus and His love for all people.

God serves us at His rest stop as we read His Word. And He offers refreshment through His sacraments, Baptism and the Lord's Supper.

We can do all things in all situations with His help!

_____Let's talk: Talk to your family and friends about working in a fund-raiser for your church or community.

_____Let's pray: Dear caring Christ, please give us strength to show Your love to others in all that we do and say. Amen.

A. S.

10 july

Read from God's Word

"Do not let your hearts be troubled. Trust in God; trust also in Me. In My Father's house are many rooms; if it were not so, I would have told you. I am going there to prepare a place for you. And if I go and prepare a place for you, I will come back and take you to be with Me that you also may be where I am. You know the way to the place where I am going." John 14:1–4

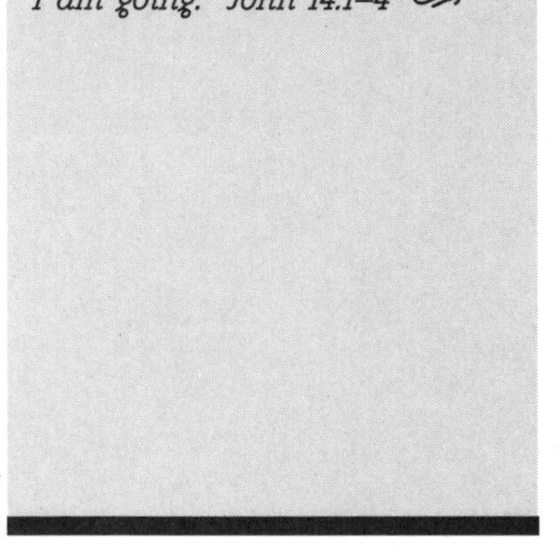

Butterfly Messenger

"Another butterfly hatched!" Mrs. Bangert excitedly told her class.

Eager students, looking through the viewing windows of the large box, saw three pretty butterflies. The butterflies flew around the flowers Mrs. Bangert had placed in the box. Then the butterflies rested on the flowers, sipping the sugar water on them.

The next sunny day, Mrs. Bangert and the students took the box of butterflies outside. It was time to set them free. The excited students watched as the butterflies flew toward the beautiful blue sky.

Later, Mrs. Bangert told the children about heaven. "Jesus went there to prepare a place for us," she said. The butterfly is a reminder that we are going to heaven to be with Jesus. The butterfly comes out of its cocoon just like we leave our bodies when we die and go to heaven. We'll join our Savior in heaven. We have faith that Jesus died for us and rose again on that first Easter.

Butterflies are wonderful messengers from God. They remind us that our loved ones who have died are in heaven with our heavenly Father. Someday our family and all believers will be together in that special place.

_____Let's do: Draw a picture or write a story about what you think heaven looks like. Talk about it with family and friends.

_____Let's pray: Dear heavenly Father, we praise You for the butterflies. They remind us of the good news of Easter and heaven. In our Redeemer's name we pray. Amen.

A. S.

God's "People Wash"

Read from God's Word

And this water symbolizes baptism that now saves you also—not the removal of dirt from the body but the pledge of a good conscience toward God. It saves you by the resurrection of Jesus Christ, who has gone into heaven and is at God's right hand—with angels, authorities and powers in submission to Him. 1 Peter 3:21–22

"Watch out, Dad," called Rodney. Allen and Rodney were helping their father wash the car. Allen, who was younger, had just discovered he could spray the water from the hose. The water drenched Rodney and their dad. They all laughed.

Together the team scrubbed the car with soap and water, rinsed it, and wiped it dry. When they were finished, they admired their work.

"It sure is shiny and clean! Good job, boys," said Dad.

Water can be used in many ways. We enjoy splashing in it when we go swimming. We use it to wash cars, take baths, and clean dishes.

God uses water and His Word in a special way when we are baptized into Christ. Through the water and the Word, we become members of God's family. It isn't the water alone, but the water applied in connection with God's promise that gives us God's forgiveness and salvation.

1 Peter 3:21–22 says: "This water symbolizes baptism that now saves you also—not the removal of dirt from the body but the pledge of a good conscience toward God. It saves you by the resurrection of Jesus Christ, who has gone into heaven and is at God's right hand."

We can be glad that God makes us clean from sin and unites us with our Savior forever.

_____Let's talk: If you are baptized, do you know your Baptism birthday?

_____Let's pray: Heavenly Father, thank You for making me part of Your family. Keep me safe in Your love always, for Jesus' sake. Amen.

K. L. M.

Read from God's Word

Go to the ant, you sluggard; consider its ways and be wise! It has no commander, no overseer or ruler, yet it stores its provisions in summer and gathers its food at harvest. ... "Four things on earth are small, yet they are extremely wise: Ants are creatures of little strength, yet they store up their food in the summer; coneys are creatures of little power, yet they make their home in the crags; locusts have no king, yet they advance together in ranks; a lizard can be caught with the hand, yet it is found in kings' palaces." Proverbs 6:6–8; 30:24–28

Going Buggy for God

Chris and his mother would often walk to the little grocery store for bread or milk. The store was only two blocks away, but sometimes it seemed that these journeys took half a day instead of a few minutes. The reason for the slow progress was bugs.

Chris was really into insects. He liked to stop and inspect the ants, spiders, and any other tiny critters that went marching by. The bugs always seemed to know exactly where they were going.

The Bible tells us we can learn some lessons from these marvelous creatures God made. In Proverbs 6:6 we read: "Go to the ant, you sluggard; consider its ways and be wise!"

Take some time to watch an ant for a while. If you put something in its path, it doesn't just give up. The ant will either go around the obstacle or over it as it does its job. God is telling us that we can learn about work, persistence, and patience from the ant.

God has made us far superior to insects, however. In all our work, and even in our play, we want to serve Him who made Himself lowly to snatch us from sin, death, and the devil. Yes, Jesus is our main reason for "going buggy" in serving the Lord.

_____Let's do: Read about insects in an encyclopedia or a book from the library. You'll be amazed at some of the things they do.

_____Let's pray: Dear Lord, thank You for creating all things. Help me to appreciate the many insects in the world and to learn from them. Above all, I praise You that I am Your child because of Jesus. Amen.

J. A. D.

Chameleon Kids

When Vanika was with the church group, she seemed to be honest and sincere. But when she was with her friends in the neighborhood, she joined them in making fun of God and church. Vanika was a real "chameleon kid."

A chameleon is a lizard that can change the color of its skin to match its surroundings. It may be green or yellow one minute and brown or black the next.

At times we're all like the chameleon. We might say what people want to hear instead of what we really think. We laugh at things that aren't funny because everyone else is laughing. We let other people and situations control what we do and say. We all become chameleon kids.

Being honest and sincere in all circumstances is hard work. We can do it, but only when we depend entirely on God's strength.

Read from God's Word

Jesus Christ is the same yesterday and today and forever. Hebrews 13:8

Fortunately, our Lord is not like a chameleon. No matter what we do, God doesn't change the way He feels about us. God always loves us and forgives us.

From the beginning of the world our Lord has never changed, and He never will. We can trust Him to save us completely.

_____Let's talk: Think about situations where you might behave like a chameleon kid. How can you change your behavior and stand up for what you believe? How do you get the power to do this?

_____Let's pray: Lord, thank You for never changing how You feel about me. Help me be honest and sincere in what I do, and forgive me when I act like a chameleon. Amen.

J. A. D.

Read from God's Word

Jesus answered, "I am the way and the truth and the life. No one comes to the Father except through Me. If you really knew Me, you would know My Father as well. From now on, you do know Him and have seen Him." John 14:6–7

The Loch Ness Hoax

Have you heard of the Loch Ness monster? According to legend, this monster lives in a lake in Scotland. A photo published in 1934 helped create interest in it. People come to catch a glimpse of this mysterious sea serpent.

In 1994, researchers revealed that the photo wasn't real. Two friends dreamed up this practical joke. One man made a long giraffelike neck and a small head, then attached it to a toy submarine. When finished, it resembled a sea serpent.

The other man took the photo. This photo was published in newspapers all around the world, and many persons believed the lie.

Whom can we trust to tell the truth? There is only one who knows the truth about everything. That one is our God and Savior, who actually *is* the truth.

You can believe it when God says He loves you. You can believe it when God says you have eternal life through faith in Jesus. He gave everything He had, even His life, to rescue you. You can believe it when Jesus says He will always be with you.

We can't always believe what people say. People may go back on their promises. But we can always believe what our Savior says. He is the way, the truth, and the life.

_____Let's talk: Why can you depend on the Lord to be truthful about the way to eternal life?

_____Let's pray: Thank You, Lord God, for telling us the truth about sin and about Your great love for us. Help us always to believe Your truth. In Jesus' name. Amen.

M. J. G.

Precious Things

Write five things that are precious to you.

Did you list an expensive bike or a sweatshirt with a team logo on it? Did you list jewelry or money? Did you list a favorite pet or toy? If you were to go on a long trip, what precious things would you take with you?

The apostle Peter uses the word *precious* many times in his letters. Scan the verses in today's Bible reading. Then write Peter's list of precious things next to your list of precious things. What kinds of things are on both lists?

Peter's list includes Jesus' blood, Jesus, faith, and the promises given in God's Word.

Jesus' blood is more precious than gold or silver. All the money in the world isn't enough to pay the cost of redeeming us from our sins. Only Jesus' blood was precious enough.

Jesus Himself is precious. Peter says Jesus is precious in the Father's sight. Jesus is also precious to those who believe, to you and me.

True faith is more precious than gold because it brings honor and glory to Jesus. God's great and precious promises help us escape evil in the world and live our lives for Him.

Read from God's Word

These have come so that your faith—of greater worth than gold, which perishes even though refined by fire—may be proved genuine and may result in praise, glory and honor when Jesus Christ is revealed. ... For you know that it was not with perishable things such as silver or gold that you were redeemed, ... but with the precious blood of Christ, a lamb without blemish or defect. ... For in Scripture it says: "See, I lay a stone in Zion, a chosen and precious cornerstone, and the one who trusts in Him will never be put to shame." Now to you who believe, this stone is precious. But to those who do not believe, "The stone the builders rejected has become the capstone." 1 Peter 1:7; 1:18–19; 2:4–7

His divine power has given us everything we need for life and godliness through our knowledge of Him who called us by His own glory and goodness. 2 Peter 1:3

_____Let's talk: Why is Jesus precious to you? Why are His promises precious to you? Remember, you, too, are precious to God. What would you put on your list of precious things now?

_____Let's pray: Dear God, thank You for Jesus' precious blood given for me. Help me remember that I am precious to You. In Jesus' name. Amen.

M. J. G.

Read from God's Word

"Are not two sparrows sold for a penny? Yet not one of them will fall to the ground apart from the will of your Father. And even the very hairs of your head are all numbered. So don't be afraid; you are worth more than many sparrows." Matthew 10:29–31

Humble yourselves, therefore, under God's mighty hand, that He may lift you up in due time. Cast all your anxiety on Him because He cares for you. 1 Peter 5:6–7

All Problems, Great and Small

Mario took his favorite toy, a set of building blocks that snapped together, to day camp. At recess, Mario and his friends built houses and cars with the set.

But one girl picked up some of the blocks and threw them. Mario found most of the blocks, but some were still missing.

After camp, Mario told his mother about the missing blocks. She suggested that they pray about it. "God cares about our little problems too," she said. The next day, Mario found all the pieces. He learned an important lesson—that God cares about the small problems he faces every day.

We know we can trust God for big concerns, like salvation and heaven. He has provided these marvelous gifts for us through Jesus. We can also trust the Lord to help us with less important matters.

Read what Jesus said about the sparrow. If our heavenly Father takes care of a little bird, He will take good care of us too.

1 Peter 5:7 tells us to give all our problems to the Lord. He cares about the things that happen to us. He wants us to tell Him all the problems in our lives—big and small. We can trust Him because He loves us.

_____Let's talk: Why can you trust God with your small problems as well as the big ones?

_____Let's pray: Thank You, Jesus, for giving us salvation and the hope of heaven. Help us bring all our problems to You, the small ones as well as the big ones. Amen.

M. J. G.

Consult Me

Consult Me is an advice book. It's a collection of information about cooking, home remedies, removing stains, playing card games, and even eliminating bedbugs.

Because *Consult Me* was written in 1866, some of the advice sounds silly today. For instance, the cure for a headache is to "keep your feet in warm water for a quarter of an hour before you go to bed, for two or three weeks." Or you could "order a teakettle of cold water to be poured on your head every morning in a slender stream." Treat a sore throat by "rubbing the soles of the feet before the fire, with garlic and lard well beaten together, overnight."

God's version of *Consult Me* is the Bible. In it He offers advice about every problem we face. God loves us so much that He wants us to consult Him about everything that makes us sad or confused. Although the Bible is much older than *Consult Me*, its advice is never old-fashioned. Look at today's Bible verses for some advice God gives us about living healthy, happy lives.

Will we still have problems and heartaches if we do the things God asks us? Yes, we will because we live in a sinful world. But what wonderful hope we have because of our faith in Jesus as our Savior!

Read from God's Word

Speak to one another with psalms, hymns and spiritual songs. Sing and make music in your heart to the Lord, always giving thanks to God the Father for everything, in the name of our Lord Jesus Christ. Ephesians 5:19–20

For I am convinced that neither death nor life, neither angels nor demons, neither the present nor the future, nor any powers, neither height nor depth, nor anything else in all creation, will be able to separate us from the love of God that is in Christ Jesus our Lord. Romans 8:38–39

_____Let's do: Draw a picture of the images suggested in Romans 8:38–39. Keep the picture where you can see it often as a reminder of how much God loves you.

_____Let's pray: Father, I thank You that nothing can separate me from Your love, which led You to send Jesus to save me. Amen.

J. R.

Read from God's Word

Open for me the gates of righteousness; I will enter and give thanks to the LORD. This is the gate of the LORD through which the righteous may enter. I will give You thanks, for You answered me; You have become my salvation. The stone the builders rejected has become the capstone; the LORD has done this, and it is marvelous in our eyes. Psalm 118:19–23

A Warm Welcome

One winter we had day after day of below-zero weather. Even worse, there were bitter winds and frequent snow flurries. People were warned not to go out unless it was absolutely necessary.

One day we had to go out of town. We let our dog out before we left, but no one remembered to let her in again. Amber, our dog, leads a comfortable life. She does what she wants to do. Mostly that means lying around sleeping or begging for dog treats.

Can you imagine how we felt when we came home that evening and found that Amber had been outside all day? Her paws were caked with ice. She had ice balls in her fur. She couldn't stop shivering.

After we had done this to her, she still loved us! Amber jumped all over us, tail wagging and tongue licking.

It's heartwarming for a pet to welcome us when we've been so thoughtless. And isn't that what Jesus does? We act like we don't care about the Lord. We say and do things we know are wrong. But He still loves us and welcomes us with open arms. In fact, He loves us so much that He died for us so we could live with Him in heaven. Doesn't that make you feel warm all over?

_____Let's talk: Can you think of something you did today that was thoughtless? Think about how much Jesus loves you. Then smile.

_____Let's pray: Lord Jesus, thank You for loving me even when I act like I don't love You. Help me remember that because You love me, I have a very good reason to smile! Amen.

J. R.

Thankful in All Things

Read from God's Word

Be joyful always; pray continually; give thanks in all circumstances, for this is God's will for you in Christ Jesus. 1 Thessalonians 5:16–18

Anika and her family had just returned home from a vacation. On their way home, they hit two deer with their brand new minivan. The front end was completely ruined. They have to wait a whole month for it to be fixed. But Anika was thankful.

Here is why. No one was hurt. No other vehicles were involved. The accident happened at the end of their vacation instead of the beginning. And they were only 20 minutes from home when it happened, although they had traveled hundreds of miles during their trip.

Anika understood what God means when He encourages us to "give thanks in all circumstances." God desires that we be thankful in all circumstances. That's not the same as being thankful *for* all circumstances. Anika didn't thank God for their ruined minivan, but she recognized that even during the most unhappy and frustrating events of life, there is always reason to praise God.

Take another look at today's Bible reading. It is a good reminder of how we can face each day's events. See if you can memorize these words. Share them with a friend or a member of your family. Ask that person to remind you of these words the next time you're feeling sad or ungrateful.

_____Let's talk: What are some reasons we can joyfully thank God for the death of His Son on the cross?

_____Let's pray: Heavenly Father, because Jesus hung on the cross for my sins, I know that I am Your child. Thank You for loving me so much that You allowed Jesus to suffer and die for me. In the name of my risen Savior. Amen.

J. R.

Read from God's Word

Jesus called them together and said, "You know that the rulers of the Gentiles lord it over them, and their high officials exercise authority over them. Not so with you. Instead, whoever wants to become great among you must be your servant, and whoever wants to be first must be your slave—just as the Son of Man did not come to be served, but to serve, and to give His life as a ransom for many." Matthew 20:25–28

Living as a Guest

Do you know what a bed-and-breakfast is? It is like a motel but is a private home. People prepare rooms in their homes that are just for other people to spend the night in. In the morning, the guests receive breakfast as part of the cost of staying overnight.

In one bed-and-breakfast, the hostess places notes in the bedrooms that explain the history and decorations in the home. She also includes information about activities in the area that may interest guests. She sometimes sleeps in the guest rooms and tries to imagine what guests would want to know and what would make them comfortable. She knows that to be a good hostess, she has to know what it was like to live as a guest.

Isn't that what God did for us? He prepared a beautiful home for us in heaven. In order to bring us there, He sent Jesus to earth to live as one of us. Jesus, our heavenly guest, felt our sorrow and experienced our temptations. He knew what it was to be hungry, homeless, and lonely.

Because God knows what it's like to be one of us, we can come to Him with any problem and He will understand. Because Jesus lived and died for us, we can be certain that heaven will truly be our home someday.

_____Let's do: Spend some time today making your room reflect the care God wants you to have for the possessions He has given you.

_____Let's pray: Dear Jesus, I know You are always present in my room. Be present in my heart too. Amen.

J. R.

Our Heavenly Deposit

Read from God's Word

Now we know that if the earthly tent we live in is destroyed, we have a building from God, an eternal house in heaven, not built by human hands. Meanwhile we groan, longing to be clothed with our heavenly dwelling, because when we are clothed, we will not be found naked. For while we are in this tent, we groan and are burdened, because we do not wish to be unclothed but to be clothed with our heavenly dwelling, so that what is mortal may be swallowed up by life. Now it is God who has made us for this very purpose and has given us the Spirit as a deposit, guaranteeing what is to come. 2 Corinthians 5:1–5

Every month Devon receives in the mail a report from the bank. The report tells how much money was deposited that month in Devon's account and how much was taken out.

Devon is saving his money. Sometimes he gets money for his birthday. Once his neighbor paid Devon for watering his garden while he was on vacation. Devon saves part of his allowance each week. All the money he saves goes into the bank and is reported on his monthly statement.

Devon can't see his money. He knows it's in the bank, though, because he has a report that proves where his money is.

Just as Devon can't actually see the money he has in the bank, so we can't see heaven. But God tells us in His Word that we can be sure of a home in heaven because He has given us His Holy Spirit as a "deposit."

The Spirit uses God's Word to create faith in Jesus, our Savior. The Holy Spirit makes our faith grow. The Spirit helps us talk to God and comforts us when we're sad. God has promised us that the Spirit's presence is our proof that He loves us and has a home waiting for us in heaven.

_____Let's talk: Another name for the Holy Spirit is the "Comforter." Why is that a good name for God's Spirit? During the next week, keep a list of the ways you see the Holy Spirit working. Then thank God for all the ways the Spirit acts as your Comforter and Helper.

_____Let's pray: Heavenly Father, thank You for opening my eyes and heart to the work of Your Holy Spirit. In Jesus' name. Amen.

J. R.

Read from God's Word

"I am the good shepherd; I know My sheep and My sheep know Me—just as the Father knows Me and I know the Father—and I lay down My life for the sheep. I have other sheep that are not of this sheep pen. I must bring them also. They too will listen to My voice, and there shall be one flock and one shepherd. The reason My Father loves Me is that I lay down My life—only to take it up again. No one takes it from Me, but I lay it down of My own accord. I have authority to lay it down and authority to take it up again. This command I received from My Father." John 10:14–18

Taken or Given?

Robby was always late for dinner. He had a watch, but he would still forget.

One morning his mother said in a firm but loving way, "Be home in time for dinner or you'll be in trouble." Robby was still late.

When he came home, everyone had a plate full of roast beef and all the trimmings—everyone except Robby. On his plate was a piece of dry bread. Robby hung his head and quietly cried.

Then Robby's father smiled and said, "Son, we love you and forgive you." Dad gave his own plate to Robby and took the dry bread for himself. Robby hugged his father. "I'm sorry for disobeying you. I'll ask God to help me do better."

Robby's dad exchanged the plates out of love. Robby didn't deserve it. That's called grace. Jesus tells us He is the Good Shepherd who lays down His life for the sheep. We are the sheep; we receive grace and forgiveness because Jesus took all our sins to the cross and died for them.

Sometimes Christians call this the "great exchange." No one took His life from Him. Jesus willingly gave it up for all sinners. Knowing that, we pledge to do His will and ask God to help us trust and obey.

_____Let's do: You may have a friend who needs some help. Think about a way you can help that friend without even being asked.

_____Let's pray: Lord Jesus, help me live in an unselfish way like You lived. Hear me for Your sake. Amen.

B. D.

Give God a Chance

Read from God's Word

Pray also for me, that whenever I open my mouth, words may be given me so that I will fearlessly make known the mystery of the gospel, for which I am an ambassador in chains. Pray that I may declare it fearlessly, as I should. Ephesians 6:19–20

During his first year of college, Brian was asked to help with a chapel service. Brian was very excited because he could show everyone how confident he was.

Suddenly, he felt a terrible wave of fear. Brian couldn't finish. He panicked. "How can I be a pastor if I am afraid to read or speak in public?"

Brian wanted to quit right then. The college president, knowing he was discouraged, said he should hang in there and see if God would change things. But the fear remained. Brian's parents said he should pray and trust that God would help him.

One day his mother wrote him a letter about Paul, whose preaching put him in danger of death just for telling about Jesus. Look at today's Bible reading again. Paul wrote these words while chained to a Roman guard.

In school many teachers helped Brian with his fear of public speaking. The Holy Spirit comforted him and helped him give God a chance to work in his life.

Now Brian preaches without fear at all. He can tell anyone who will listen that God, in the person of Jesus, came to this world to live in holiness, die innocently, and rise from death, so we all might be part of His kingdom now and forever.

____Let's do: List the people God sends you to help you. Doctors, teachers, police officers, and pastors are some of God's special helpers. You can look on them as people God sends and uses to help you in hard times.

____Let's pray: Holy Spirit, thank You for sending many people into my life as Your helpers. I pray in Jesus' name. Amen.

B. D.

A Traitor Forgiven

Read from God's Word

When they had finished eating, Jesus said to Simon Peter, "Simon son of John, do you truly love Me more than these?" "Yes, Lord," he said, "You know that I love You." Jesus said, "Feed My lambs." Again Jesus said, "Simon son of John, do you truly love Me?" He answered, "Yes, Lord, You know that I love You." Jesus said, "Take care of My sheep." The third time He said to Him, "Simon son of John, do you love Me?" Peter was hurt because Jesus asked him the third time, "Do you love Me?" He said, "Lord, You know all things; You know that I love You." Jesus said, "Feed My sheep." John 21:15–17

A boy went to camp where he had a great time. When he got home, someone asked him how camp was. He replied, "Great! The whole time I was there no one ever found out I go to church."

What this boy did was deny and betray Jesus.

In some way we all deny Jesus. Perhaps it happens when we behave badly. It may be when we do nothing to show that Christ is our Redeemer. That even happened to Peter, a disciple.

Peter vowed to defend the Lord with his own life. But later when Peter was afraid, he said he didn't know Jesus. Peter betrayed his Lord. When Jesus appeared to the disciples after His resurrection, Peter wondered what Jesus might say.

Jesus asked Peter, "do you truly love Me?"

"Yes, Lord," Peter said, "You know that I love You." Jesus said, "Feed My lambs." Jesus had not come to condemn Peter. He knew how sorry Peter was. Peter was forgiven because Jesus rose on Easter in victory over sin.

Christ knows how often we betray Him. As Christ died for Peter, He died on the cross also for our forgiveness. Although we deny and hurt our Savior, He forgives us. He calls us to His service and invites us to show friends and family God's love.

_____Let's do: Invite some of your friends who do not know Jesus to join you and your family for church. After church, talk about the service.

_____Let's pray: Lord Jesus, how often I have denied You. Forgive me, and grant me courage to tell others. Hear my prayer for Your name's sake, O Savior. Amen.

B. D.

Forgiveness Math

Read from God's Word

Then Peter came to Jesus and asked, "Lord, how many times shall I forgive my brother when he sins against me? Up to seven times?" Jesus answered, "I tell you, not seven times, but seventy-seven times." Matthew 18:21–22

How many times should you forgive someone? Do you know?

The people of God have always wondered about forgiveness. One day the disciples asked Jesus about it. They asked how often they should forgive someone. How many times did Jesus say? "Jesus answered, 'I tell you, not seven times, but seventy-seven times.' " Jesus meant there was no end to giving forgiveness.

Why is it so hard to forgive? It's because our human nature is sinful—filled with thoughts of revenge and getting back rather than letting something go and forgiving.

Because of sin we were divided from God. Jesus came to earth and solved this problem. His math works like this. When Jesus died on the cross, He took away, or subtracted, the punishment for sins that was really ours. He added forgiveness of those sins and life everlasting.

Our response to His love can be one of multiplication. We can forgive others over and over. This is God's math.

_____Let's do: Go to someone with whom you have had a disagreement. Pray that God's Spirit will help you find forgiving words.

_____Let's pray: Holy Spirit, I am so quick to get angry and stay angry. Direct my eyes to Jesus' cross, that day by day I might know the high price He paid for my forgiveness. Amen.

B. D.

Faith Moves Mountains

Read from God's Word

He replied, "Because you have so little faith. I tell you the truth, if you have faith as small as a mustard seed, you can say to this mountain, 'Move from here to there' and it will move. Nothing will be impossible for you." When they came together in Galilee, He said to them, "The Son of Man is going to be betrayed into the hands of men. They will kill Him, and on the third day He will be raised to life." And the disciples were filled with grief. Matthew 17:20–23

In the 1860s a railroad was built through the mountains in Canada. Some people said it couldn't be done. But those who knew better responded, "Have faith."

With the abilities God gave them, the workers actually moved mountains by tunneling right through them.

Today's Bible lesson is a promise. Faith moves mountains. Mountains are the things that stand in the way of a closer walk with God and a happy life. What mountains do you face? Fear of a school bully? Trouble with schoolwork? Divorced parents? Jesus says nothing is impossible.

How does faith get into the human heart? Consider the workers who had the knowledge and equipment to build that railroad. They moved mountains to do it. So it is in our walk with God.

God gives us "the means of grace," which are His Word and the sacraments of Baptism and Holy Communion. These are ways He reaches our minds and hearts. When we were baptized, we were given faith. When people read the Bible or go to Holy Communion, faith is strengthened.

But faith in what? We receive faith that Jesus takes us to heaven. We can't be good enough to do it ourselves. Jesus' life and death tunneled the way to God and provided the way for us to believe. God will move every mountain in our life.

_____Let's do: Make a list of the ways God has helped you conquer the mountains of trouble in your life.

_____Let's pray: Lord God, You alone give me faith. Let me read Your Word and remember my Baptism so my faith and love for You might grow every day. I pray in Jesus' name. Amen.

B. D.

When People Are Different

Frank was quite different from everyone else in school. He had an illness that made his body very heavy.

Many of the children called Frank names. In Sunday school the teacher reminded everyone to treat Frank as kindly as they would treat everyone else. But even some kids from church and Sunday school teased him. Frank felt lonely and sad. He had no real friends.

Today's Bible reading talks about Jesus being a true friend to someone who was different. The man had a terrible disease called leprosy. When lepers walked down the street, they had to wear a bell and shout "Unclean! Unclean!" This man heard Jesus was a friend of all and asked Jesus to heal him.

Jesus cured the leper, but He did even more for the man. He died on the cross for the forgiveness of his sins. Now that's what I call a friend!

Jesus is your special Friend, too, and above all, your Savior from sin. Maybe you're like Frank—someone who looks different from other people. Or maybe you know someone like Frank. Remember that God doesn't see our outward appearance, but our heart. He sees our faith in Jesus as Savior and Friend.

Read from God's Word

When He came down from the mountainside, large crowds followed Him. A man with leprosy came and knelt before Him and said, "Lord, if You are willing, You can make me clean." Jesus reached out His hand and touched the man. "I am willing," He said. "Be clean!" Immediately he was cured of his leprosy. Then Jesus said to him, "See that you don't tell anyone. But go, show yourself to the priest and offer the gift Moses commanded, as a testimony to them." Matthew 8:1–4

But the LORD said to Samuel, "Do not consider his appearance or his height, for I have rejected him. The LORD does not look at the things man looks at. Man looks at the outward appearance, but the LORD looks at the heart." 1 Samuel 16:7

_____Let's talk: How have you treated people who are different from you? Do you stay away from them or, like Jesus, do you make them your friend?

_____Let's pray: Dear Jesus, please forgive me for the times I have failed to make someone a friend because they are different. Help me not to ignore them or fear them. Let Your cross remind me that You died and rose for all people. Then let me follow Your example of true friendship. Amen.

B. D.

Read from God's Word

I waited patiently for the LORD; He turned to me and heard my cry. He lifted me out of the slimy pit, out of the mud and mire; He set my feet on a rock and gave me a firm place to stand. He put a new song in my mouth, a hymn of praise to our God. Many will see and fear and put their trust in the LORD. Psalm 40:1–3

"Therefore everyone who hears these words of Mine and puts them into practice is like a wise man who built his house on the rock. The rain came down, the streams rose, and the winds blew and beat against that house; yet it did not fall, because it had its foundation on the rock." Matthew 7:24–25

The Rock for All Ages

A boy and his grandfather were fishing when it began to storm. The boy fell overboard, but he managed to swim to a large rock. He climbed onto the rock and stayed there all night.

The next morning a search crew found him. Someone asked him how he felt during the long, stormy night. He replied, "I shook all night long, but the rock never moved." The rock was his safe place.

In the Bible, God is often called the Rock. Think about today's Bible reading. Each of us needs this Rock for our life. That's what Jesus meant in Matthew 7:24–25. We are wise to build our life on Jesus.

So what does it mean to build our lives on Jesus or to set our feet upon God, our Rock? It means we believe that Jesus lived a perfect life for us, died to save us from all sin, and rose for us. Now we can look forward to life everlasting. That is faith!

There may be times when you are in fearful situations. No Christian is promised a trouble-free life. But we are promised the Lord's strength, who by His Spirit dwells in our hearts and directs our lives. We can know for sure that God's love is solid as a rock!

_____Let's do: Read the words of the hymn "Rock of Ages, Cleft for Me" (*Lutheran Worship,* 361). Ask your parents or pastor to help you understand those words.

_____Let's pray: Lord Jesus, help me to believe that You are the Rock of my life. In Your holy name I pray, dear Savior. Amen.

B. D.

No Fear in Darkness

Read from God's Word

Your word is a lamp to my feet and a light for my path. I have taken an oath and confirmed it, that I will follow Your righteous laws. Psalm 119:105–6

Many years ago, a Russian pianist named Vladimir Horowitz was giving a solo piano concert at Carnegie Hall in New York City. Right in the middle of his concert the lights went out and the hall went dark.

Mr. Horowitz kept on playing as though nothing had happened. Why was he able to play so well in the dark? Because he had practiced in the light all his life.

God gave His Word that points us to Jesus, the Light of the world. Through the Word we see Him dying on the cross and rising from death. We see that God is good and merciful. By His light we see Jesus is the way to heaven.

His Word is also the light because His will and commandments show us the way to live. As children of God, we desire to show that we believe in Jesus. We also desire to share this light with others.

So we read the Word for light—light to show the way to heaven and light to know the way to live on earth. Remember the piano player? Practice trusting in Jesus when days are bright. When the darkness of trials comes to you, remember to keep on trusting Jesus. He is the true light.

_____Let's do: Memorize today's Bible verse. Some night when it's really dark in your room, remember Jesus' promise.

_____Let's pray: Lord Jesus, without You I cannot find the way to heaven. Thank You for giving me Your Word that I might live a life pleasing to You. Amen.

B. D.

30 july

Read from God's Word

You yourselves are our letter, written on our hearts, known and read by everybody. You show that you are a letter from Christ, the result of our ministry, written not with ink but with the Spirit of the living God, not on tablets of stone but on tablets of human hearts.
2 Corinthians 3:2–3

Living Letters

Letters carry words of love, hate, peace, joy, sadness, and many other matters.

What do you think it means to be a living letter? It means that our lives speak a great deal about what we believe and whom we serve—God or ourselves. We use our words and actions to say something to other people.

Jesus was the Master of all letters. He came to this world to show and tell us about God. The Bible says of Him, "The Word became flesh and made His dwelling among us. We have seen His glory, the glory of the One and Only, who came from the Father, full of grace and truth" (John 1:14). When Christ healed the sick, He said, "God wants you to be well." When Jesus died on the cross, He said, "God wants to forgive your sins and take you to heaven."

We desire to write better letters with our lives. We start by asking God for forgiveness. Then with a new spirit we write new letters to our family, our friends, our church, and the world. The power to rewrite letters comes from the Lord. He uses the Bible and the sacraments of Baptism and Holy Communion to change our hearts and lives. He alone can make us into His letter of love.

_____Let's do: Each day for one week, write a note to someone that describes the good God is doing through his or her life.

_____Let's pray: Lord Jesus, You have written of Your love by Your life and put the message into my heart. Let me follow in Your way with Your help, and so speak words of caring in all I say and do. Amen.

B. D.

In Days of Youth

Read from God's Word

Remember your Creator in the days of your youth, before the days of trouble come and the years approach when you will say, "I find no pleasure in them." Ecclesiastes 12:1

Even to your old age and gray hairs I am He, I am He who will sustain you. I have made you and I will carry you; I will sustain you and I will rescue you. Isaiah 46:4

Can you imagine the Niagara Falls ever stopping? One winter that is exactly what happened. Ice blocked the river upstream and the falls slowed to a trickle. It's often called the day Niagara Falls was turned off.

With days of youth generally come days of strength. There are few responsibilities. Young people often feel like Niagara Falls—so strong that nothing can block their energy.

God does not mean to say that there will be no hard times during our younger years. When there are, we can be assured that God's love is greater than Niagara Falls.

Jesus went through youth. Luke 2:52 says, "And Jesus grew in wisdom and stature, and in favor with God and men." This reminds us that the study of God's Word was one of the sources of His strength to obey God. Jesus needed the constant strength only His Father in heaven could give.

We can be sure the flow of God's grace will never be blocked by any obstacle on the river of life. That's important. If we live to an old age, we will also need the "Niagara Falls" of God's power. He will not fail us. So whether in youth or in days of old age, we can always rely on God, whose love is never blocked from us.

_____Let's do: Take some Christian friends and use your youthful energy to visit people who are old and possibly lonely.

_____Let's pray: O Lord my God, I thank You for these days of my youth and strength. Guide me to use them for the good of others. Amen.

B. D.

a u g u s t

Contributors for this month:

Christine Weerts

Gail Pawlitz

Phil Lang

James Klawiter

Gene Friedrich

Who's Coming to Lunch?

Read from God's Word

In the sixth month, God sent the angel Gabriel to Nazareth, a town in Galilee, to a virgin pledged to be married to a man named Joseph, a descendant of David. The virgin's name was Mary. The angel went to her and said, "Greetings, you who are highly favored! The Lord is with you." Mary was greatly troubled at his words and wondered what kind of greeting this might be. But the angel said to her, "Do not be afraid, Mary, you have found favor with God. You will be with child and give birth to a son, and you are to give Him the name Jesus. He will be great and will be called the Son of the Most High. The Lord God will give Him the throne of His father David, and He will reign over the house of Jacob forever; His kingdom will never end. ..." "I am the Lord's servant," Mary answered. "May it be to me as you have said." Then the angel left her. Luke 1:26–38

One day our family was enjoying a picnic by a river in the Great Smokey Mountains. Suddenly our father told us to get into the car. He was very serious.

Why were we leaving our lunch half-eaten? The serious tone in Dad's voice meant no arguing. As we scrambled into the car, we saw two black bears at our picnic table. They came for lunch. This was clearly a dangerous situation. Later, I thought how important it was that we immediately obeyed my father. Our obedience brought us a blessing.

I didn't always obey my dad. Sometimes I asked "Why?" or "Do I have to?" I would even whine, "That's not fair." While it's okay to occasionally ask our parents for an explanation, there are also times that we need to simply trust and obey, not knowing why.

You may wonder why the Bible reading for August is part of the Christmas story. Let's look at Mary's actions and words. She showed absolute obedience to God. Her faith was shown in her response to the angel's announcement. A wonderful blessing came because of it.

Jesus gives us another example of obedience. He obeyed His Father by suffering and dying on the cross for our sins. Through His obedience, a wonderful blessing came our way: everlasting life.

_____Let's do: Next time one of your parents tells you to do something, say okay without arguing. Both of you may be surprised at the results.

_____Let's pray: Heavenly Father, forgive me for the times I argue with You. Help me trust and instantly obey, knowing You want what is best for me. In Jesus' name. Amen.

C. W.

Read from God's Word

The LORD said to Samuel, "... I am sending you to Jesse of Bethlehem. I have chosen one of his sons to be king. ... Do not consider his appearance or his height. ... The LORD does not look at the things man looks at. Man looks at the outward appearance, but the LORD looks at the heart." ... Jesse had seven of his sons pass before Samuel, but Samuel said to him, "The LORD has not chosen these." So he asked Jesse, "Are these all the sons you have?" "There is still the youngest," Jesse answered, "but he is tending the sheep." Samuel said, "Send for him. ..." So he sent and had him brought in. He was ruddy, with a fine appearance and handsome features. Then the LORD said, "Rise and anoint him; he is the one." So Samuel took the horn of oil and anointed him in the presence of his brothers, and from that day on the Spirit of the LORD came upon David in power. Samuel then went to Ramah. 1 Samuel 16:1–13

Where to Find Beauty

Every culture seems to define beauty by physical appearance. Even in ancient Israel, looks were valued. Saul was described as "without equal among Israelites" (1 Samuel 9:2). His good looks, however, did not mean he was always wise. His disobedience and faithlessness displeased the Lord, so another king was chosen.

The prophet Samuel went to find the next king the Lord had chosen. He visited with Jesse and his sons. One by one, seven of Jesse's sons passed in front of Samuel. The Lord had chosen none of those seven. He had chosen David, the youngest son.

God valued David's faith and trust in Him. David loved the Lord. In the psalms, we read about the hope David had in the Lord. Through David's family a beautiful blessing came our way. Our Savior, Jesus Christ, was born.

The way we look on the outside makes us individuals, but we often place too much emphasis on outward appearances. Clothes, height, weight, looks—they all seem to matter too much.

God doesn't judge our beauty by our looks. God looks inside for a deeper and lasting beauty. He searches our hearts. Our beauty is in Jesus. Other people can see the beauty of our love for Jesus as we serve them and share the story of God's love.

_____Let's do: Memorize 1 Samuel 16:7. Say it next time you look in a mirror.

_____Let's pray: Precious Lord, give me a clean heart. Renew a right Spirit within me. In Jesus' name. Amen.

C. W.

Our Daily Bread

The litte boy was staying with friends. There were lots of fun activities planned, from swimming to sightseeing. Right after lunch, the boy asked, "Are we going to eat again today?"

His question wasn't the typical "What's for dinner?" question. Instead, it was a question asked by a child who often went to bed hungry. This boy's mother provided for her children the best she could. But sometimes there was no money for food.

Three meals a day seems like a basic "right" but many people have no guarantee that food will always be on the table. Think of the prayer people often pray before meals. This prayer invites Jesus to be a guest and thanks Him for the food He gives us.

Think about how we might sometimes say this prayer. Maybe we say it so quickly that we don't think about the meaning of the words. Perhaps we even forget that food is not a "right;" it is a gift from God.

The next time you have a guest at your house for dinner, set an extra plate for Jesus. Talk about Him. At the end of the meal, give thanks to God for food, family, friends, and faith in our Savior.

Read from God's Word

If there is a poor man among your brothers in any of the towns of the land that the LORD your God is giving you, do not be hardhearted or tightfisted toward your poor brother. Rather be openhanded and freely lend him whatever he needs. Be careful not to harbor this wicked thought: "The seventh year, the year for canceling debts, is near," so that you do not show ill will toward your needy brother and give him nothing. He may then appeal to the LORD against you, and you will be found guilty of sin. Give generously to him and do so without a grudging heart; then because of this the LORD your God will bless you in all your work and in everything you put your hand to. There will always be poor people in the land. Therefore I command you to be openhanded toward your brothers and toward the poor and needy in your land. Deuteronomy 15:7–11

_____Let's do: Make a donation to your local food bank. Give up snacks for a week and use the money to buy food for others.

_____Let's pray: Come, Lord Jesus, be our guest, and let Thy gifts to us be blessed. Amen.

C. W.

Read from God's Word

Now He had to go through Samaria ... and Jesus, tired as He was from the journey, sat down by the well. ... When a Samaritan woman came to draw water, Jesus said to her, "Will you give Me a drink?" ... The Samaritan woman said to Him, "You are a Jew and I am a Samaritan woman. How can you ask me for a drink?" (For Jews do not associate with Samaritans.) Jesus answered her, "If you knew the gift of God and who it is that asks you for a drink, you would have asked Him and He would have given you living water." "Sir," the woman said, "You have nothing to draw with and the well is deep. Where can You get this living water? ..." Jesus answered, "Everyone who drinks this water will be thirsty again, but whoever drinks the water I give him will never thirst. Indeed, the water I give him will become in him a spring of water welling up to eternal life." John 4:4–14

Can't Live without It

Imagine floating on a fat inner tube in a quiet lake. The sun sparkles on the blue-green water. On a hot day, nothing feels as good as a dip in cool water.

What a creative God we have! He made water fun and refreshing. What would our favorite drinks be without water? He made water useful for cooking, bathing, and washing. He made water life-giving. Plants, animals, and people die without it.

In today's reading, the Samaritan woman was getting water from the well—an essential daily task. She was surprised that Jesus, a Jew, would ask her for water. Jews did not associate with Samaritans. Jesus invited her to get "living water." This means He invited her to believe in Him as her Savior.

Remember how thirsty you feel when it's hot and there's no water? Jesus says, "Come to Me and drink" (John 7:37). Our souls thirst for Jesus. We need a Savior to satisfy our thirst. Just as we need water to live, we need Jesus Christ for an abundant life. In Baptism, the water and God's Word give us the gift of eternal life, forgiveness of sins, and the power of the Holy Spirit.

We can't live without water. We can't live eternally without Jesus.

_____Let's do: Name the ways you used water today. As you drink a glass of water, think of how Jesus is "living water" to you.

_____Let's pray: Dear Jesus, Your gift of living water quenches my thirst, now and forever. Thank You. Amen.

C. W.

Aroma Signals

Jasmine hovered over the pan of freshly baked brownies on the counter, savoring the wonderful smell.

"I love the aroma of brownies too," her mother said as she stood next to Jasmine. "It fills the whole house."

What is your favorite aroma? Is it a new basketball, sweet honeysuckle, or spicy pizza? Whatever it may be, your favorite smells send your brain a happy signal.

Can a person be an aroma? The Bible says Christians are aromas. They are the "aroma of Christ among those who are being saved."

How can Christ be a fragrance? The aroma is in the actions we do and the words we say. It is in kindness, joy, patience, gentleness, love, forgiveness, and much more. As you see these actions in others, you are seeing Christ at work in them.

Perhaps you have noticed times when this Christlike aroma is missing. It happens when we lie, say mean things, or grumble about chores. At those times we need Christ to come to us with His sweet gift of forgiveness. Christ's death and resurrection are the aroma of His love for us. He gives that love freely to us. The aroma is ours to share.

Next time your favorite smell travels to your nose, think of Christ, the life-saving aroma.

Read from God's Word

For we are to God the aroma of Christ among those who are being saved and those who are perishing. 2 Corinthians 2:15

_____Let's do: Bake a pan of brownies or a favorite treat. Enjoy the aroma. Share the goodies.

_____Let's pray: Dear Father, thank You for the blessing of Christ in my life. Help me to share this aroma with others. Amen.

G. P.

Samson, Ezekiel, John, and You

Read from God's Word

And He said to me, "Son of man, eat what is before you, eat this scroll; then go and speak to the house of Israel." So I opened my mouth, and He gave me the scroll to eat. Then He said to me, "Son of man, eat this scroll I am giving you and fill your stomach with it." So I ate it, and it tasted as sweet as honey in my mouth. Ezekiel 3:1–3

Did you know you can eat something today that is identical to something people ate more than 3,000 years ago?

It's honey. Samson found it in a lion's carcass (Judges 14:5–9). Ezekiel compared it to the Word of the Lord (Ezekiel 3:1–3). John the Baptist ate it with locusts (Matthew 3:1–4).

Amazingly, honey has not changed in all these centuries. It is still made the same way God designed: bees gather nectar from flowers and turn that flower "syrup" into a sweet golden liquid.

Far more important than the gift of honey is the gift of faith in Christ, which you share with the people of God. Samson was chosen by God to help deliver Israel from her enemies. Ezekiel was chosen to prophesy to the Israelites. John was chosen to prepare the way for Jesus Christ. These men had faith in God without seeing the salvation that was to come in the death and resurrection of Jesus. Like they were, we are sinners who need Jesus for our salvation.

Next time you spread honey on a slice of bread, imagine Samson enjoying honey and sharing it with his parents. Think of John the Baptist eating honey while in the desert. Remember that the Bible, God's precious Word, is "as sweet as honey," as Ezekiel said.

_____Let's do: Find out who else ate honey. Check out Genesis 43:11; 1 Samuel 14:25–30; and 2 Samuel 17:26–29.

_____Let's pray: Saving Lord, help me to read and cherish Your Word, which is sweeter than honey and candy and ice cream. Amen.

C. W.

The Scientist Who Loved God

George was born into slavery during the Civil War. He was owned by the Carver family. Mrs. Carver taught George to read. His first book was the Bible.

Eventually George went to college. After graduating from college, George went to Booker T. Washington's Tuskegee Institute in Alabama. He built a science laboratory and an experimental garden. George taught students and local farmers to produce better crops by rotating their plants. This meant switching from cotton, which hurt the soil, to soil-nourishing plants like sweet potatoes and peanuts. Soon there were too many peanuts on the market, and the farmers had a new problem.

George took the problem to God. In his laboratory, which he called "God's little workshop," he discovered more than 300 uses for peanuts.

George Washington Carver, a famous African-American scientist, was a deeply religious man. He saw God in science and shared his faith with students and others. His favorite Bible verse was today's reading from Genesis 1. With faith and hope in God, George would tackle problems. He would say, "God has work for me to do." He would get out his beakers and microscope and go to work. He trusted God to lead him and answer his prayers. You can too.

Read from God's Word

Then God said, "I give you every seed-bearing plant on the face of the whole earth and every tree that has fruit with seed in it. They will be yours for food. And to all the beasts of the earth and all the birds of the air and all the creatures that move on the ground—everything that has the breath of life in it—I give every green plant for food." And it was so. God saw all that He had made, and it was very good. And there was evening, and there was morning—the sixth day. Genesis 1:29–31

_____Let's do: Take a walk, as George Washington Carver did daily, and look at the plants God made.

_____Let's pray: Gracious Savior, thank You for men and women of faith. Help me to learn to say, "God has work for me to do." Amen.

C. W.

Read from God's Word

Are not five sparrows sold for two pennies? Yet not one of them is forgotten by God. Indeed, the very hairs of your head are all numbered. Don't be afraid; you are worth more than many sparrows. Luke 12:6–7

Our Feathered Friends

One morning my husband and I heard a loud squawking coming from our fireplace. Removing the grate, we found three baby chimney swifts. Pieces of their broken nest were lying around them.

These babies were not able to fly. My husband, wearing gloves, scooped up the nest and placed the baby birds in a flowerpot, then hung the pot in a tree. We hoped the mother would reclaim her chicks, but she didn't.

We took the orphans to a veterinarian who worked with wildlife. She said the babies would probably fly in a week and would care for them until they could.

Chimney swifts are not very pretty birds. They look as though they are covered in soot. Jesus chose another lowly bird, the sparrow, to show God's love for us. God cares for each sparrow. Not one is forgotten. He did not forget His chimney swifts that landed at our feet either.

The baby birds were helpless, crying, and hungry. Without care they would die. We, too, are helpless, covered with the soot of sin. Without Jesus' salvation, we would die. God loves us so much that He sent Jesus to clean our lives from sin and give us eternal life. God, who knows every bird, knows you too.

____Let's do: Watch the birds, especially the sparrows, and remember God is watching over you and caring for you.

____Let's pray: Your eye is on the sparrow, Lord, and I know You also watch over me. Thank You for loving me. In Jesus' name. Amen.

C. W.

X-Ray Eyes

Read from God's Word

Even the darkness will not be dark to you; the night will shine like the day, for darkness is as light to you. Psalm 139:12

During the day, Emily loved the big oak tree outside her window. She spent hours climbing its branches. She'd lie under its shade, watching clouds.

At night, Emily's tree turned into a monster. Its branches made shadows that frightened her.

Emily's father tried to comfort her. He bought her a night-light, but its tiny glow was no match for her fear of the tree monster.

One night when her cousin Patti was staying with her, the wind began howling. The tree monster came to life. "That big ole tree sounds like a chargin' rhinoceros." Patti tried to comfort Emily, so she went on. "I used to be scared of our neighbor's dog at night too. It howled and barked. My mom had me memorize a psalm to help me. Wanna hear it?" Emily nodded a hopeful yes.

Patti continued as the wind howled. "'Even the darkness will not be dark to You; the night will shine like the day, for darkness is as light to You.' God can see everything, all the time, and He cares for us."

Emily smiled, feeling God's peace. "It's like He's got x-ray eyes. He can see through the dark," she said. The girls felt a lot better.

"Come on," said Patti, "let's get a flashlight and check out that tree monster!"

_____Let's do: What scares you in the dark? Memorize today's Bible passage.

_____Let's pray: Dear God, thank You for Your x-ray eyes watching over me day and night. I love You! Amen.

C. W.

Read from God's Word

As Jesus was getting into the boat, the man who had been demon-possessed begged to go with Him. Jesus did not let him, but said, "Go home to your family and tell them how much the Lord has done for you, and how He has had mercy on you." So the man went away and began to tell in the Decapolis how much Jesus had done for him. And all the people were amazed. Mark 5:18–20

Tongue Twisters

Try saying this tongue twister: *Silent snakes slithered slowly southward.* Now try this one: *She sells seashells by the seashore.*

Our tongues are very important. They help us speak clearly and rapidly—most of the time.

Jesus spoke clearly while He was a man here on earth. Many of His words were written in the Bible for our instruction. For instance, Jesus said, "Be perfect, therefore, as your heavenly Father is perfect" (Matthew 5:48).

Being perfect on our own is impossible. We make mistakes. We break God's commandments. In other words, we sin. So it's good to hear Jesus say, "I am the way and the truth and the life. No one comes to the Father except through Me" (John 14:6).

Jesus was perfect for us. He is our Savior from sin, Satan, and death. God the Father sees us as perfect through Him. However, people who don't know Jesus or trust Him to be their Savior won't be saved.

That's why Jesus said, "Tell ... how much the Lord has done for you, and how He has had mercy on you" (Mark 5:19). We can use our tongues to tell others about Jesus. Then, through the power of God's Spirit, they can become *sinners who see their Savior from sin and Satan.*

______Let's talk: What other tongue twisters can you say? Can you make up one about Jesus?

______Let's pray: Dear God, thank You for my tongue and all the tricks it can do. Thanks, especially, that I can use it to tell others about Your love. In Jesus' name. Amen.

C. W.

Tenting Tonight

Read from God's Word

By faith Abraham, when called to go to a place he would later receive as his inheritance, obeyed and went, even though he did not know where he was going. By faith he made his home in the Promised Land like a stranger in a foreign country; he lived in tents, as did Isaac and Jacob, who were heirs with him of the same promise. For he was looking forward to the city with foundations, whose architect and builder is God. Hebrews 11:8–10

Can I set up our tent in the backyard?" pleaded Max.

"That sounds like fun. Go ahead," Mom replied.

"Then can Brian and I sleep in it tonight? We'll use our sleeping bags and pretend that we're camping out. Pleeeeease?" begged Max.

"As long as you don't stay up late or bother the neighbors," Mom said.

Later, inside the tent, Max said, "Tents sure are fun."

"I like them for campouts," Brian agreed, "if the weather is good. But still, there's no place like home."

"I guess I wouldn't want to live in a tent all the time either," said Max. "I'd have to give up too many things. I wonder how Bible people like Abraham did it?"

The Bible says Abraham realized that living on earth was like living in his tent. It was temporary. Through God-given faith, Abraham looked forward to his permanent home in heaven. The world is only a temporary home for all of us.

Jesus lived temporarily in a human body while He was on earth. He came to live with us save us by taking our sins to the cross and then take us to our eternal home with God. Isn't that great?

_____Let's talk: What's your favorite tenting experience? Why does it feel good to come home after a trip? What's going to be great about heaven?

_____Let's pray: Dear Jesus, thank You for "tenting" with us and leading us home. Amen.

P. L.

Read from God's Word

At the end of forty days they ... gave Moses this account: "We went into the land to which you sent us, and it does flow with milk and honey! ... But the people who live there are powerful, and the cities are fortified and very large. ... And they spread among the Israelites a bad report about the land they had explored. They said, "The land we explored devours those living in it. All the people we saw there are of great size. ... We seemed like grasshoppers in our own eyes, and we looked the same to them." Numbers 13:25–33

As Small As Grasshoppers

Have you ever looked through a telescope backwards? Instead of things looking larger, they look much smaller.

Some people look at themselves that way. Such people were the Israelites. They had just been told what a good land God was going to give them. Caleb and Joshua said that although powerful people lived there, God would help them move in.

Others said that the people who lived in Canaan were giants. "In fact," they said, "next to them we were as small as grasshoppers." And then they added, "We also seemed that way to ourselves."

Often we look like grasshoppers to ourselves too. Other people are bigger, smarter, faster, richer. We compare ourselves to them by looking through the wrong end of the telescope.

Caleb and Joshua saw the giants, but they saw that God was bigger and more powerful. They knew God had promised to help them.

Although we may be small in our own eyes, we know that God stands beside us. He has been standing there ever since our Baptism. He forgave us then, and He does so now.

With God next to us, holding onto us with His love, we see ourselves as He does—as His precious sons and daughters.

_____Let's talk: Why do people get upset when others have more than they have or are able to do more than they can do? Why should this not bother God's children? How do you know that God loves you despite what you have or don't have?

_____Let's pray: Heavenly Father, I know that I am small. But I thank You for loving me. Thank You for sending Jesus to make me Your child. Help me always remember who I am and how much You love me. Amen.

J. K.

Offering Ourselves to the Lord

Torrey was in church with his family. His parents had given him two quarters to put into the plate. But Torrey wanted to keep the money for himself.

So he pretended to drop the quarters into the plate, but he kept them in his hand.

Later that day, Torrey's dad asked, "Did you see who was in church today?"

Torrey began to squirm. "I didn't see anyone," he said.

"That someone was Jesus," said Dad. "One day Jesus saw rich people putting many coins into the offering. He also saw a poor woman put in only two pennies. It was the poor widow that He praised."

"Why?" gulped Torrey.

"Because she put in all the money she had. She trusted God to give her what she needed. I wonder what Jesus thought of your offering today."

"He probably didn't like it," confessed Torrey. "I'm sorry I did that. Here are the two quarters. I really want to put them in the plate next Sunday."

"I'm happy to hear you say that," answered Dad. "You see, Jesus isn't looking just for coins in the offering. He's looking for a heart willing to give the coins. When you put your quarters in, they show you have a willing heart."

Read from God's Word

As He looked up, Jesus saw the rich putting their gifts into the temple treasury. He also saw a poor widow put in two very small copper coins. "I tell you the truth," He said, "this poor widow has put in more than all the others. All these people gave their gifts out of their wealth; but she out of her poverty put in all she had to live on." Luke 21:1–4

_____Let's talk: How much did God put into His offering for you? What kind of offering does God's gift of Jesus inspire you to make?

_____Let's pray: Dear Jesus, I'm sorry for the times I haven't given You my best offering. Please forgive me for thinking of myself first. Thank You for thinking of me when You offered Yourself on the cross. Amen.

J. K.

Read from God's Word

The apostles gathered around Jesus and reported to Him all they had done and taught. Then, because so many people were coming and going that they did not even have a chance to eat, He said to them, "Come with Me by yourselves to a quiet place and get some rest." So they went away by themselves in a boat to a solitary place. Mark 6:30–32

Vacationing with Jesus

When people go on vacation, they usually want to rest and do something different. Many people plan all year for their vacation.

Did Jesus ever go on a vacation? Our reading for today seems to say He did. Jesus knows that once in a while people get tired or frustrated and need some time away. In today's Bible reading the disciples went away to a quiet spot. But notice that Jesus went with them.

Wherever you go or whatever you do, Jesus can be a traveler with you. As you vacation, you'll have time to talk with Him in prayer. You can take time to read about Him in the Bible. You might also do something you hardly ever get a chance to do: just sit and think about Jesus and yourself.

What can you think about? Try meditating on why you're a follower of Christ. He chose you from eternity to belong to Him. He came to earth, lived a perfect life, and then gave up His life for you. Now He lives again as your Lord and Savior forever.

Devote some of your vacation time to praising Jesus for His amazing grace.

____Let's talk: Why was Jesus' "trip" to earth not a vacation for Him? Why was He happy to make that trip?

____Let's pray: Lord Jesus, please go with me when I go on vacation. Help me talk to You more and more and hear what You tell me in Your Word. Help me have fun and keep me safe. Amen.

J. K.

Banging Your Head

As I write this, I'm sitting in the woods of Tennessee. In the distance I hear many birds. One bird I hear isn't singing. His sound is rat-a-tat-tat. He's a woodpecker and he's pecking an old tree, looking for bugs.

Jesus once told His disciples, "Look at the birds of the air; they do not sow or reap or store away in barns, and yet your heavenly Father feeds them." You've probably seen sparrows and robins finding their food, which God provides. But have you ever thought how God provides for the woodpecker?

God provides the woodpecker's food inside a tree, and he has to bang his head to get it. For the woodpecker, that is God's way.

God gives food to His creatures and to His children in many ways. For us, His greatest gift came by way of the tree of the cross of Jesus. Jesus suffered and died on a tree so we can go free.

God takes loving care of all His creatures. We don't have to bang our heads in worry over what we need. God provides for us without that. Only the woodpecker must bang his head for a meal, and he doesn't mind.

Read from God's Word

"Therefore I tell you, do not worry about your life. … Look at the birds of the air; they do not sow or reap or store away in barns, and yet your heavenly Father feeds them. Are you not much more valuable than they? Who of you by worrying can add a single hour to his life? And why do you worry about clothes? See how the lilies of the field grow. … not even Solomon in all his splendor was dressed like one of these. If that is how God clothes the grass of the field, … will He not much more clothe you, O you of little faith? So do not worry. … But seek first His kingdom and His righteousness, and all these things will be given to you as well. Therefore do not worry about tomorrow, for tomorrow will worry about itself. Each day has enough trouble of its own." Matthew 6:25–34

_____Let's talk: Although God provides for His creatures, He expects them to work for their food. What are some methods birds and animals use to find their food? How does God provide food and clothing for you?

_____Let's pray: Dear Father, thank You for the daily food You give us. Thank You for the many ways You care for us. We praise You also for birds and animals, which remind us of how well You care for them and us. Thank You for hearing this prayer for Jesus' sake. Amen.

J. K.

Read from God's Word

"Now learn this lesson from the fig tree: As soon as its twigs get tender and its leaves come out, you know that summer is near. Even so, when you see these things happening, you know that it is near, right at the door. I tell you the truth, this generation will certainly not pass away until all these things have happened. Heaven and earth will pass away, but My words will never pass away." Mark 13:28–31

Signs of the Future

In a few weeks in many parts of the country, the leaves will be changing color. This is a sign that fall has arrived and winter is coming.

Jesus used the fig tree to teach about signs. He said that when the fig tree sprouts leaves, summer is near. Jesus wasn't teaching about signs of the coming season. He was teaching about His coming. Yes, there are signs that tell us Jesus will return.

Jesus tells about these signs in Mark 13. Some signs are wars, troubles in nature, lack of food, and lack of love. These signs are unpleasant events. Yet they tell us Jesus is coming in glory, and for us that is good news.

These signs are almost the opposite of back-to-school times. Buying new things for school is mostly fun, although going back to school may not be. Seeing the signs of Jesus' coming may be frightening, but seeing Him when He returns will be the biggest joy of all.

Our Savior says, "When these things begin to take place, stand up and lift up your heads, because your redemption is drawing near" (Luke 21:28). Jesus won our redemption when He destroyed the power of sin and death. Soon we'll have the full enjoyment of Christ's victory.

_____Let's talk: How might people who don't believe that Jesus is their Savior feel when they hear that Jesus is coming soon? What can you do to help a non-Christian get ready for the final judgment?

_____Let's pray: Dear Jesus, thank You for the good news that You will be returning soon. Help me stay ready by listening to Your Word, by praying to You, and by speaking to others about You. Lord Jesus, come back soon because I can hardly wait. Amen.

J. K.

Above the Clouds

Up, up, and away. Jim was in the air, flying to his grandparents' home for a summer vacation.

Over the Midwest he could look down on a thick, cottony blanket of stratus clouds. When the clouds scattered into separate cumulus clouds, he could see the shadow each cloud cast on the ground below.

Some people on the ground were in shadows and some were in rain. Up in a jet plane, high above the clouds, it was all sunshine.

That's when he thought of Jesus. He said, "I am the light of the world." The Son of God, Jesus, is our eternal sun, shining His light on us constantly. However, Satan rolls in the clouds of sin and doubt and self-centeredness. The evil one would like to cloud our minds with darkness and fear. He would like to blot out our view of the "sun" of God, Jesus.

However, light overcomes darkness, just as Jesus overcame Satan on Easter morning. Now, with His Holy Spirit, He lifts us up. The Savior raises us above the cloudy problems of life to soak up the rich rays of His love and salvation.

Read from God's Word

When Jesus spoke again to the people, He said, "I am the light of the world. Whoever follows Me will never walk in darkness, but will have the light of life." John 8:12

_____Let's talk: Have you experienced God's sunshine in your life? Do you know someone with whom you can share the "sun" of God? Let your light shine.

_____Let's pray: Dear Jesus, light of the world, shine on me. Chase the clouds of sin away, and let me be a light in the world by showing Your love to others. Amen.

J. K.

Read from God's Word

God is our refuge and strength, an ever-present help in trouble. Therefore we will not fear, though the earth give way and the mountains fall into the heart of the sea, though its waters roar and foam and the mountains quake with their surging. There is a river whose streams make glad the city of God, the holy place where the Most High dwells. God is within her, she will not fall; God will help her at break of day. Nations are in uproar, kingdoms fall; He lifts His voice, the earth melts. The LORD Almighty is with us. ... Come and see the works of the LORD. ... He makes wars cease to the ends of the earth. ... "Be still, and know that I am God; I will be exalted among the nations, I will be exalted in the earth." The LORD Almighty is with us; the God of Jacob is our fortress. Psalm 46

How God Speaks to Us

It was a terrible thunderstorm. Lightning crackled. Thunder boomed. Wind and the rain crashed down on the old farmhouse on the hill.

Sarah was sobbing and clutching her grandmother's hand. They were standing at the upstairs window. The lightning made the barn and fields look as bright as day.

"I'm scared, Grandma!" wailed Sarah. "Why doesn't God stop this awful storm?"

"Shh! Be still!" comforted Grandma. "God is working. He's telling the wind to rain on the fields so the corn will grow. God just talks kinda loud."

God may talk loudly in thunderstorms, but when we're afraid, He talks like Grandma. God told the people of Israel, "Be still," when the king of Egypt frightened them. In our reading God says, "Be still, and know that I am God."

One day Jesus told the wind and the rain, "Be still!" He did this because His disciples were frightened in a storm on the Sea of Galilee.

Jesus says to us, "Be still!" when we're afraid of storms, troubles, and people. Only God can stop storms, sickness, evil, and the unhappiness sin brings.

When Jesus gave His life for us, that was the loudest "Be still!" we will ever hear. "Be still, and know that I am God," says the Lord. He forgives and He cares.

_____Let's talk: How many ways can you think of that God makes Himself known on earth? Why does God want us to be still when He acts?

_____Let's pray: Dear Father, You control both the rain and the sunshine. Through everyday happenings help me see how great You are. Help me thank You for even the storms and rain in my life. Help me trust You in all things. Amen.

J. K.

Can You Float?

Cesar was taking swimming lessons. One of the first things the instructor taught him was floating on the water. His instructor supported him as he lay on his back on the water. As she removed her hands, Cesar started to sink.

"Just arch your back," she said. Cesar did but sank like a brick.

"Arch your back and relax," the instructor said. "Trust the water to hold you up." What a thought! The water hadn't held him up before, so why should it now?

Eventually, Cesar learned to float. The water held him up. What a difference relaxing and trusting the water made!

Relying on Jesus for eternal life is like learning to float. The harder we try to gain salvation by ourselves, the faster we sink. When we tense up, thinking that we have to keep the commandments, to do better, to work harder to please God, we sink.

Jesus wants us to think of Him holding us up the same way the water holds up a swimmer. Just let the water of life, Jesus, hold you afloat. Jesus did all the work for us. He obeyed God's laws for us. He took our punishment for us. Relax and float. Jesus won't let you sink.

Read from God's Word

"Lord, if it's you," Peter replied, "tell me to come to You on the water." "Come," He said. Then Peter got down out of the boat, walked on the water and came toward Jesus. But when he saw the wind, he was afraid and, beginning to sink, cried out, "Lord, save me!" Immediately Jesus reached out His hand and caught Him. "You of little faith," He said, "why did you doubt?" And when they climbed into the boat, the wind died down. Then those who were in the boat worshiped Him, saying, "Truly You are the Son of God." Matthew 14:28–33

_____Let's talk: Why is it good to know how to swim? Think of a recent time when you trusted Jesus to take care of a problem. Thank Him for His support.

_____Let's pray: Dear Jesus, help me relax and trust Your loving arms to support me. Amen.

P. L.

Read from God's Word

To some who were confident of their own righteousness and looked down on everybody else, Jesus told this parable: "Two men went up to the temple to pray, one a Pharisee and the other a tax collector. The Pharisee stood up and prayed about himself: 'God, I thank you that I am not like other men—robbers, evildoers, adulterers—or even like this tax collector. I fast twice a week and give a tenth of all I get.' But the tax collector stood at a distance. He would not even look up to heaven, but beat his breast and said, 'God, have mercy on me, a sinner.' I tell you that this man, rather than the other, went home justified before God. For everyone who exalts himself will be humbled, and he who humbles himself will be exalted." Luke 18:9–14

Are You a Straw?

Where do you think the idea of drinking straws came from? People learned they could cut a wheat stem and suck liquid through it. They were drinking through the hollow straw stem, thus the name "straw."

Have you tried to use a straw that had something stuck in it? Sometimes a milkshake is so thick it can't move through the straw. Maybe you were drinking lemonade and a seed got stuck in the straw so the lemonade couldn't get through. A straw has to be empty to be useful.

God wants us to be like straws. He wants us to empty ourselves so He can use us. We need to empty out our pride, selfishness, worry, and doubt. When we confess our sins to the Lord and ask for His mercy, we become empty. God fills us with His love, joy, and peace.

Imagine trying to drink through a straw clogged with mud! We would have to clean the mud out first. In a similar way, God cleans out our lives. He sent Jesus to wash away our sins. Now God sends His Holy Spirit to us each day to clean our lives (forgive us) so we can be filled with the good gifts of God.

_____Let's talk: What kind of straw are you? Are you "cleaned out" (forgiven) by the mercy of God? Share with others your good gifts from God.

_____Let's pray: Dear God, make me useful. Clean me each day by Your Spirit, and fill my life with Your good blessings. Help me share those blessings with others. In Jesus' name. Amen.

P. L.

Footprints in the Sand

"Let's go to the beach," suggested Laura.

"Yeah, we can get wet and cool off," replied Laisa.

Later at the beach the sisters were walking along the hot sand. "It's too hot to walk barefoot on this burning sand," complained Laisa.

"Then let's walk on the wet sand where the waves wash up," suggested Laura. "Hey, look! My feet sink into this wet sand and leave a trail of footprints."

Laisa yelled, "Watch out! Here comes a wave!"

"Oh, it feels good to get my feet wet," Laura said. "Look—all our footprints are washed away. The sand fills the holes back up."

The girls made more footprints and watched as the waves came and erased them. Finally Laisa said, "Do you know what Dad would say if he saw this?"

"What?"

"He would say the waves are just like Jesus. They constantly erase the footprints, just like Jesus constantly erases our sins."

"Oh, I see. We mess up by disobeying God, but He forgives all our sins. He loves us."

"Yes, it's good to know that Jesus loves us enough to wipe out all we do wrong."

"Wow!" concluded Laura. "We've had a pretty good devotion out here on the beach."

Read from God's Word

Surely I was sinful at birth, sinful from the time my mother conceived me. Surely You desire truth in the inner parts; You teach me wisdom in the inmost place. Cleanse me with hyssop, and I will be clean; wash me, and I will be whiter than snow. Let me hear joy and gladness; let the bones You have crushed rejoice. Hide Your face from my sins and blot out all my iniquity. Psalm 51:5–9

_____Let's talk: Have you ever made footprints at the beach? What sins in your life has Jesus washed away? How can you share Jesus with your friends?

_____Let's pray: My Savior, thank You for washing away all the wrongs I have done. Help me always stay close to You. Amen.

P. L.

Read from God's Word

Thomas said to Him, "Lord, we don't know where You are going, so how can we know the way?" Jesus answered, "I am the way and the truth and the life. No one comes to the Father except through Me." John 14:5–6

Straight to Heaven!

Have you ever wondered why the length of a ruler, 12 inches, is called a foot?

Many years ago, people used their feet to measure distances. In some countries, the length of the king's foot was the official length of one foot. In the 1300s, England made the official length of the foot 12 inches.

How does your foot measure up? Place your foot on your ruler. Is it longer or shorter than the ruler? Whether we have short feet or long feet, the important thing is they get us where we want to go.

We go many places: soccer games, the dentist, Grandma's house. But we will not always be on earth. Eventually we will die and go to heaven. How will we get there? The psalmist says, "Teach me your way, O LORD; lead me in a straight path" (Psalm 27:11). In John 14:6, Jesus says, "I am the way and the truth and the life."

Get the message? God's Word leads you to know Jesus. The way to heaven is a straight path through Him. When we try to get to heaven by ourselves, it won't work. Jesus is our ruler. He suffered the punishment of our sins and creates for us the way—the only way, the straight way—to heaven.

_____Let's do: Use your ruler to make straight lines on a piece of paper. Let those straight lines remind you of what Jesus has done for you.

_____Let's pray: Dear Jesus, thank You for being our ruler. Thank You for keeping us on the straight path to heaven. Amen.

G. F.

Our Best Friend

Read from God's Word

"A new command I give you: Love one another. As I have loved you, so you must love one another. By this all men will know that you are My disciples, if you love one another." John 13:34–35

Holly was excited. It was the first day of school. She would get to see her friends again!

As she entered her classroom, Holly saw April, Sarah, and Alyssa. The girls talked happily until the bell rang. Holly could hardly wait until recess to talk to her friends again. When the bell rang, her teacher, Mrs. Smith, said, "Holly, I'd like to see you for a moment."

"We have a new girl in class," Mrs. Smith said. "Her name is Megan. I would like you to help her feel at home." In the excitement of seeing her friends, Holly hadn't even noticed the new girl. Holly introduced Megan to her friends.

Later that night, Holly told her mother, "Mrs. Smith asked me to be friends with a new girl in class, and you know what? She lives right next door!"

As she made friends with Megan, Holly was following God's command. Read the Bible passage for today. Holly did just that. Mrs. Smith had asked her to be a friend to Megan because she knew Holly had the love of Jesus in her heart. She knew Holly would let that love flow out to Megan. And she was right!

_____Let's do: Is there someone in your class who needs God's love? Find ways to share the Good News of Jesus with them!

_____Let's pray: Dear Jesus, thank You for being our friend. Let Your love shine out of us to others. Amen.

G. F.

Read from God's Word

"Now, brothers, I know that you acted in ignorance, as did your leaders. But this is how God fulfilled what He had foretold through all the prophets, saying that His Christ would suffer. Repent, then, and turn to God, so that your sins may be wiped out, that times of refreshing may come from the Lord, and that He may send the Christ, who has been appointed for you—even Jesus. He must remain in heaven until the time comes for God to restore everything, as He promised long ago through His holy prophets. For Moses said, 'The Lord your God will raise up for you a prophet like me from among your own people; you must listen to everything He tells you. Anyone who does not listen to Him will be completely cut off from among His people.'" Acts 3:17–23

Two Kinds of Erasers

Tyler's teacher asked the class to write about summer vacation. Tyler started this way: "My sumer was nice." Then he noticed he had misspelled the word summer. Tyler erased sumer and wrote summer.

Later that day, Tyler made other mistakes. He added 2 + 2 and got 5. He changed his answer to 4. He used his eraser again when he forgot to begin a sentence with a capital letter. Tyler learned that when he used his pencil lightly, it was easy to erase a mistake. When he pressed hard with his pencil, the eraser couldn't completely get rid of his mistake.

That evening, Tyler complained to his mother, "I need a really good eraser that will erase all of my mistakes."

"If you want a perfect eraser for your paper," his mother said, "I'm afraid you won't find one. But you have another kind of perfect eraser."

Tyler was curious.

"Because we are sinners," his mother explained, "we all make mistakes. We need a sin eraser to make us right with God. Jesus erased all our sins when He died for us."

Whether they are little sins written lightly or big sins written boldly, Jesus has completely erased them. There is no trace left. So the next time you use your eraser, say a prayer of thanks for Jesus!

_____Let's do: What mistakes have you made today? Ask God to erase them!

_____Let's pray: Dear Jesus, thank You for dying on the cross to erase all of our sins. Amen.

G. F.

The Right Prayer

After a day of canoeing, swimming, and fishing, the family was ready to eat. Don said the prayer: "Thank You, Lord, for giving us a fantastic day. Thank You for Your protection. Please bless this food to nourish our bodies and be with us in our meal. In Jesus' name. Amen."

As everyone dove for the food, four-year-old Devin began to cry. His mother asked Devin why he was crying. "He didn't say the right prayer, Mommy."

Devin's mom understood. They prayed together, "Come, Lord Jesus, be our guest, and let these gifts to us be blessed. Amen." Devin began to eat, content that God had heard his prayer.

Although Don's prayer was a good prayer, it was confusing for Devin. Devin was used to starting each meal with "Come, Lord Jesus." He didn't feel right eating without it.

Do you ever feel like Devin? Maybe someone prays with words you don't know. Maybe you can't decide the exact words to use when you pray. If that is the case, here is good news.

The Holy Spirit will help us. God's Spirit knows what is in our heart. He knows the things that bother, worry, and frustrate us. If we don't know what to say when we pray, the Spirit comes to our rescue.

Read from God's Word

The Spirit himself testifies with our spirit that we are God's children. Now if we are children, then we are heirs—heirs of God and co-heirs with Christ, if indeed we share in His sufferings in order that we may also share in His glory. ... In the same way, the Spirit helps us in our weakness. We do not know what we ought to pray for, but the Spirit Himself intercedes for us with groans that words cannot express. Romans 8:16–17, 26

_____Let's do: What prayer do you say before a meal? Write a new prayer thanking the Lord for sending Jesus to be your Savior and for providing you with food to nourish your body.

_____Let's pray: I put my thoughts and cares into Your hands, O Lord. Thank You for always hearing me, no matter what words I use. Amen.

G. F.

Read from God's Word

"The kingdom of heaven is like a man who sowed good seed … [but] his enemy came and sowed weeds among the wheat … The owner's servants … asked him, 'Do you want us to go and pull them up?' 'No,' he answered, 'because while you are pulling the weeds, you may root up the wheat with them.'" … [Jesus said], "The one who sowed the good seed is the Son of Man. The field is the world, and the good seed stands for the sons of the kingdom. The weeds are the sons of the evil one, and the enemy who sows them is the devil. The harvest is the end of the age, and the harvesters are angels. As the weeds are pulled up and burned in the fire, so it will be at the end of the age. The Son of Man will send out His angels, and they will weed out of His kingdom everything that causes sin and all who do evil. They will throw them into the fiery furnace. … Then the righteous will shine like the sun in the kingdom of their Father." Matthew 13:24–43

Weeds in the Garden

Sweat poured from Jenny's brow as she forged her way through the thick underbrush. Mosquitoes and bugs swarmed. Finally, she saw it—her prized pepper plant!

Jenny had carefully watered and hoed the pepper plant. Then she went on vacation and wasn't home to tend her plant. Tall weeds had grown up around it. Jenny reached her plant in time to save it. She weeded, watered, and hoed her plant every day.

Finally Jenny picked her peppers. She carried a full basket onto the porch, where her father was waiting.

"Those peppers look wonderful," he said. "What a harvest! Your pepper plant reminds me of a story Jesus told. He talked about weeds growing up among the wheat plants. When it was time for the harvest, the weeds were thrown into the fire while the wheat was put into the barn. Your pepper plant is just like the wheat. And, as Jesus explains the story, the wheat is just like you.

"God planted the seed of faith in you when you were baptized. Since then, the Holy Spirit has been helping your faith grow every day. All around us, though, are unbelievers or 'weeds.' The Holy Spirit tends our faith and keeps it strong. In the end, He brings us home to Jesus."

_____Let's do: With your parents' help, pull some weeds around your house. Remember God's care for you.

_____Let's pray: Dear Lord, thank You for helping us to grow strong. Thank You for feeding us the Good News of Jesus every day. In Jesus' name. Amen.

G. F.

A Mighty Rushing Wind

Jesse and his dad went to see the Blue Angels, a group of jet fighter planes. They did all sorts of tricks, zipping close to the ground, zooming straight up in the air.

At one point, they gathered in the distance then flew in formation. Jesse and his dad could not hear the jets until they flew overhead. Then the roar of their engines blasted the crowd. The ground shook. That noise certainly got everyone's attention. Most of the noise came from the air as it was pulled into the jet engine and pushed back out at a very great speed.

That sound may have been like another mighty rushing wind. On Pentecost, the disciples were in a house in Jerusalem. Suddenly, there was a sound "like the blowing of a violent wind." Many people heard it and came to find out what it was. Tongues of fire appeared on the disciples' heads. The Holy Spirit entered their hearts. The disciples began to speak the Good News of Jesus in many languages. The power of the Spirit changed the disciples. It gave them strong faith and bold words.

As God's Spirit works through His Word and Sacraments, we change. Our faith becomes stronger; our words become bolder. We share the story of Jesus with "roaring" power.

Read from God's Word

When the day of Pentecost came, they were all together in one place. Suddenly a sound like the blowing of a violent wind came from heaven and filled the whole house where they were sitting. They saw what seemed to be tongues of fire that separated and came to rest on each of them. All of them were filled with the Holy Spirit and began to speak in other tongues as the Spirit enabled them. Acts 2:1–4

_____Let's talk: Which of your friends would you like to talk to about Jesus but are afraid to? Have you tried asking the Holy Spirit for help?

_____Let's pray: Dear Father, thank You for giving me the Holy Spirit to help me share the story of Your love with strength and boldness. Amen.

G. F.

Read from God's Word

For we were all baptized by one Spirit into one body—whether Jews or Greeks, slave or free—and we were all given the one Spirit to drink. 1 Corinthians 12:13

Mighty Drops of Water

As Joel stared out the living room window at the rain, he noticed something. The rain came down in drops. When the drops hit the ground, they ran together to form puddles. The drops acted differently than the big can of marbles in his room. If he dropped marbles into the can, they didn't run together to form one big marble. They all stayed separate. So why did the water drops run together?

In science class Joel learned the answer. "The water drops run together because of a force called cohesion," his teacher said. She explained how cohesion holds everything together.

"I don't get it," Joel told his teacher at recess.

"Don't worry, Joel," his teacher replied. "One day you will. You can think of cohesion as a mystery. It will remind you of another special cohesion. That's the cohesion in God's family. Think of each person in God's family as a raindrop. When all the raindrops are pulled together, it is the work of the Holy Spirit.

Look at today's Bible reading again. Through Baptism, the Holy Spirit produces faith and makes us members of the Christian church. Like Joel, we don't know how it happens. We just believe it does!

_____Let's do: Ask your teacher to help you do some experiments that will show cohesion. Think about how the Holy Spirit binds us together in the same way.

_____Let's pray: Thank You, Lord, for the gift of faith in each of us and for making us one in the Holy Spirit. Amen.

G. F.

The Hidden Beauty

Read from God's Word

Jesus said to her, "I am the resurrection and the life. He who believes in Me will live, even though he dies; and whoever lives and believes in Me will never die. Do you believe this?" John 11:25–26

As I pull the weeds near my driveway, I am amazed at the number of insects I find. There are ants, spiders, roly-poly bugs, and worms. There are insects everywhere. Some of these insects "bug" me, but some of them I love. My favorite is the butterfly.

The Papago Indians explained the beauty of the butterfly in a myth. They said the creator felt sorry for people when he realized they would grow old, wrinkled, and weak. Hence, he put colors from the earth, flowers, sunlight, and leaves into a magical bag for children. When the children opened the bag, colored butterflies flew out.

We know that the butterfly's beauty is not magic, as some people may have once believed. God created the butterfly as a marvelous miniature with a life-cycle lesson. The transformation of the brown chrysalis into the adult butterfly reminds us of Easter. What looks like death turns into beauty.

Jesus came to rescue us from more than growing old, wrinkled, or weak. He rescued us from sin. His love is real beauty.

The next time you spot a butterfly, thank God for sending Jesus.

_____Let's do: Make a scrapbook of the butterflies in your yard. Draw pictures of them and try to find their names.

_____Let's pray: Thank You, heavenly Father, for the gift of butterflies, which remind me of my new life in You. In Jesus' name. Amen.

G. F.

Read from God's Word

In Lystra there sat a man crippled in his feet. ... Paul ... saw that he had faith to be healed and called out, "Stand up on your feet!" At that, the man jumped up and began to walk. When the crowd saw what Paul had done, they shouted ... "The gods have come down to us in human form!" ... But when the apostles Barnabas and Paul heard of this, they tore their clothes and rushed out into the crowd, shouting: "... We too are only men, human like you. We are bringing you good news, telling you to turn from these worthless things to the living God." ... They stoned Paul and dragged him outside the city, thinking he was dead. But after the disciples had gathered around him, he got up and went back into the city. The next day he and Barnabas left for Derbe. They preached the good news in that city and won a large number of disciples. ... "We must go through many hardships to enter the kingdom of God," they said. Acts 14:8–22

The Persistent Mosquito

The buzzing grew louder then, suddenly, it stopped. Cyril was sure the mosquito had landed on his ear, so he hit himself in the head. But the mosquito just flew away and returned in a few minutes. It took Cyril a long time to get to sleep that night.

The next morning Cyril told his mother about the mosquito. "It wouldn't leave me alone!"

"Maybe you should be like a mosquito," his mother replied.

"What do you mean?" Cyril asked.

"You could try to finish things like the mosquito does when it wants something. You asked Brandon to go to church with you a few weeks ago, but he was busy. Did you ask him again?"

"No, I forgot," Cyril replied.

"That's when it's good to be like a mosquito. The apostle Paul traveled around the world bringing the Good News of Jesus to everyone who would listen. He never stopped talking about Jesus. When Paul was preaching in Lystra, the people threw stones at him until they thought he was dead. But Paul recovered and went back to Lystra! He knew everyone needed to hear about Jesus, even the people who had tried to kill him. Paul kept trying."

"Hmm, I think I'll go call Brandon," Cyril said as he buzzed off.

_____Let's do: Is there someone you know who needs to hear about Jesus? Be a good mosquito for Christ!

_____Let's pray: Thank You, Jesus, for suffering and dying for me. Help me to tell others about You. Amen.

G. F.

New Fingerprints

Read from God's Word

Therefore, if anyone is in Christ, he is a new creation; the old has gone, the new has come! 2 Corinthians 5:17

Something caught Ryan's eye as he was drinking a glass of milk. "Mom, there are funny-looking marks on this glass."

"Those are your fingerprints," his mother said. "Look closely. You will see tiny little lines in them."

Each of our fingers has a unique print, and each of us has different prints from someone else. There are three basic patterns in fingerprints. There are loops, arches, and whorls. What kind do you have? Whatever your fingerprint pattern, you are one of a kind.

Did you know we have an expert who can identify each of us by our fingerprints? That expert is our Creator, our God. He knows everything about each of us. He knows we are sinners. And He sent Jesus to solve our sin problem.

The Bible verse for today says we are a new creation in Christ. His suffering, death, and resurrection create new life in those who believe in Him. Thinking about our fingerprints is another way to remember we are special to God. Use two fingers to make a cross. There you have it. The cross is your reminder of God's fingerprint.

_____Let's do: With your parents' help, make a copy of your fingerprints on a note card. Put the card in a place where you can see it. Let it remind you of God's fingerprint on you!

_____Let's pray: Lord, You have made me different. You have made me Your child. Thank You for loving me and caring for me. Amen.

G. F.

s e p t e m b e r

Contributors for this month:

Nicole Dreyer

Tom Raabe

Mary Lou Krause

Endless Summer

Marta watched a seagull dive into the ocean and snatch a fish. Her brother, Jake, was digging in the sand.

Mom called. "Marta! Jake! Time to go!"

They didn't move.

Dad walked up to them. "Didn't you hear your mother calling?"

"Okay," Marta sighed. When they were in the car, Marta said, "I wish vacation could last forever."

Mom smiled. "I know how you feel. I'm always sad when our vacation ends. But then I think of all the things we have to look forward to in the fall."

"Like apple-picking," said Dad.

"Football and soccer," said Mom.

"School," said Jake, and everyone laughed.

"Everyone wishes special times could last forever," said Dad. "When Jesus was on earth, His disciples thought He would always be with them. They didn't understand that Jesus had to die on the cross. But because He did, their time together would last forever in heaven, like a vacation that never ends."

"You mean that because Jesus died and rose again, He will come with us on vacation?"

"Well, sort of," said Mom. "Jesus said that He will be with us always. And God has given us faith to believe in Jesus. We will live in heaven with Him forever."

"Me too?" asked Jake.

"You too," said Mom.

Read from God's Word

There is a time for everything, and a season for every activity under heaven: a time to be born and a time to die, a time to plant and a time to uproot, a time to kill and a time to heal, a time to tear down and a time to build, a time to weep and a time to laugh, a time to mourn and a time to dance, a time to scatter stones and a time to gather them, a time to embrace and a time to refrain, a time to search and a time to give up, a time to keep and a time to throw away, a time to tear and a time to mend, a time to be silent and a time to speak, a time to love and a time to hate, a time for war and a time for peace. Ecclesiastes 3:1–8

_____Let's do: Make a mobile of the four seasons. Hang your mobile as a reminder of God's love for us all year.

_____Let's pray: My Creator, You give us everything in due season. Thank You for showing us Your love in the sun and the rain, the flowers and the snow, the blowing winds and the falling leaves. Thank You most of all for Jesus. Amen.

N. D.

Family Picnic

The first Sunday in September is always a special day for my family. My parents, sister, aunts, uncles, and cousins have a big family picnic. We eat hot dogs, hamburgers, and salad. We drink iced tea and lemonade. We play catch and croquet. We take pictures of everyone having a good time.

When it gets dark, we hug and kiss each other good-bye and say, "God bless you! I love you! See you at Thanksgiving." Saying good-bye is happy and sad. We're happy that we've had a fun day, but we're sad because it will be two months until we're all together again.

Many families have special traditions. The family of God has a special tradition too. Every Sunday we gather in God's house to receive His blessings and share the peace and love of Christ. We listen to the Word of God and sing praises to Him. We tell God and one another we're sorry for our sins. We receive forgiveness from our Father in heaven and our brothers and sisters in Christ.

Although we can't see Jesus, we have His promise that He is with us. Jesus says, "I am with you always" (Matthew 28:20). We can celebrate His love with all of His family every Sunday. Isn't that a great reason for a party?

_____Let's do: Invite a friend to celebrate God's love with you in church this week.

_____Let's pray: Dear God, thank You for being my heavenly Father. Dear Jesus, thank You for being my brother. Holy Spirit, bless our family as we celebrate together. Amen.

N. D.

Labor Day

In 1894, Congress declared the first Monday in September a national holiday. They wanted to honor all of the workers in America. Today, people celebrate Labor Day in many ways, but they don't always remember why they are celebrating.

The apostle Paul and his friends Silas and Timothy did not want to forget about the hard-working Christians in Thessalonica. Paul gave thanks to God because many of the people there became believers in Jesus. The Thessalonians wanted to serve Jesus. They knew He had labored on the cross for their sin and freely gave them rest from their labors. In return, they worked hard to share Christ's love and the Good News of salvation in Him.

However, some people in their country didn't believe in Jesus. These people tried to hurt the Christians. The Christians were suffering, but they didn't give up. Paul gave them good advice. He told them to "be joyful always; pray continually; give thanks in all circumstances" (1 Thessalonians 5:16–18a).

God blessed the Thessalonian church just as He blesses everyone who serves Him. When you celebrate Labor Day, give thanks to God for all of the servants of the Lord who are hard at work spreading the Good News.

Read from God's Word

We always thank God for all of you, mentioning you in our prayers. We continually remember before our God and Father your work produced by faith, your labor prompted by love, and your endurance inspired by hope in our Lord Jesus Christ. For we know, brothers loved by God, that He has chosen you, because our gospel came to you not simply with words, but also with power, with the Holy Spirit and with deep conviction. You know how we lived among you for your sake. You became imitators of us and of the Lord; in spite of severe suffering, you welcomed the message with the joy given by the Holy Spirit. 1 Thessalonians 1:2–6

_____Let's do: What can you do today to make your mom's or dad's job easier?

_____Let's pray: Dear Jesus, bless all of the workers in our country. In Your name we pray. Amen.

N. D.

Read from God's Word

Devote yourselves to prayer, being watchful and thankful. And pray for us, too, that God may open a door for our message, so that we may proclaim the mystery of Christ, for which I am in chains. Colossians 4:2–3

Back to School

"Good morning, Ana," said Mom. "Rise and shine!"

Ana groaned and pulled the covers over her head. It was the first day of school and Ana didn't want to get up. Mom gave her a nudge. "Let's go. Luke's already up."

"That's because he *wants* to go to school," grumbled Ana.

"Luke's excited that he's finally going to school like his big sister."

"Hmph!" grumbled Ana as she climbed out of bed.

She was still grumbling when she and Luke got to the bus stop. "Hey, Ana," her friend Michelle called, "did you hear about Chucky? His family had to move because his dad lost his job."

"That's terrible," Ana said

"Chucky's big brother had to get a job during the day to help pay the bills. He's going to school at night."

Just then the school bus pulled up. Ana let Luke sit by the window.

"Are you still grumpy?" asked Luke.

"No, Luke. I'm kind of sad but kind of happy. I feel sad for Chucky. I am going to ask Jesus to help his family. I also feel happy because you and I get to go to school. I want to thank Jesus for that blessing."

"Can we pray on the school bus?" asked Luke.

"We sure can," answered Ana, and they bowed their heads.

_____Let's talk: It is hard to go back to school when summer is over. How can you make the first days of school special days?

_____Let's pray: Dear Jesus, help me to be a good listener too so I may learn all about the world our Father created. Help me to do my very best every day. Amen.

N. D.

Twice Blessed

Read from God's Word

There are different kinds of gifts, but the same Spirit. There are different kinds of service, but the same Lord. There are different kinds of working, but the same God works all of them in all men. 1 Corinthians 12:4–6

Robkrun and TaDarrol were twins. They were alike in many ways. They played the trumpet. They got A's in math and B's in science. They were acolytes in church.

Over the summer, Robkrun and TaDarrol played baseball, went to vacation Bible school, and took a trip to the Grand Canyon with their family. When it was time to go back to school, a strange thing happened. TaDarrol decided to play soccer. Robkrun decided to play football.

Although they were alike in many ways, they developed their own talents. TaDarrol was good at dribbling and kicking a soccer ball. Robkrun was good at stopping players from getting a touchdown. Both boys had skills their teams needed.

There are many things we do together as God's family. We go to Sunday school and church. We read the Bible and sing hymns. We pray every day. But God also gives different gifts to the members of His family. You are an important part of God's team, a special member of His family. It doesn't depend on your talents. Jesus died for all people—people who have many different abilities. There is always something you can do in the family of God. God will help you serve.

_____Let's do: Name several things you can do to help serve God's family.

_____Let's pray: Heavenly Father, I want to serve. Help me to know my gifts and to use them wisely. In Jesus' name. Amen.

N. D.

Read from God's Word

Your attitude should be the same as that of Christ Jesus: Who, being in very nature God, did not consider equality with God something to be grasped, but made Himself nothing, taking the very nature of a servant, being made in human likeness. And being found in appearance as a man, He humbled Himself and became obedient to death—even death on a cross! Therefore God exalted Him to the highest place and gave Him the name that is above every name, that at the name of Jesus every knee should bow, in heaven and on earth and under the earth, and every tongue confess that Jesus Christ is Lord, to the glory of God the Father. Philippians 2:5–11

You've Got Mail

Do you like to get e-mail? I do. I like sending and receiving messages from my family and friends. Getting an e-mail message from someone I love is like getting a big hug.

The names people use when they send e-mail say a lot about them. A racecar driver might use SPEEDY1. A singer could use SONG4U. Someone who likes to cook might choose STEWPOT.

We can find many different names for Jesus in the Bible—Prince of Peace, Bread of Life, Good Shepherd, just to name a few. Each name for Jesus tells us something special about our Savior.

The name I like best for Jesus is Immanuel, which means "God with us." Although we can't see Jesus, we know He is always with us. When we hear His Word, the Bible, Jesus is with us. Jesus comes to us in Baptism and the Lord's Supper. When we sing His praises, He is beside us. When we pray, Jesus is close to us, listening to everything we say. Praying to Jesus is better than e-mail. Praying to Jesus is talking to our best Friend.

_____Let's do: How many names for Jesus can you find in your Bible?

_____Let's pray: Jesus, help me to use Your name in prayer and praise every day. Amen.

N. D.

Sleep Tight

Read from God's Word

I lift up my eyes to the hills— where does my help come from? My help comes from the LORD, the Maker of heaven and earth. He will not let your foot slip—He who watches over you will not slumber; indeed, He who watches over Israel will neither slumber nor sleep. The LORD watches over you—the LORD is your shade at your right hand; the sun will not harm you by day, nor the moon by night. The LORD will keep you from all harm—He will watch over your life; the LORD will watch over your coming and going both now and forevermore. Psalm 121

"They're here!" yelled Carolyn when the doorbell rang.

Carolyn was having a party. Abigail, Elisabeth, Tabitha, and Amy were coming to spend the night. The girls came in with their sleeping bags, pajamas, and teddy bears.

"What are your plans tonight, girls?" Mom asked.

"Oh, we have so much to do, we'll be up all night," said Elisabeth.

"We're not going to sleep at all," said Abigail.

"Can we stay up all night, Mom?" asked Carolyn.

"You can try," said Mom.

"We can do it," Tabitha declared.

"It'll be easy," agreed Amy.

At 9:00 the girls had pizza and soda and listened to music. At 10:30 they drank milkshakes. At midnight they ate nachos and popcorn and played a game. Then Tabitha fell asleep. At 1:30 a.m. Abigail and Elisabeth fell asleep. At 3:00 they told silly stories. Soon Amy and Carolyn fell asleep. At 6:00 the sun came up. All the girls were asleep.

No matter how hard we try to stay awake, sooner or later we fall asleep. We have to sleep, but our God never does. He watches over us all day and all night. When the sun sets, our heavenly Father covers us with a blanket of blessing and zips us safely into His loving arms. Good night. Sleep tight.

____Let's do: Write a new bedtime prayer and say it tonight.

____Let's pray: Dear God, thank You for Your love and protection from evil. Keep us close to You always. In Jesus' name. Amen.

N. D.

Read from God's Word

"For God so loved the world that He gave His one and only Son, that whoever believes in Him shall not perish but have eternal life." John 3:16

Finders Keepers

Hannah and her brother Tommy went to the amusement park. Tommy had saved $3 to use in the arcade. Hannah had saved $5 to buy a souvenir.

They rode the rides and went to the arcade. When he had only two quarters left, Tommy played Frog Bog. His last frog landed on a lily pad. He won! Tommy's prize was a big stuffed frog.

Then they decided to ride the roller coaster before they went home. When the ride was over, they walked toward the gate to meet their parents. Suddenly, Tommy shouted, "My frog! I left him on the ride!"

They saw a boy holding Tommy's frog. "Excuse me," said Tommy politely. "That's my frog."

"Finders keepers," the boy said.

Hannah held out her money. She said, "will you give him the frog if I give you $5?" The boy grabbed the money and dropped the frog.

Tommy hugged his frog and then he hugged Hannah. "Thanks, Hannah, but now you don't have money to buy a souvenir. You can have my frog."

"That's okay, Tommy. You won him. He belongs to you."

We belong to God, but the devil tries to lead us away from Him. He loves us so much that He sacrificed His own Son to buy us back and keep us forever. We are more than His souvenir—we are His own children.

_____Let's talk: How does God keep you close to Him?

_____Let's pray: Dear God, I want to stay close to You forever. Thank You for the victory You won for me. Thank You for eternal life in You. For Jesus' sake. Amen.

N. D.

Rally Day

"Hannah! Tommy! Time to go!" called Dad. "We don't want to be late for Rally Day."

As the family drove to church, Tommy asked, "What is Rally Day?"

"A rally is a meeting where people gather for a special reason. Our rally today celebrates the start of a new year in Sunday school."

"Is it like a New Year's party?" asked Hannah.

"That's exactly what it's like," answered Mom.

When they arrived at church, the fellowship hall was decorated with streamers and balloons. Tommy's teacher gave each third-grader a Bible. Everyone in Hannah's fifth-grade class received a prayer book.

Pastor Keith played his guitar, Miss Lori played her drums, and everyone sang along. Pastor Keith asked God to bless their Sunday school, their teachers, and all the students.

Then Pastor Keith said, "I'm glad everyone is here to celebrate Rally Day. God's family has many reasons to celebrate, but the best reason is Jesus. When God sent Jesus to save us from our sins, He made it possible for us to go to heaven. On the Last Day, when Jesus comes again, we will celebrate with all the saints and the angels. It will be the greatest Rally Day ever, and the party will last forever!"

Read from God's Word

"At that time men will see the Son of Man coming in clouds with great power and glory. And He will send His angels and gather His elect from the four winds, from the ends of the earth to the ends of the heavens." Mark 13:26–27

_____Let's do: Invite your friends to celebrate Jesus with you in Sunday school or church.

_____Let's pray: Lord Jesus, let me be a messenger for You and take Your invitation to others. In Your name I pray. Amen.

N. D.

Read from God's Word

How many are your works, O LORD! In wisdom you made them all; the earth is full of your creatures. Psalm 104:24

Beautiful God

Nicki flew in an airplane across the country, from Maryland to California. She sat next to the window so she could see everything.

Nicki saw the Appalachian Mountains covered with trees and the Ohio River as it flowed toward the mighty Mississippi. She saw flat farmland and the Rocky Mountains. The mountaintops were covered with white snow and the valleys in-between were deep green. They soared above the Painted Desert and the Grand Canyon.

Finally, they flew across California. From there she caught a glimpse of the Pacific Ocean. When the plane landed, the mountains were behind them, the San Diego Bay was in front, and palm trees and cactus were all around.

When she thought about the flight, Nicki remembered how beautiful our country looked from the air. She saw many wonderful ways God formed our rivers and land. She thanked and praised God for all His creation.

This God, the Creator of all, has a beautiful plan for each of us. He calls us from sin to be His own dear children. The death and resurrection of His Son, our Savior, leads us in faith to call Him beautiful.

_____Let's do: Look at a map of the United States or a globe of the world. God created a perfect world for us. We are part of God's creation too.

_____Let's pray: Lord of all creation, we thank and praise You for our wonderful country. In Jesus' name. Amen.

N. D.

The Mission of the Mission

The Basilica San Diego de Alcala in San Diego, California, was built more than 200 years ago by Spanish missionaries. They wanted to teach Native Americans about Jesus. But some Native Americans hated the Spanish. They attacked the wooden church and set it on fire. Everything burned.

The pastor of the church, Padre Serra, rebuilt the mission using adobe, a type of clay that will not burn. Padre Serra learned from the natives how to protect the mission on the outside. The Native Americans learned from Padre Serra that Jesus' love protected them on the inside. Seventeen years after Padre Serra rebuilt the church, the missionaries in San Diego baptized 565 Native Americans.

Many years later, the church was damaged again—this time by an earthquake. The priests there rebuilt the church again. The mission's troubles weren't over yet. Soldiers used the buildings as a fort until President Abraham Lincoln gave the mission back to the church.

Many other missions were built, and thousands of people have learned about God's love. Nothing was able to separate the mission from the love of God, and nothing can separate God's children from His love in Christ Jesus. Through this love, we can spread the news of salvation in Jesus on our mission too.

Read from God's Word

For I am convinced that neither death nor life, neither angels nor demons, neither the present nor the future, nor any powers, neither height nor depth, nor anything else in all creation, will be able to separate us from the love of God that is in Christ Jesus our Lord. Romans 8:38–39

_____Let's talk: Sometimes we have a hard time getting up on Sunday mornings. Read verse 1 of Psalm 122. Why was King David so happy?

_____Let's pray: Lord of the church, help me to remember the Sabbath Day by keeping it holy. For Jesus' sake. Amen.

N. D.

Read from God's Word

To some who were confident of their own righteousness and looked down on everybody else, Jesus told this parable: "Two men went up to the temple to pray, one a Pharisee and the other a tax collector. The Pharisee stood up and prayed about himself: 'God, I thank you that I am not like other men—robbers, evildoers, adulterers—or even like this tax collector. I fast twice a week and give a tenth of all I get.' But the tax collector stood at a distance. He would not even look up to heaven, but beat his breast and said, 'God, have mercy on me, a sinner.' I tell you that this man, rather than the other, went home justified before God. For everyone who exalts himself will be humbled, and he who humbles himself will be exalted." Luke 18:9–14

God's Night-Light

In 1855 a lighthouse was built on Point Loma, a high cliff in California. It was the highest light in the United States.

The lighthouse builders thought it was perfect, but 36 years later they stopped using it. It was too high. Fog from the ocean was below the lighthouse and sailors could not see the beam of light. A new lighthouse was built at the bottom of the cliff where sailors could see the light in the fog.

Jesus told the parable of the Pharisee and the tax collector to teach us how to pray. The Pharisee thanked God that he was better than other sinners. He was so "high" on himself, he was so proud, that the light of Jesus' salvation was not visible to him.

The tax collector was much different. He knew he was a sinner and asked God for forgiveness. He bowed his head and prayed. God heard his prayer.

When we bow our heads and talk to God, He listens to us too. When we raise our heads and praise God, we light a way for others to see His glory.

The Bible says, "In the same way, let your light shine before men, that they may ... praise your Father in heaven" (Matthew 5:16).

_____Let's do: Play flashlight tag. Remember Jesus is the light of the world.

_____Let's pray: Jesus, light of the world, shine on me. Let me reflect Your light to others with my words and actions. Amen.

N. D.

Foolish Peace

Read from God's Word

"Peace I leave with you; My peace I give you. I do not give to you as the world gives. Do not let your hearts be troubled and do not be afraid." John 14:27

The year was 1520. Ferdinand Magellan and his crew were looking for a shortcut from the Atlantic Ocean to the South Sea. When Magellan finally found the shortcut, the South Sea looked so calm that he renamed it Pacific, which means "peaceful."

But the peaceful ocean fooled him. It was much bigger than he thought it was. His crew ran out of food and fresh water, and many of them died. Then, Magellan was killed in a battle. The Pacific Ocean was not as peaceful as it had looked.

When I saw the Pacific Ocean for the first time, it did look calm and peaceful from the airplane window. I went to the beach and saw the Pacific up close. While I was wading in the waves, a thick fog blew in. The water turned dark and the air got very cold. The peaceful ocean fooled me too. It was not very peaceful that day.

Jesus promises to give His peace to everyone who believes in Him. The world's peace can fool us, but the peace of God is certain. That peace will guard our hearts and keep our minds on the power, forgiveness, and love of Jesus. His peace will never fool or fail us. The God of peace will always be with us.

_____Let's talk: Read Luke 8:22–25. "'Who is this? He commands even the winds and the water, and they obey Him'" (verse 25).

_____Let's pray: Dear Jesus, even the winds and the waves obey You. Give me Your peace. Amen.

N. D.

Read from God's Word

Let us fix our eyes on Jesus, the author and perfecter of our faith, who for the joy set before Him endured the cross, scorning its shame, and sat down at the right hand of the throne of God. Hebrews 12:2

Holy Cross Day

Do you have a cross in your home? I have a beautiful silver cross necklace that my sister gave me for my confirmation. I also have a gold cross necklace and earrings, cross pins from Sunday school, and a cross on my kitchen wall.

Each cross is special, but the one that means the most to me is unusual. My favorite cross is six inches long, painted brown, and slightly crooked. I made it when I was in kindergarten. It's a very special symbol of my faith.

After Jesus died and rose again, Christians did not use the cross as a symbol. The Christians of that time had to meet in secret because it was against the law to believe in Jesus. Then a man named Constantine became emperor. He believed in Jesus and allowed Christians to worship in public. Churches were built with crosses inside and outside. Priests wore crosses on their robes. Christians began to make the sign of the cross to remember their Baptism and the promise of eternal life. Now, the cross helps Christians show others that it is an important symbol of our faith.

Today is Holy Cross Day, a special day for Christians to think about the sacrifice Jesus made for us. We remember with thanks the empty cross and the empty tomb.

_____Let's do: When you say your prayers today, make the sign of the cross by touching your head, your chest, and your left and right shoulders. Remember God's promise of eternal life.

_____Let's pray: "Give thanks to the Lord, for He is good. His love endures forever" (Psalm 136:1). Amen.

N. D.

Staying on the Path

Read from God's Word

Make level paths for your feet and take only ways that are firm. Do not swerve to the right or the left; keep your foot from evil. Proverbs 4:26–27

Anh and her sister Thanh loved to ride bikes. They rode their bikes around the neighborhood. They raced, played follow the leader, and explored.

One day, Anh, Thanh, and their mom went riding on a bike trail. It went for miles and miles through the woods. Along the edge of the trail were flowers, bushes, and trees. In the woods were squirrels, raccoons, and deer. They rode five miles to the Old Railroad Station where Mom bought treats for everyone.

Anh and Thanh wanted to get off of their bikes and explore the woods, but Mom knew the woods were dangerous. On one side of the path was a cliff with thornbushes and sharp rocks. On the other side was a steep hill with vines and poison ivy.

Anh and Thanh stayed on the path with Mom.

God wants to guide us on His path, but we are tempted to go exploring away from Him. When we don't do our homework or our chores, we've strayed off of the path. When we use bad language or talk back to our parents or teachers, we're not on God's path. But God's love is powerful, more powerful than the world or the devil. Whenever we leave the path, He is there to forgive us and put us back on track.

_____Let's talk: Have you ever been lost? Read Isaiah 53:6. How are we like sheep that have gone astray? Now read Psalm 23. How does this psalm make you feel?

_____Let's pray: Good Shepherd, may I sing Thy praise within Thy house forever. Amen. (*Lutheran Worship* 412:6)

N. D.

Read from God's Word

These twelve Jesus sent out with the following instructions: "... Go rather to the lost sheep of Israel. As you go, preach this message: 'The kingdom of heaven is near.' Heal the sick, raise the dead, cleanse those who have leprosy, drive out demons. Freely you have received, freely give. ... I am sending you out like sheep among wolves. Therefore be as shrewd as snakes and as innocent as doves. Be on your guard against men; they will hand you over to the local councils and flog you in their synagogues. On my account you will be brought before governors and kings as witnesses to them and to the Gentiles. But when they arrest you, do not worry about what to say or how to say it. At that time you will be given what to say, for it will not be you speaking, but the Spirit of your Father speaking through you." Matthew 10:5–20

Not the Underdogs

The whole family was watching football on TV. Hannah and Tommy didn't recognize either of the teams that were playing.

"Which team are you cheering for, Dad?" asked Hannah.

"I always root for the underdog," Dad answered.

"What's an underdog?" Tommy wanted to know.

"An underdog is a person or a team that isn't expected to do well," Dad explained. "I like to cheer for them so maybe they will win."

"I'll cheer for the underdog too," said Hannah.

"Let's all cheer for them," agreed Tommy.

When Jesus called His disciples, He wanted to get them ready to go out and preach His Gospel. He warned them that they would be the underdogs. "I am sending you out like sheep among wolves," said Jesus (Matthew 10:16). Jesus told them they would be arrested and beaten. Many people would not think of the disciples as winners, but Jesus told His friends not to worry or be afraid. The Spirit of God would be with them, making them winners.

We don't have to worry either because God's Spirit is with us too. He gives us courage to tell others about Jesus, to invite someone to church, or to do the right thing when our friends want us to do something wrong. With God on our team, we are always winners.

_____Let's do: Do you know classmates who need someone to cheer for them? Give them your support. Let them know you're on their side.

_____Let's pray: Almighty God, You're my biggest fan. You cheer for me even when I'm down. Give me the courage to lead cheers for You. In Jesus' name. Amen.

N. D.

Owner's Pride

Read from God's Word

But you were washed, you were sanctified, you were justified in the name of the Lord Jesus Christ and by the Spirit of our God. *1 Corinthians 6:11b*

Today was a special day for Michelle's big brother. Craig had finally saved enough money to buy his first car.

"Isn't it beautiful?" Craig asked.

Michelle stared at the car. It was old. It had scratches and dents.

Craig left to find a bucket so he could wash his car. Mom asked, "What's the matter, Michelle?"

"This car is ugly. Why does Craig think it's so beautiful?"

Mom laughed. "Craig loves this car because it's his. He worked hard to buy it. He will take good care of it because it means so much to him."

"It sure does," said Craig as he came back with the bucket and a hose. "My car will get lots of love and attention, Michelle. I'm going to wash it and fix it up. This car will be loved and cared for because it's mine."

"Can I help?" asked Michelle with a smile. "This car is going to need all the love it can get!"

Our lives look like Craig's car—scratched and dented from sin. But we belong to God. He loves us so much that He sent Jesus to wash away our sins. When Jesus died on the cross, His blood covered our dents and scratches. His love and care make us beautiful in God's eyes.

_____Let's do: Help others today without being asked. Set the table, do the dishes, or take out the trash.

_____Let's pray: Thank You, Jesus, for washing away my scratches, dents, and yucky sins with Your blood. In Your name I pray. Amen.

N. D.

Read from God's Word

Your hands made me and formed me; give me understanding to learn Your commands. May those who fear You rejoice when they see me, for I have put my hope in Your word. Psalm 119:73–74

No Lid on It

Play dough is fun. You can squeeze it and roll it to make shapes. If you make a mistake, just smash it flat and start over. When you're finished, stick the play dough in the can and seal the lid so it will be ready when you want to play again.

When God created a perfect world, He didn't make mistakes. God made Adam and Eve and put them in the beautiful garden. God gave them everything they needed.

But Adam and Eve sinned. And because they disobeyed God, sin came into the world.

God's creation wasn't perfect anymore. He could have smashed it like play dough. God could have flattened it and started over. But He didn't. God loved His creation so much that He saved it. He sent His own Son to take our sin. Jesus was "smashed" by the soldiers, "flattened" on the cross, and "sealed" in the tomb.

But the devil couldn't keep the "lid" on Jesus. On the third day our Savior burst from the tomb. Sin, Satan, and death were defeated. We are still sinful and make mistakes. But God doesn't put the lid on us. He forgives our sins. He saves us. That is Good News and we can't keep a lid on it!

_____Let's do: Use play dough to make a cross. Let it dry completely. When the cross is hard, put it in a special place where everyone can see it.

_____Let's pray: Dear God, I'm glad You loved us so much that You sent Jesus to be our Savior. Thank You for listening to our prayers and forgiving our sins. Amen.

N. D.

Bulb Secrets

Read from God's Word

For by Him all things were created: things in heaven and on earth, visible and invisible, whether thrones or powers or rulers or authorities; all things were created by Him and for Him. Colossians 1:16

"Whatcha doin', Mom?" asked Marta.

"I'm planting flowers."

"But it's fall, not spring time. Why are you planting?"

"God made these flowers in a special way. I plant the bulbs in the ground now and the soil covers them through fall and winter. The fertilizer I give them now, together with moisture from the rain and snow, will feed them. In the spring, they will grow."

"Cool!" said Marta. "What kind of flowers will these be?"

"In February we'll have crocuses."

"February? What if it's snowing?" asked Marta.

"That's what's so wonderful about these bulbs," explained Mom. "The crocuses will grow even if it's snowing."

"It's like a miracle," said Marta.

"It is God's plan," Mom told her. "Daffodils and tulips that bloom in March and April, colorful leaves in autumn, snow in winter—each season is a gift from God that reminds us of His great love and plan for us."

"I get it!" Marta said. "God loves His creation and made it beautiful all year. And He loves us even more! God sent Jesus as part of His beautiful plan to save us all year round, all life long."

"Exactly!" agreed Mom. "Now, I've got a plan. How about helping me plant the rest of the bulbs?"

_____Let's do: Draw some flowers on construction paper and cut them out. In the middle of each flower write, "God loves you." Now, hide them around your home. See how long it takes for all of them to "bloom."

_____Let's pray: Lord God, You give us so many signs of Your love. Help me to see You wherever I look. Amen.

N. D.

Read from God's Word

Then Jesus declared, "I am the bread of life. He who comes to Me will never go hungry, and he who believes in Me will never be thirsty." John 6:35

Which Food?

Kristen, come here. Hurry!" called Luke. "There's a squirrel in our bird feeder. It's eating the bird seed!"

Kristen and Luke told Mom and Dad about the squirrel. "If we grease the pole," said Mom, "it should be too slippery for the squirrel to climb." But as soon as Mom got back into the house the squirrel was back in the feeder.

Dad had another solution—a clear plastic shield. "We'll put this baffle on the pole. That should keep that squirrel out," declared Dad.

For a little while, the baffle worked. A few days later, Kristen looked outside. That tricky squirrel figured out how to get around the shield!

Mom gave Grandma a call. When she hung up, Mom was smiling. "Grandma says we're using the wrong food. If we use safflower seeds instead of sunflower seeds, the squirrel will stay away."

"Hooray!" Luke and Kristen shouted.

Our sinful ways lead us to the wrong food, like the squirrel getting into the bird feeder. When we hear and listen to God's Word, our hearts and souls are fed with stories about God and promises of God. We get strength and help to serve the Lord. In God's Word we are reminded of His forgiving love. God's Word is the right "food" for us.

_____Let's talk: Whom can you tell about Jesus, the bread of life?

_____Let's pray: Dear Jesus, help me to fill up on Your words so I can worship You with a full and happy heart. In Your name I pray. Amen.

N. D.

Who's Less Sinful?

Read from God's Word

If we claim to be without sin, we deceive ourselves and the truth is not in us. If we confess our sins, He is faithful and just and will forgive us our sins and purify us from all unrighteousness. 1 John 1:8–9

David and Sam were brothers who argued about everything. One day they argued about which of them was less sinful. Sam said he was less sinful because he always obeyed their parents and his teachers.

"I obey right away," David said.

"I obey better than you do," Sam said. "I deserve to go to heaven more than you."

Just then their mother walked into the room. "Mom," David asked, "does Sam deserve to go to heaven more than I do?"

"No," Mom said.

"Ha!" David said. "I told you."

"David," Mom continued, "you don't deserve to go to heaven either. In fact, nobody deserves to go to heaven. If we depend on how good we are, we will never go to heaven."

Although that was bad news for the boys, their mother had good news too: "The moment you realize you're a sinner, God's Spirit shows us Jesus as our Savior from sin and He forgives us."

"How?" Sam asked.

"God helps us feel sad about our sins and honestly confess them," Mom said. "God forgives and forgets them. When Jesus died, He took all our sins away, even those of the worst sinner."

The Bible says: "If we confess our sins, [God] is faithful and just and will forgive our sins." That's a promise we can count on!

_____Let's talk: When you say your daily prayers, how do you confess your sins, even those you may not be aware of? Why is that important?

_____Let's pray: Lord, we know that we are sinners. Help us always rely on Your great love and mercy through Jesus to save us. Amen.

T. R.

Read from God's Word

For I am convinced that neither death nor life, neither angels nor demons, neither the present nor the future, nor any powers, neither height nor depth, nor anything else in all creation, will be able to separate us from the love of God that is in Christ Jesus our Lord. Romans 8:38–39

Don't Trust in Feelings

Nicole was worried. She knew she sinned often and she confessed her sins in her prayers every day. But sometimes she felt forgiven and sometimes she didn't.

Her father noticed her concern. Nicole explained: "I am sorry for my sins and I ask for forgiveness. But I don't feel any more forgiven when I get done praying than when I started."

"If forgiveness depended on whether you feel forgiven," her father said, "you'd be in trouble. Feelings are misleading. How you feel doesn't change the most important thing about forgiveness."

"What's that?" Nicole asked.

"The most important thing about forgiveness is that you are forgiven, no matter how you feel. God forgives your sins for Jesus' sake."

Nicole was still puzzled. "But how do you know?" she asked. "If you can't feel it, what proof do you have?"

Her father replied, "You know it because the Bible talks about forgiveness for everyone who believes. Everything the Bible says is true. You believe God's promises, right? His love for us is shown through Jesus, who forgives our sins no matter how we feel."

Nicole thought about that. Knowing her forgiveness didn't depend on how she felt made her very happy and secure.

_____Let's talk: How do you feel after you pray? Does knowing you are forgiven through Jesus make you feel more confident and secure?

_____Let's pray: Lord, help us always remember that Your promise to forgive our sins overshadows any of our feelings. Amen.

T. R.

God Finds Us

Have you ever looked for God? Have you ever looked into the sky and wondered how far up you would have to travel to find God? Maybe you have looked for God in the world He created—in flowers and trees and other wonders of nature.

God is everywhere. We can look for God our whole lives, but it will not do us much good unless we look for Him in the Bible. God has revealed Himself to us in His Word. And as we look into His Word, we find that all our searching and striving to find Him does no good at all.

The fact is, we cannot find God. Like the sheep in the Bible reading, we are lost. God finds us. When He sent His Son into the world to die on the cross for us, He saved us from eternal death. He rescued us from a life without hope and gave us the hope of glory. He found us for eternity.

The next time you look for God, don't turn to the telescope or the microscope. Don't look to the highest heavens or the deepest seas. God helps you look to the cross. There you see God's mercy and grace.

Read from God's Word

Then Jesus told them this parable: "Suppose one of you has a hundred sheep and loses one of them. Does he not leave the ninety-nine in the open country and go after the lost sheep until he finds it? And when he finds it, he joyfully puts it on his shoulders and goes home. Then he calls his friends and neighbors together and says, 'Rejoice with me; I have found my lost sheep.' I tell you that in the same way there will be more rejoicing in heaven over one sinner who repents than over ninety-nine righteous persons who do not need to repent." Luke 15:3–7

_____Let's talk: Why is it necessary for God to find us, and not the other way around? What difference does it make to you that Jesus came to rescue you?

_____Let's pray: Lord, please remind us always that You help us look to Jesus for the joy of eternal salvation. Amen.

T. R.

Read from God's Word

I will exalt You, O LORD, for You lifted me out of the depths and did not let my enemies gloat over me. O LORD my God, I called to You for help and You healed me. O LORD, You brought me up from the grave; You spared me from going down into the pit. Sing to the LORD, you saints of His; praise His holy name. For His anger lasts only a moment, but His favor lasts a lifetime; weeping may remain for a night, but rejoicing comes in the morning. Psalm 30:1–5

Rejoice in the Morning

It's morning again! Oh, what happiness! Boys and girls everywhere are awaking from sleep. Their eyes are shining, and they are starting another brand-new, wonderful day. Oh, joy of joys—it's morning!

But wait a minute. What's that you're saying? The only joyful mornings are those when you can sleep in?

Even if you do not like to get up early, you can have joy in the morning. You can rejoice in every day that offers the joys of living.

David, the author of Psalm 30, felt joy in the morning. He had known the darkness of night, but in a different way—a spiritual way. He knew what it was like to experience great shame and guilt.

When David said, "Weeping may remain for a night, but rejoicing comes in the morning," he was talking about more than a sunrise. He was talking about the weeping that will end when the darkness of sin is gone for good. He saw the bright rays of eternal life.

For David, the joy of forgiveness on earth was a beautiful reminder of the joy he would experience in heaven. And so it is for us too. Because of Jesus we know that our guilt and shame are forever removed.

Rejoice in the morning! Rejoice in the thought of heaven!

_____Let's talk: What is the saddest feeling you've ever had?
What makes our sadness turn into joy?
How can morning remind us of heaven?

_____Let's pray: Our Father, we rejoice in the morning of Your forgiveness. Amen.

T. R.

Pray and Watch

Read from God's Word

But when Sanballat, Tobiah, the Arabs, the Ammonites and the men of Ashdod heard that the repairs to Jerusalem's walls had gone ahead and that the gaps were being closed, they were very angry. They all plotted together to come and fight against Jerusalem and stir up trouble against it. But we prayed to our God and posted a guard day and night to meet this threat. Nehemiah 4:7–9

The Israelites were very disobedient toward God. Because of their sins, they were taken into captivity for 70 years in Babylon.

When they were released, they returned home to Jerusalem. One of their goals was rebuilding the walls of the city. To lead them in this task, the Lord sent Nehemiah. Nehemiah found that people who were not believers tried to defeat the project. Opponents threatened, bullied, ridiculed, and even organized an army.

With trouble all around, Nehemiah did two things: he prayed and he posted a guard. He realized that without God's support he could not succeed, so he prayed that God would be on their side. By posting a guard, he told his enemies that he was not afraid and he prevented a sneak attack.

What threatens us in our lives? Temptation. Sin is always about us, urging us to give in to its demands.

God guided Nehemiah's strategy and He guides our strategy against temptation. We pray that God will deliver us from temptation, and then we set up our guard against it. When it does strike, with God's help we'll be able to fight it off.

Remember that Jesus was tempted as we are in all ways. He didn't yield; He overcame sin for us. Through Him we, too, are conquerors.

____Let's talk: How does prayer help you fight against temptation? How does watching help you defeat temptation?

____Let's pray: Lord, help us in Jesus to say no to sin. Amen.

T. R.

Read from God's Word

People were also bringing babies to Jesus to have Him touch them. When the disciples saw this, they rebuked them. But Jesus called the children to Him and said, "Let the little children come to Me, and do not hinder them, for the kingdom of God belongs to such as these. I tell you the truth, anyone who will not receive the kingdom of God like a little child will never enter it." Luke 18:15–17

Trusting Like a Child

Donell and his grandfather always did something together on Saturdays. They played ball. They went to the park.

But the most fun for Donell was when they went fishing. Grandpa baited Donell's hook and set Donell's bobber just right. Grandpa told Donell where to cast his line and when to reel in the fish.

"Why do you want to go fishing with me, Grandpa," Donell asked one day when the fish weren't biting, "especially when you have to help me with so much work?"

Grandpa replied, "Because you depend on me so much, Donell."

In our Scripture reading Jesus teaches us we can depend on Him. When He took little children on His knee and blessed them, He was telling us that we are to trust in Him and depend on Him just as a child depends on a parent or grandparent.

It's often easy for us to trust in our own intelligence or in our own good works, thinking that they make us good in the eyes of God. When we do that, we aren't trusting in Jesus. Faith in Jesus and His sacrifice on the cross saves us—nothing else. God helps us trust Him with the faith of a little child.

_____Let's talk: How does a child trust parents and elders? Why is it important that we trust in Jesus in the same way?

_____Let's pray: Dear Savior, may we always see You with the eyes of a child, trusting that Your words and promises are true. We love You because You first loved us. Amen.

T. R.

What Is Happiness?

Read from God's Word

David says the same thing when he speaks of the blessedness of the man to whom God credits righteousness apart from works: "Blessed are they whose transgressions are forgiven, whose sins are covered. Blessed is the man whose sin the Lord will never count against him." Romans 4:6–8

Happiness is an A on a test.
Happiness is a B on a test when you expected a C.
Happiness is having no homework over the weekend.
Happiness is making the winning basket in a championship basketball game.
Happiness is having a dog that meets you after school.
Happiness is having your science experiment work.
Happiness is the clock stopping during recess and none of the teachers noticing it.
Happiness is a brother or sister who helps you with your homework.
Happiness is having all your homework done.
Happiness is having a brother or sister you are proud of.

All these things can make you happy. But that kind of happiness fades eventually. True happiness is spiritual happiness. It's knowing and trusting in a God who loves you and forgives your iniquities, who covers your sins and will not count your sins against you. It's having a Savior who suffered all the punishment you ever deserved.

That sort of happiness will last forever.

_____Let's do: Make a list of things that make you happy. At the bottom of the list write, "Happiness is Jesus as my Savior." Put the list where you can see it every day.

_____Let's pray: Lord, thank You for not counting my sins against me because Jesus took them away. I will be grateful forever. Amen.

T. R.

Read from God's Word

"Now, brothers, I know that you acted in ignorance, as did your leaders. But this is how God fulfilled what He had foretold through all the prophets, saying that His Christ would suffer. Repent, then, and turn to God, so that your sins may be wiped out, that times of refreshing may come from the Lord, and that He may send the Christ, who has been appointed for you—even Jesus. He must remain in heaven until the time comes for God to restore everything, as He promised long ago through His holy prophets." Acts 3:17–21

Correcting Our Mistakes

The difference between good math students and not-so-good math students isn't that good students make fewer mistakes. All students make mistakes.

The difference is in what good students do when they make a mistake. When they realize that they've made it, they immediately fix it.

Some students check their work. Other students have the knack of knowing when they've made an error. Something doesn't feel right about their work. So they stop right where they are and correct it. This can keep them out of trouble later in the problem.

Repentance is a part of God's way of fixing spiritual mistakes in our lives. None of us is perfect. All of us sin. If it's allowed to remain uncorrected, it will ruin our lives. It makes our salvation impossible.

Jesus offers us forgiveness for every sin we commit. He grants us free and full forgiveness through faith in His atoning sacrifice on Calvary's cross.

The forgiven sinner is one who realizes that he or she is sinning and is willing to let God correct that sin through repentance. We tell God that we're sorry for our sins. We trust in His pardon, given to us because of Jesus' perfect life, death, and resurrection. The forgiven sinner is filled with peace and joy.

_____Let's talk: Why is forgiveness always a gift?

_____Let's pray: Lord, give us faith in Your redeeming work, which cancels all sins. Amen.

T. R.

Are You a Servant?

Read from God's Word

Sitting down, Jesus called the Twelve and said, "If anyone wants to be first, he must be the very last, and the servant of all." He took a little child and had him stand among them. Taking him in His arms, He said to them, "Whoever welcomes one of these little children in My name welcomes Me; and whoever welcomes Me does not welcome Me but the one who sent Me." Mark 9:35–37

Jesus considered Himself a servant for us. He also tells us to be servants to one another.

But being a servant is contrary to human nature. Who wants to serve others? Nobody goes into a restaurant and cooks his own meal. You don't take the water pitcher from the waiter and fill everybody's glass. That's the waiter's job. Society tells us that the one who is being served is greater than the one who serves.

Today's reading says that the one who serves is greater. To emphasize His point, Jesus tells us that His job on earth is not to be served but to serve (Mark 10:45).

Is Jesus our servant? It seems odd for the sinless Son of God to be our servant. In love He chose to be our Suffering Servant. He took our sins and carried them to the cross, where He died for us—the greatest act of servanthood in history. And because He did that for us, we are free of our sins.

Jesus' love for us shows as we serve other people. We reflect His gifts. And when we serve others, we demonstrate our love and gratitude for the One who served us.

_____Let's talk: What are some ways you serve other people? What is your reason for serving others? How can you serve with your whole life?

_____Let's pray: Lord God, move us by Your Spirit to go and serve others joyfully. Amen.

T. R.

Read from God's Word

"I have given them Your word and the world has hated them, for they are not of the world any more than I am of the world. My prayer is not that You take them out of the world but that You protect them from the evil one. They are not of the world, even as I am not of it. Sanctify them by the truth; Your word is truth." John 17:14–17

When the Heat Is On

Isn't it great to get a dessert like baked Alaska? The ice cream is placed in a hot oven to bake, but it doesn't melt. The secret is that the meringue frosting acts like insulation, keeping the heat away from the ice cream.

The devil offers many temptations. The heat is on when friends ask us to join them in a mean trick. Perhaps you were gossiping last week or giggled about an inappropriate note.

The heat of hell threatens to destroy all sinners forever. Thank God that Jesus took the heat for us. He gave His life to keep the punishment of hell from touching us. He is our insulation.

Jesus knows all about the ugly temptations we face every day. In John 17 He prayed that God would keep His followers from the evil one. He wants us all to enjoy the glory of heaven with Him.

The devil uses all kinds of excuses to entice us to sin: "Everybody's doing it"; "It's not that bad"; "So what—I'm not hurting anyone"; "I only did it once." We need the strong protection that God offers against these temptations. Studying God's Word helps us remain strong in the Lord. God answers our prayers for help.

With the Holy Spirit's help we can beat the heat of temptation!

_____Let's talk: How could thinking of Jesus on the cross help you when temptations come?

_____Let's pray: Heavenly Father, thank You for sending Jesus to bear the heat of hell for me. Amen.

M. L. K.

october

Contributors for this month:

Richard P. Lieske

Christine Dehnke

Carolyn Sims

Jeanette A. Dall

Read from God's Word

I lift up my eyes to the hills—where does my help come from? My help comes from the LORD, the Maker of heaven and earth. He will not let your foot slip—He who watches over you will not slumber; indeed, He who watches over Israel will neither slumber nor sleep. The LORD watches over you—the LORD is your shade at your right hand; the sun will not harm you by day, nor the moon by night. The LORD will keep you from all harm—He will watch over your life; the LORD will watch over your coming and going both now and forevermore. Psalm 121

A Place of Safety

German bombs fell on England every night for months during 1941. Many people were hurt or killed.

One night a father and son ran from a building that had been hit by a bomb. The father jumped into a shell hole for protection and called for his son to follow. The boy could hear his father but couldn't see in the dark. He was very scared and cried out.

The father could see his son against the glow from the burning buildings. "You can't see me, but I can see you. Jump!"

The boy trusted his father and jumped to the safety of his arms.

We cannot see what is ahead. We don't know what will happen after a friend moves away or Mom and Dad divorce. We may be scared about getting braces or changing schools. People may disappoint us. We may feel like we have nowhere to turn.

Our heavenly Father calls us to trust His voice. He calls us to turn to Him and His love and care. He offers us strength to make it through difficulties. He gives us a safe place in the middle of troubles.

Today's reading offers us these words of hope: "The Lord will keep you from all harm—He will watch over your life."

_____Let's do: Think about a time that you wished you had a safe place to go. Write a prayer or draw a picture that tells how God offers you safety in Jesus' love for you.

_____Let's pray: Dear Jesus, because You died on the cross and rose again, I always have hope in You. I have a place to turn to—someone who will keep me safe. Help me trust Your voice. Amen.

R. P. L.

The Real Thing

I made a new friend. Her name is Vinh. She's a Buddhist," Carmella told her mother when she came home from school.

"That's interesting," her mother replied. "Did you talk much about your faith?"

"Sure, Mom," said Carmella. "I just think it's really exciting to learn about other religions and cultures."

"That's great, honey," her mom said. "I'm glad you made friends with Vinh. Your father and I want you to learn and explore, but we also want you to stay firmly grounded in the real thing."

"What do you mean?" asked Carmella.

Her mom got out a dollar bill. "You know what counterfeit money is?" Carmella nodded. "U.S. Treasury agents can spot fake money because they know about real money. They know the real thing and can't be fooled."

"I think I see what you mean," said Carmella, taking the bill to look at it more closely. "I need to know about Jesus so I can know whether other beliefs are true or false."

"Right!" her mom said. "We want the real Savior, the real thing. Why don't you invite Vinh to come over sometime?"

Carmella agreed and then added, "Who knows? Maybe God will use us to help her learn about Jesus!"

Read from God's Word

Dear friends, do not believe every spirit, but test the spirits to see whether they are from God, because many false prophets have gone out into the world. This is how you can recognize the Spirit of God: Every spirit that acknowledges that Jesus Christ has come in the flesh is from God, but every spirit that does not acknowledge Jesus is not from God. This is the spirit of the antichrist, which you have heard is coming and even now is already in the world. 1 John 4:1–3

_____Let's talk: How would you tell someone from another country what you believe about Jesus? How can the Holy Spirit use you to witness about Jesus, the real thing?

_____Let's pray: Dear Father, thank You for friends from other lands. Help us trust Your Son, our Savior Jesus, as the real thing. Move us to share Jesus with our new friends. Amen.

R. P. L.

Read from God's Word

The Spirit of the Sovereign LORD is on me, because the LORD has anointed me to preach good news to the poor. He has sent me to bind up the brokenhearted, to proclaim freedom for the captives and release from darkness for the prisoners, to proclaim the year of the LORD's favor and the day of vengeance of our God, to comfort all who mourn, and provide for those who grieve in Zion—to bestow on them a crown of beauty instead of ashes, the oil of gladness instead of mourning, and a garment of praise instead of a spirit of despair. They will be called oaks of righteousness, a planting of the LORD for the display of His splendor. Isaiah 61:1–3

Potato-Chip Dust

Randy, Kordell, and Rashan ate lunch together at school. They liked to trade things in their lunches for something they liked better.

One day Kordell found his potato chips all crumbled. "Potato-chip dust!" he said sadly.

"I'll trade my chips for your candy bar," Randy said. But Randy's chips were smashed too.

They both looked at Rashan's bag of chips. "Wait a minute, guys. Melissa dropped her math book on my lunch and ..."

Before he could finish, his friends had torn open his bag. Together they said, "Dust!"

Mr. Zehnder, their teacher, came upon the unhappy three and asked what happened.

"Our chips!" said Randy.

"I've got a big bag," said Mr. Zehnder.

"You'd trade your chips for our smashed ones?" asked Rashan.

"You could call it a trade," said Mr. Zehnder. "But it's really more of a gift. Kind of like God giving us His Son. There's nothing we can trade to God for the wonderful blessings of forgiveness and eternal life He gave through Jesus."

Mr. Zehnder ate some potato-chip dust as he went back to his desk. Then Rashan had an idea. "Say, Mr. Zehnder, my sandwich is smashed too."

"Forget it, Rashan," said his teacher, smiling. "God's grace is endless, but my lunch isn't!"

____Let's talk: How do our lives become like potato-chip dust?
How does Jesus trade His perfect chips for our broken ones?

____Let's pray: Dear Jesus, thank You for taking away my sin and guilt and giving me Your love and forgiveness. Amen.

R. P. L.

Words Can Hurt You

Read from God's Word

May the words of my mouth and the meditation of my heart be pleasing in Your sight, O LORD, my Rock and my Redeemer. Psalm 19:14

Two boys were sitting at a table in a fast-food restaurant. One boy was holding a small device in his hand. He pressed a button and out came horribly foul words. They both giggled.

A woman at another table said, "Please put that away." The boy pressed the button again and more foul words came out. She looked at them with an angry expression.

The other boy said, "You shouldn't play that in here. Put it away."

Sometimes just a disapproving look can confront others with sin. Words of Jesus' forgiveness are also needed.

An old saying goes, "Sticks and stones may break my bones, but words can never hurt me." That may be true about words others say to you. But the words you say certainly can hurt you, even if you "say" them by pressing a button.

How can we speak Jesus' name in one breath and use it to curse in the next? How can we claim to love our neighbor and insult him at the same time?

If not for the gracious forgiveness we have in Jesus, we would all be under God's anger. Because we're free from punishment, we can praise God's name and honor Him with our speech. May our words be acceptable in His sight because of Jesus.

_____Let's talk: Why do people use foul language? How do God's love, forgiveness, and power help keep our speech pure?

_____Let's pray: Lord, open my lips and let my mouth show forth Your praise! Amen.

R. P. L.

Read from God's Word

My command is this: Love each other as I have loved you. Greater love has no one than this, that he lay down his life for his friends. John 15:12–13

My Best Friend Is …

Jet, a 16-year-old Doberman pinscher, belonged to Candy Sangster. Once when Candy passed out and slipped into a diabetic coma, Jet ran into the yard, unlatched the gate, and ran next door. She barked and ran through the house, prompting the neighbor to call 911.

Leo, a four-year-old poodle, saved two children from a rattlesnake attack. Sean Callahan stumbled over a diamondback rattler while playing with his sister. Leo jumped between the boy and the snake just as it struck, and the poodle was bitten several times. After hovering near death for several days, Leo recovered.

Dogs are sometimes called our "best friends." These heroic acts make many people love them even more, but dogs can't be our best friends.

Jesus is the best friend we can ever have. He saves us from sin and death and hell. He loves us even when we do not love Him, and He offers Himself for those who do not yet call on His name.

If you asked 100 people, "Who is man's (or woman's) best friend?" they would probably say, "Dog." The answer is really the same letters in reverse: God! Specifically, the name is Jesus, Son of God, Savior of the world.

If your dog is like Jet and Leo, he wouldn't mind being called "second-best" friend.

_____Let's talk: What do you look for in a friend? How is Jesus your best friend?

_____Let's pray: Father, thank You for blessings like pets. Help me see Your love reflected in all the blessings You have given me. Amen.

R. P. L.

Haunted House—NOT!

Read from God's Word

There is no fear in love. But perfect love drives out fear, because fear has to do with punishment. The one who fears is not made perfect in love. 1 John 4:18

There once was a boy who was afraid to go to church. This little boy grew up to be one of the most adventurous, powerful men in history. He rode with cowboys in the Wild West, led troops into battle, hunted big game, and became president of the United States. But as a young boy he was terrified to go to church.

The boy was Teddy Roosevelt.

His mother was puzzled. Then she found out that Teddy was terrified of something called "zeal." He said it was crouched in the dark corners of the church, ready to jump at him. He didn't know what it looked like, but he was sure he heard the minister read about it in the Bible.

His mother looked up every passage in the Bible that used the word zeal. In John 2:17, in the King James Version, she read the answer: "The zeal of Thine house hath eaten me up"!

The Bible assures us that "perfect love drives out fear." God's house is not scary. It is filled with His Spirit of love, forgiveness, and joy. We may express God's love, joy, and forgiveness with harmless zeal. Jesus, our risen Redeemer, has defeated sin, death, and the devil himself.

_____Let's talk: What danger might there be in focusing on evil things at Halloween? How might Halloween be celebrated in wholesome ways?

_____Let's pray: Lord God, grant me Your Spirit that I may always love You and be Your child. Give me true zeal to honor You in all things. In Jesus' name. Amen.

R. P. L.

Read from God's Word

Then He got into the boat and His disciples followed Him. Without warning, a furious storm came up on the lake, so that the waves swept over the boat. But Jesus was sleeping. The disciples went and woke Him, saying, "Lord, save us! We're going to drown!" He replied, "You of little faith, why are you so afraid?" Then He got up and rebuked the winds and the waves, and it was completely calm. The men were amazed and asked, "What kind of man is this? Even the winds and the waves obey Him!" Matthew 8:23–27

Best Place in a Storm

Many years ago a tornado was about to hit a small town. A man made his family lie on the floor and covered them with a mattress. But he didn't get under the mattress with them.

The man's young son peeked out from under the mattress. He saw his father standing by an open window, keeping an eye on the twister.

The little boy struggled out of his mother's arms and ran to hold on to his father's leg. "Something told me," he said years later, "that the safest place was next to my father."

Our heavenly Father keeps us safe in the middle of dangerous times. He keeps watch over us because we're dear to Him. As we trust in Him, we desire to be nearer to Him. We read His Word, worship in His house, and talk to Him often.

The best place to be in the storms of life is right next to our heavenly Father. He didn't spare His own Son but gave Him up to protect us from eternal destruction. In Jesus, He offers life and hope even when death is at hand. We can count on God to protect us from other dangers as well.

_____Let's talk: How can we stand close to our heavenly Father? What leads us to depend on Him each moment?

_____Let's pray: Dear Father, we know that many storms of life will come to us. Because You gave Your Son, Jesus, to save us forever, we trust You to keep us safe in Your arms. Amen.

R. P. L.

Discovering Thanksgiving

In October we remember the discovery of America by Christopher Columbus in 1492. This week is also Thanksgiving for citizens of Canada. These may seem like very different holidays, but the two can blend together nicely.

Many people say we should not celebrate the "discovery" of America by Columbus. Native people had lived here for hundreds of years. The coming of Columbus started a chain of events that led to many sad things. Native people were deceived, driven out, and even killed.

All people in all times and places have sinned. Sin is sin no matter who does it or when. So how can we celebrate something that may include sin and the devil?

God wants us to celebrate His love for us. He wants us to trust in Him to work through any bad circumstances and even some terrible rulers. We are grateful for all His blessings, especially forgiveness through Jesus. We give thanks for what God has done.

We "discover thanksgiving" on Columbus/Thanksgiving Day. We rejoice in the goodness of God. In the person of Jesus, He came among us and made us citizens of the heavenly kingdom. We have so much to give thanks for!

Read from God's Word

Then Peter began to speak: "I now realize how true it is that God does not show favoritism but accepts men from every nation who fear Him and do what is right. You know the message God sent to the people of Israel, telling the good news of peace through Jesus Christ, who is Lord of all." Acts 10:34–36

_____Let's talk: What are some of the blessings God has given you in your native country? What can you celebrate the most today?

_____Let's pray: Father God, thank You for the country in which I live. Help me discover Your goodness even when people do sinful things. Send Your Spirit to create faith in Jesus Christ in the hearts of all people so we can share true peace. Amen.

R. P. L.

Read from God's Word

Do you not know that in a race all the runners run, but only one gets the prize? Run in such a way as to get the prize. Everyone who competes in the games goes into strict training. They do it to get a crown that will not last; but we do it to get a crown that will last forever. 1 Corinthians 9:24–25

Cross-Country Running

Cross-country runners do not run on a track. They have a course to run up and down hills and around corners. Flags, barrels, or cones mark the route. The meet is held if it is sunny or if it rains or even snows. The run goes on for nearly three miles. Runners put in long hours of hard work as they train for meets.

When most of the runners on a team run well, that team may win a trophy. But what about other teams? Was all their training wasted?

Most runners say their training is fun. They may say the workout is good for them because it strengthens their bodies. Most runners discover that winning isn't everything.

Christians are in training for a cross-life course. This course runs indoors and outdoors in all kinds of weather. The markers along the way come from the Bible. As Christian runners hear, read, and share God's Word, He helps them stay on course.

The trophy at the end of our race is the prize of eternal life with Jesus. We don't win the prize on our own. The One who "crossed over" into our "country" and died on the cross in our place gives it to us. Thanks be to Jesus! He makes us all winners!

_____Let's talk: According to the Bible reading, what's the main difference between running in a sporting event and running in the Christian life? What determines who gets the heavenly prize?

_____Let's pray: Lord, bring us by Your mercy to the goal of eternal joy in Your presence. Amen.

C. D.

Candy for Sale!

On the first day of the sale, the candy just sat in the box, unnoticed. On the second day, one student came into the office with a message. She saw the candy and asked if students could buy it. The third day, the student came in after school to buy a candy bar.

After a few weeks, the person selling the candy as a fund-raiser was refilling the box daily. Did the candy sell well because of posters around the school? Was it because of an advertisement in the school newsletter? Was it because the secretary encouraged students to buy some?

The candy sold well because the first student who noticed it told her friends. This "word of mouth" was all that was needed.

The sweet message of God's love in Jesus is spread in much the same way. God doesn't light up the sky with Bible verses. He doesn't advertise His gift of salvation. But He does use people who believe in Him to tell others that the gift is available.

Those who have received the precious prize of eternal life by faith in Jesus point the way to God's Word, where others can find it. It isn't hidden, but it does need to be shared.

Read from God's Word

Having brought the apostles, they made them appear before the Sanhedrin to be questioned by the high priest. "We gave you strict orders not to teach in this name," he said. "Yet you have filled Jerusalem with your teaching and are determined to make us guilty of this Man's blood." Peter and the other apostles replied: "We must obey God rather than men! The God of our fathers raised Jesus from the dead—whom you had killed by hanging Him on a tree. God exalted Him to His own right hand as Prince and Savior that He might give repentance and forgiveness of sins to Israel. We are witnesses of these things, and so is the Holy Spirit, whom God has given to those who obey Him." Acts 5:27–32

_____Let's talk: Do you know someone who needs to hear the sweet message of God's love? How can you tell in your own words that "God loved the world so much that He gave His only Son, so that everyone who believes in Him may not die but have eternal life" (John 3:16 TEV)?

_____Let's pray: Dear God, help me be an enthusiastic sharer of the Good News of Your love. Amen.

C. D.

Read from God's Word

Then Peter, filled with the Holy Spirit, said to them: "Rulers and elders of the people! If we are being called to account today for an act of kindness shown to a cripple and are asked how he was healed, then know this, you and all the people of Israel: It is by the name of Jesus Christ of Nazareth, whom you crucified but whom God raised from the dead, that this man stands before you healed. He is 'the stone you builders rejected, which has become the capstone.' Salvation is found in no one else, for there is no other name under heaven given to men by which we must be saved." Acts 4:8–12

Knowing What to Expect

October is Fire Prevention Month. Many classes have discussions about fire safety. Some schools schedule tours of fire stations and fire trucks. Firefighters visit schools, giving talks about their important work.

The firefighters who came to our school showed the students how they put on their equipment, right down to the air tank on their back and the mask on their face. When one firefighter asked if his dressed-up partner looked frightening, the students shook their heads no.

However, as the firefighter crawled around the students seated on the floor, they backed away. He would look frightening to someone just awakened in the middle of the night. Of course, the only reason a firefighter wakes people is to save them from their burning home.

Knowing what to do or what to expect if you're in a fire is very important. However, there's even more urgency in knowing what God will do when His people die. Because God sent the greatest Rescuer to take our punishment on Himself, we will be saved. Because Jesus died for us and rose again to prepare a place for us in heaven, we can expect to be there with Him someday.

As today's Bible reading states, there is no other name on earth that means salvation except the name of Jesus. Jesus is our rescuer.

_____Let's talk: Why is it important to have fire-safety drills? Why is it important to know what will happen after you die?

_____Let's pray: Dear Jesus, thank You for rescuing me from sin, death, and hell. Help me share with others Your saving power so they will be rescued also. Amen.

C. D.

Life Is Risky

When Uncle Ray came to visit, he brought a gift. "Hey, Steve," he called, "happy birthday!" It was a silver scooter with neon green wheels—just what Steven wanted.

Steven grabbed his helmet and rushed out the door. The sidewalk became his training ground. His skills improved with each pass by his house.

Finally he tried a stunt. He didn't notice that his wheels had turned while he was airborne. He landed off balance with a crash. His helmet took most of the shock, but his knees and elbows were skinned and bloody.

"Life is full of risks," said Mom. "I don't want you to be afraid to try new things. God was taking care of you, and He kept your body from being hurt badly. Even if you had gotten hurt, God would still protect your soul."

This story helps us remember God is with us each day, through hurts, sadness, and embarrassment. Even if our bodies would be seriously hurt, our souls would be safe.

"So, Steven," asked Uncle Ray, "what did you learn today?"

Steven thought for a moment. "I learned that God takes care of me in ways I can see and in ways I cannot see."

Read from God's Word

If you make the Most High your dwelling—even the LORD, who is my refuge—then no harm will befall you, no disaster will come near your tent. For He will command His angels concerning you to guard you in all your ways; ... "Because he loves Me," says the LORD, "I will rescue him, for he acknowledges My name. He will call upon Me, and I will answer him; I will be with him in trouble, I will deliver him and honor him. With long life will I satisfy him and show him My salvation." Psalm 91:9–16

_____Let's talk: Is there any activity you should not try because it is unwise and dangerous? Name some times God protected you. Thank Him.

_____Let's pray: Dear Jesus, thank You for protecting me. Please give me courage to do whatever You want me to do. Amen.

C. S.

Our God Is for the Birds

Read from God's Word

"Are not two sparrows sold for a penny? Yet not one of them will fall to the ground apart from the will of your Father. And even the very hairs of your head are all numbered. So don't be afraid; you are worth more than many sparrows." Matthew 10:29–31

Noel was a beautiful white dove that lived in the third grade classroom. She loved to perch in a basket on the teacher's desk and coo happily.

One day Noel flew out of the room through an open door and into the sky. The children tried chasing and calling to Noel, but she was gone.

The teacher reminded her tearful class that God cares for the birds. They prayed that Noel would be safe and that, if it was God's will, she would return. The children made posters. "Missing bird," they said. They scanned the sky, but no dove appeared.

On the last day of school Arielle heard a familiar cooing sound. There on the sidewalk was Noel! She scooped the bird up into her arms and ran back to her classroom shouting, "Noel is back!" The children celebrated the return of their much-loved pet.

God loves the students even more than they love Noel. He sent Jesus to be their Savior and to make them part of His family forever.

In our Bible reading we learn how much God cares for us. No one is too small or too unimportant to receive God's love.

_____Let's talk: How has He shown His love for you?

_____Let's pray: Dear God, thank You for loving and caring for all Your creatures. Thank You for loving and caring for me! Amen.

C. S.

Where's God?

Read from God's Word

O LORD, You have searched me and You know me. You know when I sit and when I rise; You perceive my thoughts from afar. You discern my going out and my lying down; You are familiar with all my ways. Before a word is on my tongue You know it completely, O LORD. ... You have laid Your hand upon me. ... If I go up to the heavens, You are there; if I make my bed in the depths, You are there. If I rise on the wings of the dawn, if I settle on the far side of the sea, even there Your hand will guide me, Your right hand will hold me fast. Psalm 139:1–10

A popular series of books features pictures of many people and asks you to find one character named Waldo. You are to look for Waldo on each page. Some people spend a lot of time looking for God. They become distracted and forget God is always with them.

When Chris's grandpa was sick, she wondered where God was. Shouldn't He make Grandpa well again? Was God in the picture? Yes, He was. He comforted the whole family with His Word. He took Chris's grandpa to live with Him in heaven.

When Evan's parents got divorced he wondered where God was. Shouldn't He have been there to make his parents love each other again? Was God in the picture all along? Yes, He was. He comforted Evan with the assurance of His own love and the continuing love of his parents.

When you have trouble finding God in your life, remember that God has found you and made you His own. He sent Jesus to die for you on the cross. His Word is clear. He keeps track of you even when your view of Him is clouded by sadness or sin.

Where is God? He is in His Word, in your heart, and in your life just as He promised.

_____Let's do: What book clearly shows you where God is and what He is like? List some people who help you understand more about God and His ways.

_____Let's pray: Dear God, thank You for being with me all the time. Please help me see You at work in my life. Amen.

C. S.

Read from God's Word

As the rain and the snow come down from heaven, and do not return to it without watering the earth and making it bud and flourish, so that it yields seed for the sower and bread for the eater, so is My word that goes out from My mouth: It will not return to Me empty, but will accomplish what I desire and achieve the purpose for which I sent it. You will go out in joy and be led forth in peace; the mountains and hills will burst into song before you, and all the trees of the field will clap their hands. Isaiah 55:10–12

A Useful Toy

Jerome likes to play with his yo-yo. It took a lot of practice, but now Jerome can do lots of tricks with his yo-yo.

Yo-yos were invented to be used as weapons. Warriors would send out a rock tied on a string to strike an enemy and then draw it back. Then they could use it over and over. The name "yo-yo" means "come back." It is a powerful tool in the hand of one who knows how to use it.

You are like a yo-yo in God's hand. He sends you out over and over to accomplish the work He wants you to do. Just like Jerome's yo-yo can do nothing by itself, you can achieve nothing on your own. God gives you the power—the words and actions you need. When you are sent out and given power by God, nothing is impossible.

God called you as His own at your Baptism. The Holy Spirit created faith in you. Now God holds you in His loving hand. And from Him you go out each day to your family or school or neighborhood as a blessing to speak His Word and to share His love and forgiveness. You give God great joy, and He uses you to be a blessing to many others.

_____Let's talk: Tell about a time God used you to help someone. How do you know that you belong to God? What gifts has God given you to use for Him?

_____Let's pray: Dear God, thank You for making me Your own and for sending me out into Your world. Please show me ways I can do Your work wherever I am. Amen.

C. S.

Speaking Up

Jimmy loved his grandfather and liked to do things with him. But one thing they didn't do together was go to church.

His mother explained, "Grandpa never learned about Jesus when he was little. Now it's hard for Grandpa to change his mind."

When his grandfather became very sick, Jimmy asked his mother if Grandpa would go to heaven. "The Bible says Jesus is the only way to heaven," answered his mother. "Keep praying for another chance to tell your grandfather." And Jimmy did.

Not long after that Jimmy's teacher gave the class this assignment—to write about Jesus. Jimmy wrote how God loves us and how He sent Jesus, His Son, to die for the sins of the world. He wrote about the gift of faith and the hope of heaven. He included a prayer thanking God for His love and asking Him to put faith in his grandpa's heart.

That evening, Jimmy visited his grandfather in the hospital and read his assignment to him. Grandpa smiled, nodded his head, and grabbed Jimmy's hand. Jimmy felt that his grandpa finally believed in Jesus. That night Jimmy's grandfather died. God used Jimmy's words to speak His Word.

Is there someone you know who needs to hear about Jesus? You could be the one to tell the Good News.

Read from God's Word

For, "Everyone who calls on the name of the Lord will be saved." How, then, can they call on the one they have not believed in? And how can they believe in the one of whom they have not heard? And how can they hear without someone preaching to them? And how can they preach unless they are sent? As it is written, "How beautiful are the feet of those who bring good news!" Romans 10:13–15

_____Let's do: How are you sure you will be in heaven with Jesus? Write what you believe about Jesus and the way to heaven. Read your story to others.

_____Let's pray: Dear Jesus, please help me tell others about You. Bring me and those I know and love to live with You forever. Amen.

C. S.

Read from God's Word

"For God so loved the world that He gave His one and only Son, that whoever believes in Him shall not perish but have eternal life. For God did not send His Son into the world to condemn the world, but to save the world through Him." John 3:16–17

God's Opinion

Kim was in serious trouble at school. She had stolen money from her teacher's desk and then lied about it. Now she had to face the principal and take the consequences.

"You know what is right and what is wrong," said the principal. "How do you feel about what you have done?"

"I feel so guilty," Kim sobbed. "I asked God to forgive me for taking the money."

"And did He?" asked the principal.

"I hope so," Kim replied. "I wish He would make His opinion clear."

Then the principal had the chance to comfort Kim. He assured her that God had forgiven Kim's sin. God did make His opinion clear on the cross. Jesus died for Kim's sins. He wants her to know that she has been forgiven.

God's forgiveness does not eliminate the fact that Kim sinned. Kim faced an earthly consequence to help her learn from her mistake. But His grace allows her to move on with her life. Her heavenly gift was that nothing would separate her from God's unconditional love and forgiveness.

God wants you to be sure of that too. Every time you see a cross, remember that Jesus took your sin there and suffered the consequences once and for all. In His opinion, you are free!

_____Let's talk: What makes you feel guilty? How can you be sure you are forgiven? How does knowing you are forgiven make a difference in how you treat other people?

_____Let's pray: Dear Jesus, thank You for forgiving all of my sins and making me right in Your sight. Now fill me with Your Holy Spirit so I can keep on trying to live in ways that please You. I pray in Your name. Amen.

C. S.

Attitude Check

Samuel watched the birds in the feeder outside his window. They ate until a squirrel climbed up the pole and scared them away. There was plenty of food. Why couldn't they take turns? *Stupid animals,* thought Samuel.

Then he remembered how he had grabbed the cereal box out of his younger sister's hand earlier that morning, making her squeal. And last night his older sister snatched the TV remote away from him. When he hit her in the arm and yelled at her, Dad sent both of them to their rooms.

Samuel remembered that he and Joey lost most of their recess yesterday because they had been shoving at the water fountain. Each wanted to be first in line.

Letting others be first is hard—until we remember what Jesus gave up for us. He gave up His throne in heaven to come to earth as a human being. He gave up His time to help others in need. He gave up His life so others could live forever.

God encourages us to have that same attitude. Think of the difference the love of Jesus makes in your life, family, and school. When you are sure of God's love, you become more eager to share it with others.

Read from God's Word

If you have any encouragement from being united with Christ, if any comfort from His love, if any fellowship with the Spirit, if any tenderness and compassion, then make my joy complete by being like-minded, having the same love, being one in spirit and purpose. Do nothing out of selfish ambition or vain conceit, but in humility consider others better than yourselves. Each of you should look not only to your own interests, but also to the interests of others. Your attitude should be the same as that of Christ Jesus: Who, being in very nature God, did not consider equality with God something to be grasped, but made Himself nothing, taking the very nature of a servant, being made in human likeness. And being found in appearance as a man, He humbled Himself and became obedient to death—even death on a cross! Philippians 2:1–8

_____Let's talk: Who could you let go first in your life at school? at home? Why would you want to?

_____Let's pray: Dear heavenly Father, thank You for giving me so much. Please make me always willing to share Your gifts cheerfully with others because I love You. For Jesus' sake. Amen.

C. S.

Read from God's Word

When you were dead in your sins and in the uncircumcision of your sinful nature, God made you alive with Christ. He forgave us all our sins, having canceled the written code, with its regulations, that was against us and that stood opposed to us; He took it away, nailing it to the cross. And having disarmed the powers and authorities, He made a public spectacle of them, triumphing over them by the cross. Colossians 2:13–15

Eat Your Vegetables

Have you ever heard of cruciferous (krew-SIF-er-us) vegetables? They include foods such as broccoli, cauliflower, and cabbage. Does cruciferous sound familiar? It probably reminds you of the word crucify, which means to put someone on a cross.

If you cut the stem of a cruciferous vegetable and look at it, you will see the shape of a cross there. That's how cruciferous vegetables got their name.

Cruciferous vegetables are very good for you. They are packed with vitamins and minerals that keep your body healthy and strong. They provide life-giving nutrition.

The cross of Jesus gives life—not just earthly life, but spiritual health and wholeness to all who believe. We were not able to save ourselves, but Jesus died for us and made us strong. He gives us sight to recognize Him as our Savior. This new sight allows us to see the needs of others. He makes our hearts beat with love for Him and His people. He gives our muscles power to work in His kingdom. He provides energy to live for Him and puts in our minds the understanding of His Word.

The next time your parents remind you to eat your cruciferous vegetables, remember the power of Jesus' cross in your life and thank Him for taking care of your body and soul.

_____Let's talk: Why is it important to take care of your body? Why is it important to take care of your soul? How do you receive the gifts God has to give?

_____Let's pray: Dear heavenly Father, thank You for giving me my body and soul and for caring for them. Help me appreciate all of Your gifts and use them in Your service. Amen.

C. S.

Special Needs

Amber had some special needs. She could not walk and used a wheelchair. Amber's classmates looked out for her and helped her. Two "buddies" pushed her chair from class to class. When she couldn't keep up, her friends walked more slowly. Amber's problem was obvious to anyone who saw her.

Mariah also had some special needs, but her problems were not so visible. Mariah had trouble getting along with others. Sometimes she made remarks that sounded strange. Sometimes she cried if she didn't get her way. Mariah needed help just like Amber did, but no one understood that people who look like everyone else may not be able to control how they act.

We all have a disability that may not be easy to see. This disability keeps us from doing what is right. It keeps us from caring perfectly about other people. It keeps us from pleasing God. It is called sin, and we cannot deal with it alone.

Read from God's Word

I do not understand what I do. For what I want to do I do not do, but what I hate I do. And if I do what I do not want to do, I agree that the law is good. As it is, it is no longer I myself who do it, but it is sin living in me. I know that nothing good lives in me, that is, in my sinful nature. For I have the desire to do what is good, but I cannot carry it out. For what I do is not the good I want to do; no, the evil I do not want to do—this I keep on doing. Now if I do what I do not want to do, it is no longer I who do it, but it is sin living in me that does it. ... What a wretched man I am! Who will rescue me from this body of death? Thanks be to God—through Jesus Christ our Lord! Romans 7:15–20, 24–25a

Jesus died on the cross to take care of our special need. He is with us every day to overcome the difficulties caused by our sin. He never gives up. He is our constant helper.

When you see someone with a special need, remember how God cares for you, and then share His patient love with others.

_____Let's talk: Why is it easier to help a person with a physical disability than it is to be kind to a person who acts strangely? When are you the hardest to help? Why does God keep on helping you?

_____Let's pray: Dear Jesus, thank You for loving me just as I am, with all my problems and sinfulness. Help me to care about others in the same way for Your sake. Amen.

C. S.

Read from God's Word

This is how we know what love is: Jesus Christ laid down His life for us. And we ought to lay down our lives for our brothers. If anyone has material possessions and sees his brother in need but has no pity on him, how can the love of God be in him? Dear children, let us not love with words or tongue but with actions and in truth. 1 John 3:16–18

People Are More Important

Juan's father could hardly wait to take his family on their first vacation in their brand new car.

Dad packed the luggage as the rest of the family climbed into the car and buckled up. Juan's dad climbed behind the wheel, but he didn't notice that Juan had forgotten to close the door and he began to back up.

The open door hit the fence post with a crash. The expensive new car was not perfect any more. Juan watched nervously as Dad silently looked at the damage.

"Dad," he said, "I am so sorry. I've ruined everything."

"It's a mess all right," sighed Dad, "but I'm glad you weren't hurt. This car is only important because of what it can do for our family. We'll get it fixed when we get back from our trip. I love you, Juan, much more than I love this car. Now let's go!"

It was the best vacation ever. Besides all the fun their family had, every time Juan looked at the car door, he remembered his father's words. Juan's family shows that people are more important than things.

In God's family, people are always valuable. Jesus paid for us with His own blood. Heaven is now our gift. That makes us more valuable than any thing.

_____Let's talk: Which of your possessions is most valuable to you? Why? What would cause you to give it up? Who sees you as the most valuable person in the world?

_____Let's pray: Dear Jesus, thank You for loving me more than You loved Your own life. Always remind me that people are more important than things. Amen.

C. S.

Getting Even

Gerald constantly picked on Angela and teased her. Angela thought Gerald was annoying and wanted to get rid of him. "He's the sand in the chewing gum of life," she said.

Many people know someone like Gerald who is irritating and says and does hurtful things. Often our first reaction to such a person is to get even.

The religious leaders were "sand" in the chewing gum of Jesus' earthly life. But He didn't get even by zapping them with His godly power. Instead, Jesus showed love to His enemies. It is hard for us to understand that He could pray for the people who nailed Him to the cross, but He did! Jesus invites us to do the same thing—"Love your enemies and pray for those who persecute you" (Matthew 5:44).

It isn't easy to love our enemies. With our own strength and in our own way it would never happen. So how does it happen? It happens when we take our eyes off of ourselves and God helps us look to Jesus on the cross. He loves us so much that He died for our sins. Without Jesus, we are helpless and sinful. God's forgiveness shows us how to love and forgive others. Now that's a great way to "get even"!

Read from God's Word

"You have heard that it was said, 'Love your neighbor and hate your enemy.' But I tell you: Love your enemies and pray for those who persecute you, that you may be sons of your Father in heaven. He causes His sun to rise on the evil and the good, and sends rain on the righteous and the unrighteous." Matthew 5:43–45

_____Let's talk: Who's the "sand in the chewing gum" of your life? How do you react to him or her? What are some ways you can show love to that person?

_____Let's pray: Dear Jesus, help me to follow Your example and show love and forgiveness to my enemies. In Your name I ask this. Amen.

J. A. D.

Read from God's Word

Keep your lives free from the love of money and be content with what you have, because God has said, "Never will I leave you; never will I forsake you." So we say with confidence, "The Lord is my helper; I will not be afraid. What can man do to me?" Hebrews 13:5–6

The Dog and the Shadow

Aesop told stories using clever, foolish, greedy, and generous animals. These animals acted in ways that people often do. Each story had a moral—a lesson to learn.

One of Aesop's fables is "The Dog and the Shadow:" "A dog was crossing a river with a piece of meat in his mouth. When he looked down, he saw his reflection in the water. He thought the reflection was another dog carrying a piece of meat in its mouth. The dog dropped his meat to grab for the other dog's meat. Of course, his own piece of meat fell into the water and was swept away by the river. Both pieces disappeared and the dog ended up with nothing." The moral of the story is don't be greedy.

We sometimes want what someone else has. Like the dog in the fable, we can be selfish and greedy.

That doesn't mean we should never buy anything newer, bigger, or better. What it does mean is that we can be satisfied with what God provides. He loves us and gives us just what we need at just the right time. Our Savior put us first when He died for our sins. Now we have forgiveness and eternal life. Nothing is better than that!

_____Let's talk: Are you content with what you have? Why or why not? God gives you what you need. What is the difference between having what you "need" and what you "want"?

_____Let's pray: Gracious God, thank You for giving me everything I need now and forever. Help me to be content with what I have. In Jesus' name. Amen.

J. A. D.

Job List

Read from God's Word

And whatever you do, whether in word or deed, do it all in the name of the Lord Jesus, giving thanks to God the Father through Him. ... Whatever you do, work at it with all your heart, as working for the Lord, not for men, since you know that you will receive an inheritance from the Lord as a reward. It is the Lord Christ you are serving. Colossians 3:17, 23–24

"I hate cleaning out the goat pens!" moaned Heather. "It's the smelliest, yuckiest job on the whole farm."

"Well, my arms are going to fall off," said her sister Holly. "Raking the leaves is the pits. There must be a zillion of them. And they just keep falling!"

"Why all the fussing?" Mom asked.

"We're tired of chores," Heather mumbled. "We have to do them over and over."

"Me too," said Mom, "but when I'm bored or tired, I remember Colossians 3—'Whatever you do, work at it with all your heart, as working for the Lord, not for men.' Even yucky or boring jobs are done for Jesus."

Jesus values all the things you do because you are His creature. He especially values you because He chooses to love you, not because you are good or worthwhile. He showed His love by doing a difficult job for you—dying on the cross. God loves and cares for us, protects us, forgives our sins, and gives us a home in heaven.

As the girls thought more about God's love and care, they saw their chores differently. Their jobs hadn't changed, but their hearts had.

_____Let's talk: What are some things you dislike doing? How can remembering what God has done for you make those jobs easier to do?

_____Let's pray: Lord, there are some jobs I don't like to do, such as _____________. Please help me to do those jobs without complaining. Help me remember that I have a chance to work for You. In Jesus' name. Amen.

J. A. D.

Read from God's Word

Shout for joy to the LORD, all the earth. Worship the LORD with gladness; come before Him with joyful songs. Know that the LORD is God. It is He who made us, and we are His; we are His people, the sheep of His pasture. Enter His gates with thanksgiving and His courts with praise; give thanks to Him and praise His name. For the LORD is good and His love endures forever; His faithfulness continues through all generations. Psalm 100

A Racecar Day

Three-year-old Connor jumped out of his dad's car and ran up the sidewalk, shouting all the way. "Grammy, Grammy! Guess what!" he yelled, charging through the door.

Connor didn't wait for his grandmother to respond or even to say hello. He was so excited that a hug was definitely out of the question. Connor hopped around the kitchen as he rattled on about all the things he had done that day.

When Connor finally stopped to catch his breath, she said, "Wow! It sounds like you and Dad had a super time together."

"I had soooo much fun," Connor said. "It was a racecar day!" Racecars are Connor's all-time favorite. So this was the best way he could describe a wonderful day.

Racecar days aren't mentioned in the Bible, but it does tell of special days worth shouting about. The puzzle below describes one of those days. Figure out the code by printing the letter that comes *after* the letter given (Z=A).

SGHR HR SGD CZX SGD KNQC GZR LZCD; KDS TR QDINHBD ZMC AD FKZC HM HS (ORZKL 118:24).

Have a racecar day!

_____Let's talk: What makes a day special for you? How can you make a day special for someone else? How does thinking about God make every day special?

_____Let's pray: Dear God, thank You for every day—the wonderful days, the ordinary days, and even the bad days. Knowing that Jesus loves and forgives me makes every day special. Amen.

J. A. D.

The Soap Solution

Read from God's Word

"But the things that come out of the mouth come from the heart, and these make a man 'unclean.' For out of the heart come evil thoughts, murder, adultery, sexual immorality, theft, false testimony, slander." Matthew 15:18–19

My parents didn't tell dirty jokes or use bad language and didn't allow us to say them either. Sometimes ugly words just seemed to pop out anyway, so Mom and Dad had a solution. If they heard us say naughty words, they washed out our mouths with soap!

Soap doesn't really clean out bad language because words don't start in our mouths. They start in our hearts, our thoughts, and our feelings. When we are angry, we may say bad words. Sometimes we use bad language because our friends do.

In today's Bible reading, Jesus lists bad things that start in the heart and come out of the mouth. David spoke of an excellent use for the mouth in Psalm 19:14: "May the words of my mouth and the meditation of my heart be pleasing in Your sight, O LORD."

Think about all the great things God has done for you. He loves you and cares for you. Most important, God sent Jesus to be your Savior. Your sins are forgiven and heaven is waiting for you. When our thoughts and hearts are filled with these things, great words come from our mouths. We use our mouths to praise and thank God, to speak kind and loving words, and to tell others about Jesus. No soap needed!

_____Let's talk: When are you tempted to use bad language? What causes this? How can you change bad language into good language?

_____Let's pray: Dear God, I'm sorry for using my mouth and voice in ways that aren't pleasing to You. Please help me use my words in a kind way and to praise You. In Jesus' name. Amen.

J. A. D.

Read from God's Word

Ruth replied, "Don't urge me to leave you or to turn back from you. Where you go I will go, and where you stay I will stay. Your people will be my people and your God my God. Where you die I will die, and there I will be buried. May the LORD deal with me, be it ever so severely, if anything but death separates you and me." When Naomi realized that Ruth was determined to go with her, she stopped urging her.
Ruth 1:16–18

Greater Than Super Glue

Certain types of glue are guaranteed to stick anything together forever.

In today's Bible reading, Ruth seems to be "super-gluing" herself to Naomi. Ruth had married Naomi's son but he had died. Naomi's husband had also died. Now Naomi was moving back to her own land. She thought Ruth should stay with her own family in Moab. Ruth disagreed and gave Naomi a list of reasons for going with her. When Ruth said, "Your God will be my God," Naomi didn't argue anymore. Ruth stayed with her mother-in-law instead of her own parents.

It's great to have a friend who always sticks with us. We know we can count on such friends no matter what happens. But there are times when the glue of friendship fails. We move away from our friends or they move away from us. Friendship glue isn't always so super.

God's love for us is the greatest glue ever. It has more strength than super strong glue. The Bible tells us, "Neither death nor life, neither angels nor demons, neither the present nor the future, nor any powers, neither height nor depth, nor anything else in all creation, will be able to separate us from the love of God that is in Christ Jesus our Lord" (Romans 8:38–39).

_____Let's talk: Do you know someone who sticks by you, no matter what? How about you—are you a loyal and committed friend?

_____Let's pray: Eternal God, I am so happy that You always stick by me. Thank You for never letting anything separate me from Your love and forgiveness in Jesus. Amen.

J. A. D.

A Mighty Fortress

Read from God's Word

God is our refuge and strength, an ever-present help in trouble. Therefore we will not fear, though the earth give way and the mountains fall into the heart of the sea, though its waters roar and foam and the mountains quake with their surging. Psalm 46:1–3

About 500 years ago, Martin Luther hid in a German castle for a year. This was to protect him from being arrested by his enemies. They were angry because Luther disagreed with some of the teachings of the church. Luther was especially upset that the church said you could buy forgiveness with money. He knew the only way to have forgiveness was faith in Jesus as your Savior.

Luther wrote many songs and hymns so people could sing about their faith. Perhaps Luther was thinking of the castle where he was locked up when he wrote "A Mighty Fortress Is Our God." This hymn became the "theme song" for many people who believed what Luther taught. The inspiring words were sung by soldiers going into battle and by martyrs as they went to their death. The hymn has been translated into almost every language.

The words of this hymn are just as true today as they were when Luther wrote them. You can face life and death because of Jesus, your Savior. He won the battle against sin and Satan when He died for your sins and rose again. You are forgiven, loved, and cared for as God's child. That's worth singing about!

_____Let's talk: Have you ever sung this hymn? How did the words make you feel? If you wrote a hymn, what would it tell about God?

_____Let's pray: Dear God, thanks for being a "mighty fortress" and for loving me. I will thank and praise You all my life for taking all my sins away. Amen.

J. A. D.

Read from God's Word

Christ redeemed us from the curse of the law by becoming a curse for us, for it is written: "Cursed is everyone who is hung on a tree." He redeemed us in order that the blessing given to Abraham might come to the Gentiles through Christ Jesus, so that by faith we might receive the promise of the Spirit. Galatians 3:13–14

Redeem before Expiration

When I go grocery shopping I take along "money-off" coupons that I've clipped from the newspaper. I give the coupons to the cashier. Then the amount of the coupons is subtracted from my bill. Sometimes I have "double" coupons so even more is taken off my bill. It's like getting bonus money!

When I redeem, or trade in, these coupons, they are valuable. But there's one problem. Most coupons include this line: "Must be redeemed before expiration date." I don't always use them before the deadline and then they are useless—just pieces of paper.

To redeem something means to buy it back or trade a useless thing for something valuable. The person who does the buying back or trading is called the redeemer. Jesus is often called our Redeemer because He bought us back from sin and Satan. Jesus didn't use coupons to redeem us—He used His very own blood. We were redeemed by Jesus' death on the cross for our sins. Now we are forgiven and free to be God's child.

And guess what? There's no expiration date on being redeemed by Jesus. It lasts forever because after we die we will be with Jesus, our Redeemer, in heaven.

_____Let's talk: The word redeem can mean to buy back, trade a thing for something valuable, or free someone from prison or harm. How does Jesus, the Redeemer, fit each of these definitions? How can knowing that Jesus redeems you help you in your life?

_____Let's pray: I know that my Redeemer lives! What comfort this sweet sentence gives! He lives, He lives, who once was dead; He lives, my everliving head! (*Lutheran Worship* 264:1)

J. A. D.

Shooting Free Throws

"I'll never get it!" Jared bounced the basketball so hard it almost hit the backboard.

"There's nothing to shooting free throws," his younger brother Mike said. To prove his point, Mike swished one through the net.

"Go away!" Jared hated to admit it, but his little brother was better at shooting free throws than he was. Not that Jared was a terrible athlete, he just couldn't shoot free throws. He always did something wrong.

"Keep at it, Jared," Dad advised. "That's the only way you'll improve. Think about how badly you want to be able to shoot free throws. That will help you keep at it until it seems as easy as breathing." With determination, Jared picked up the basketball and started practicing.

Keeping at something and not giving up is called perseverance. It means sticking with something that may take a long time and be lots of hard work. The writer to the Hebrews encourages us to "run with perseverance the race marked out for us" (Hebrews 12:1).

When you feel like giving up, think of the perseverance of God. He never gives up on you. God always offers His love, care, forgiveness, and eternal life.

Read from God's Word

Therefore, since we have been justified through faith, we have peace with God through our Lord Jesus Christ, through whom we have gained access by faith into this grace in which we now stand. And we rejoice in the hope of the glory of God. Not only so, but we also rejoice in our sufferings, because we know that suffering produces perseverance; perseverance, character; and character, hope. And hope does not disappoint us, because God has poured out His love into our hearts by the Holy Spirit, whom He has given us. Romans 5:1–5

_____Let's talk: Think of something you persevered at doing. What kept you going? How did you feel after you accomplished what you were trying to do?

_____Let's pray: Dear God, thank You for not giving up on me and for always giving me Your love and forgiveness. I am really having trouble persevering at __________. Please help me to stick with it and not give up. In Jesus' name. Amen.

J. A. D.

Read from God's Word

But as for you, continue in what you have learned and have become convinced of, because you know those from whom you learned it, and how from infancy you have known the holy Scriptures, which are able to make you wise for salvation through faith in Christ Jesus. All Scripture is God-breathed and is useful for teaching, rebuking, correcting and training in righteousness, so that the man of God may be thoroughly equipped for every good work. 2 Timothy 3:14–17

B-I-B-L-E

I get lots of e-mail. Some of it brings family news from all over the country. Some of the e-mail includes information for my job. Some of it is silly jokes or things I really don't want to know about. But occasionally, e-mail really makes me think. Like this:

B asic
I nstruction
B efore
L eaving
E arth

I wrote that short e-mail on a piece of paper and use it as a bookmark in my Bible. It reminds me that the Bible is the true Word of God. By reading the Bible, we learn that God created the world and everything in it. We can find out how God worked in the lives of the people in the Bible. We can also learn how He works in our lives now and how we can live as His children. The Bible tells us about God's love, protection, and care for each of us.

The most important thing we can find in the Bible is how much God loves us. He loves us so much that He sent Jesus to die for the sins of all people. Because of Jesus' death, our sins are forgiven and we are part of God's family. Now we know that after leaving the earth, we will live with Jesus forever in heaven.

_____Let's talk: What are your favorite parts of the Bible? Why? How can reading the Bible help you in your life?

_____Let's pray: Triune God, thank You for telling me about Yourself in the Bible. I especially say thanks for the good news of Jesus' death and resurrection for me. Now I know I am forgiven and will live in heaven someday. What wonderful news! Amen.

J. A. D.

november

Contributors for this month:

Kathy A. Schutz

Phil Lang

Gail Pawlitz

Jewel L. Laabs

Judy Williams

Valerie Schultz

Read from God's Word

Gideon, Barak, Samson, Jephthah, David, Samuel and the prophets, who through faith conquered kingdoms, administered justice, and gained what was promised; who shut the mouths of lions, quenched the fury of the flames, and escaped the edge of the sword ... Others were tortured and refused to be released, so that they might gain a better resurrection. Some faced jeers and flogging, while still others were chained and put in prison. They were stoned; they were sawed in two; they were put to death by the sword. They went about in sheepskins and goatskins, destitute, persecuted and mistreated—the world was not worthy of them. They wandered in deserts and mountains, and in caves and holes in the ground. ... God had planned something better for us so that only together with us would they be made perfect. Hebrews 11:32–40

Are You a Saint?

Yesterday was Halloween. Did you dress up in a costume? If you did, people did not see you as you really are. They saw you as something you pretended to be.

The day after Halloween is All Saints' Day. This day had its beginning in the year 360. It has been a time to remember Christians who have died. On this day we also look forward to joining them in heaven.

You may wonder what Halloween and All Saints' Day have in common. On Halloween you dress up as something you are not. On All Saints' Day you celebrate the "costume" you received when you were baptized.

Before you became a child of God at your Baptism, God saw your ugly, scary sin. But when the pastor put water on your head and spoke God's Word of forgiveness, you became clothed with Christ's righteousness. You "put on" Jesus' perfect, sinless life.

Because you are covered in this way, God no longer sees your sin. He sees you as if you had no sin. He doesn't see your sin because it has been removed by Christ. In sin's place is Christ's righteousness.

You can celebrate All Saints' Day because you, too, are a saint. You have on the costume of Jesus' perfect life.

_____Let's talk: What are your sins covered with? Why are you a saint? Who are some saints you knew who have joined the Lord in heaven?

_____Let's pray: Dear Jesus, thank You for Your holiness, which removes my ugly sin. I'm honored and grateful to be one of Your saints. Amen.

K. A. S.

Yes-s-s!

When was the last time you had such a perfect time that you said, "Yes-s-s!"? Was it the day you got all A's or when you were picked first for the team? When was it? Where was it? That moment is like a tiny taste of heaven.

Draw a picture of that memory. Now imagine that every moment of every day is like that "perfect" picture. Your God, the one who created you, has a perfect heaven waiting for you. And it will last forever!

You might think that you don't deserve it. You are absolutely right! You don't deserve a perfect home in heaven because every thought, word, and deed hasn't been perfect. However, Jesus, the Son of God, did the perfect thing for you. He takes every imperfect thought, word, and deed away and gives you His goodness in its place. All the guilt and bad feelings from talking back, grumbling about homework, or saying unkind things are gone. In their place, Jesus' perfect moments give us a perfect forever.

The perfect forever will not be like the last time you said, "Yes-s-s!" The perfect forever will not be just a picture you draw. God makes the perfect forever a permanent reality.

Read from God's Word

Then I saw a new heaven and a new earth, for the first heaven and the first earth had passed away, and there was no longer any sea. I saw the Holy City, the new Jerusalem, coming down out of heaven from God, prepared as a bride beautifully dressed for her husband. And I heard a loud voice from the throne saying, "Now the dwelling of God is with men, and He will live with them. They will be His people, and God Himself will be with them and be their God. He will wipe every tear from their eyes. There will be no more death or mourning or crying or pain, for the old order of things has passed away." Revelation 21:1–4

____Let's do: Can you share your "Yes-s-s!" picture with someone and talk to them about heaven and God?

____Let's pray: Dear Jesus, thank You for being perfect in my place so I might have a perfect home with You forever. Amen.

P. L.

Read from God's Word

Therefore, there is now no condemnation for those who are in Christ Jesus, because through Christ Jesus the law of the Spirit of life set me free from the law of sin and death. For what the law was powerless to do in that it was weakened by the sinful nature, God did by sending His own Son in the likeness of sinful man to be a sin offering. And so He condemned sin in sinful man, in order that the righteous requirements of the law might be fully met in us, who do not live according to the sinful nature but according to the Spirit. Romans 8:1–4

Bible Math

"There's something wrong with your math, Mr. Sage," Billy said.

"I'm glad you noticed," smiled Mr. Sage. "Your math books would give different answers, but today I want to teach you some Bible math."

"What's that?" the whole class asked.

"Bible math gives you a new way to look at God's loving plan for all people."

"Let's start with 100 – 1 = 0. The 100 stands for 100 percent perfect. In the beginning, God created people to be perfect. But we are all sinners. Even the smallest mistake is taken from the 100 percent and we end up with nothing, zero. We have a zero percent chance to be in heaven on our own.

"Now let's check out the next problem, 0 + 1 = 100. God takes our zero percent chance and adds 1 to it. He adds His one Son, Jesus, who lived a 100 percent perfect life in our place. He filled our empty chances with His loving gift. So God takes our zero chance and adds Jesus, our one and only Savior. With Him, we are 100 percent saved."

God looks at Jesus and sees the answer to our sin problem. God's solutions help us to reach out with His love and forgiveness to others.

_____Let's do: Can you create a Bible math problem? Share it with a friend.

_____Let's pray: Dear God, thank You for subtracting my sins by adding Jesus to my life. Amen.

P. L.

Bible Riddles

1. When was medicine first mentioned in the Bible?
2. Where is tennis found in the Bible?
3. Who was the greatest entertainer in the Bible?

The answer to number 1 is Moses. He received the two "tablets" at Mount Sinai. The answer to number 2 is Joseph. He served in Pharaoh's court. The answer to number 3 is Samson. He brought down the house.

Here is another Bible riddle with an important lesson: How can a man be born when he is old? That's what Nicodemus asked Jesus.

Jesus had surprised Nicodemus by answering, "Unless a man is born again, he cannot see the kingdom of heaven." Jesus was talking about a spiritual birth. After listening to Jesus, Nicodemus believed in Jesus as his Savior and was baptized. He was "born again," even though he was old.

At Baptism, faith begins to grow. The Holy Spirit enters our hearts. Our journey to heaven does not depend on what we do, but completely on what Jesus has done for us through His life, death, and resurrection. We are freed from the need to pile up good behavior and actions. We are energized to serve others and share the Gospel message.

Read from God's Word

Nicodemus ... came to Jesus at night and said ... "How can a man be born when he is old? ... Surely he cannot enter a second time into his mother's womb to be born!" Jesus answered, "I tell you the truth, no one can enter the kingdom of God unless he is born of water and the Spirit. Flesh gives birth to flesh, but the Spirit gives birth to spirit. ... Just as Moses lifted up the snake in the desert, so the Son of Man must be lifted up, that everyone who believes in Him may have eternal life. For God so loved the world that He gave His one and only Son, that whoever believes in Him shall not perish but have eternal life. ... Light has come into the world, but men loved darkness instead of light because their deeds were evil. Everyone who does evil hates the light, and will not come into the light for fear that his deeds will be exposed. But whoever lives by the truth comes into the light, so that it may be seen plainly that what He has done has been done through God." John 3:1–21

_____Let's talk: What other Bible riddles do you know? Have you been baptized? What do you remember about it? What is the importance of Baptism for you? Pray about it.

_____Let's pray: Dear Jesus, thank You for being the answer to life's hardest riddle. Amen.

P. L.

Read from God's Word

The man said, "The woman you put here with me—she gave me some fruit from the tree, and I ate it." Then the LORD God said to the woman, "What is this you have done?" The woman said, "The serpent deceived me, and I ate." Genesis 3:12–13

The Blame Game

He pushed me!"

"He pushed me first!"

"Did not!" screamed Chuck. "You started it!"

"Hey!" said Mr. Potter. "Let's talk about this. You are both trying to blame the other person and excuse yourself. It is pointless to argue about who started it!"

After a pause, Kevin explained, "Actually, Mr. Potter, we both remember who started it all."

"Yeah, it was our first day in kindergarten. During recess Kevin pushed me down," laughed Chuck.

Kevin smiled and nodded.

"Wow, you guys are great at remembering. You need to be great at forgetting. I want you to forgive each other. I also want you to forget who started the pushing or whatever the problem might have been. Can you shake hands and forgive each other?"

Chuck and Kevin, Adam and Eve, you and I—we all play the blame game. We also try to get even. It is no use. It does not work; we are all sinners. We can never make things even. Jesus offers us hope. Through His perfection and love, we are set free from guilt and sin. Just as He offers us forgiveness, we are free to forgive others.

_____Let's do: What were Adam and Eve's consequences for blaming others and disobeying God? See Genesis 3. What is God's solution to the blame game? See John 3:13–21.

_____Let's pray: Dear Jesus, help me admit my mistakes without blaming others. Thank You for loving me enough to pay for all my mistakes with Your life. Amen.

P. L.

My Mama Said …

Mr. Potter watched as Mitchell cleaned mud off his shoes. Now mud was on the floor. The rest of the class noticed too.

Mr. Potter told the class a story. "When I was little, my mama gave me lots of advice. She would say, 'If you make a mess, you clean it up. If you play with toys, you put them away. If you spill food, you clean it up.'"

Mitchell got the point. "Did you tell that story so I would clean up the mess I made?"

"Yes, I did. Please use the broom and dustpan under the bookshelf to clean up the dirt."

Now that mess was gone, but Mitchell had an unseen mess. And so do we.

No amount of sweeping will clean away our sinful thoughts and actions. When we disobey God, become selfish or angry, or complain, we sin. Guilt piles up around us. We cannot clean up our own mess.

Read from God's Word

But now a righteousness from God, apart from law, has been made known, to which the Law and the Prophets testify. This righteousness from God comes through faith in Jesus Christ to all who believe. There is no difference, for all have sinned and fall short of the glory of God. Romans 3:21–23

We cannot stand before God with our pile of dirt and declare ourselves clean. Jesus is our only solution. God forgives us through our Baptism and through the faith He gives us. The dirt of our sin-stained lives is removed when God looks at Jesus—not at us. By God's grace we are freed from the mess of our sin.

_____Let's do: What does your mom tell you? What is the worst mess you have ever made? What chores do you do each day or week?

_____Let's pray: Dear Jesus, thank You for cleaning up the mess of sin in my life. Help me take good care of the world around me. Amen.

P. L.

Read from God's Word

"Therefore I tell you, do not worry about your life, what you will eat or drink; or about your body, what you will wear. Is not life more important than food, and the body more important than clothes? Look at the birds of the air; they do not sow or reap or store away in barns, and yet your heavenly Father feeds them. Are you not much more valuable than they? Who of you by worrying can add a single hour to his life? ... So do not worry, saying, 'What shall we eat?' or 'What shall we drink?' or 'What shall we wear?' For the pagans run after all these things, and your heavenly Father knows that you need them. But seek first his kingdom and his righteousness, and all these things will be given to you as well. Therefore do not worry about tomorrow, for tomorrow will worry about itself. Each day has enough trouble of its own." Matthew 6:25–34

Willy's Worries

Willy Witherspoon worried. Willy worried whether the weather would be warm and wet or windy and wonderful. Would Willy wear his warm woolies or his worn-out white Wranglers? Were Warren, Woody, and Wilma walking to school today? Would breakfast be waffles with whipped cream or wheat cereal with berries?

Willy worried about school. Would Mr. Winslow explain a lesson on wigwams or weevils? Would Willy have worksheets with word lists? Would Wilma and Winnie whisper words which would wound him? Would Warren and Woody want him on their wiffle ball team? Willy's worries were way out of whack!

This Wednesday, Willy's wise mother, Winona, had words for him. Winona said, "The Bible tells us we need not worry. Jesus also said to give all your worries to Him because He cares for you. God is in control." Winona's wisdom from God's Word comforted Willy. He now saw his worries as trouble called sin.

The same God who cares for the birds and the flowers provided a way for all people to walk away from sin. Jesus, our Savior, paid the price for each worry through His perfect life, suffering, and death. The victory He won through His resurrection turns our worries into songs of celebration and thanks.

_____Let's do: What have you worried about lately? What good does worry do? What is God's solution to worry?

_____Let's pray: What a friend we have in Jesus, All our sins and griefs to bear! What a privilege to carry Ev'rything to God in prayer! Oh, what peace we often forfeit; Oh, what needless pain we bear—All because we do not carry Ev'rything to God in prayer! (*Lutheran Worship* 516:1)

P. L.

Team Colors

Read from God's Word

You are all sons of God through faith in Christ Jesus, for all of you who were baptized into Christ have clothed yourselves with Christ. Galatians 3:26–27

The whistle blew; the season was over. The volleyball team had an 8 and 0 record; they were undefeated! They brought home the trophy. To celebrate, the girls wore their jerseys to school. They were proud to be seen in their colors.

The orange and black jerseys identified the members of the volleyball team. What identifies members of God's team? Did they earn the good-behavior trophy? Have they beaten the devil at his game and won eternal life for themselves?

The answer to these questions is no. The family of God gets its colors from the victory of Christ. He fought the battle; He won the prize. Jesus defeated Satan and rose in victory. We are identified as God's own people by the powerful but invisible sign of the cross over our forehead and heart. We are identified as God's own by the fruit of His Spirit, which He produces in us.

We cannot win by ourselves. The victory message comes in the words from Galatians. We share in His glory for we are all "sons [and daughters] of God through faith in Christ Jesus." He places on us His victory colors; He hands us the trophy He has won. We are amazed at His love and mercy.

_____Let's do: What are your school's colors? Have you ever been on a winning team? Think of a cheer to thank Jesus for His victory.

_____Let's pray: Dear Jesus, we thank You for Your suffering, death, and victory. Help us to share this wonderful victory news with others. Amen.

G. P.

Read from God's Word

Thomas said to Him, "Lord, we don't know where You are going, so how can we know the way?" Jesus answered, "I am the way and the truth and the life. No one comes to the Father except through Me. If you really knew Me, you would know My Father as well. From now on, you do know Him and have seen Him." John 14:5–7

One Way

"Mom, don't turn. That's a one-way sign!" said Gideon.

"Thanks," sighed Mom. "I made that mistake once before. It was scary to make a wrong turn and see cars coming straight at me."

"What did you do then, Mom?"

"I quickly turned into an alley before I caused an accident. I was so thankful God gave me a way out of danger."

"Look, there's another one-way sign, but it's broken. It's pointing up at the sky."

That second one-way sign pointing up can remind us of another rescue. God tells us in the Bible that the only way to heaven is through Jesus, who died on the cross for us. Left on our own to get to heaven, we might find that arrow pointing at us. That way would get us nowhere because sin is our roadblock.

God loved us so much that He saved us from going the wrong way forever by sending Jesus as our Savior. Jesus shows us the right way to heaven because He is the one and only way. He is both an arrow and a path.

Our misguided feet and our blocked path are set straight by Jesus, who says, "I am the way." With His help, we share this news with others.

_____Let's do: Draw three traffic signs. Using these signs, what message can you share about Jesus?

_____Let's pray: Dear Jesus, thank You for showing me the one way to heaven. Keep me safe as I follow You and share the news with others. Amen.

P. L.

What Does This Mean?

"Grandpa, I found this old book on your shelf. What does this mean?" asked Chris.

"This says *sola gratia, sola fide, sola Scriptura*. It's Latin. Translated into English," Grandpa said, "it says, 'grace alone, faith alone, Scripture alone.' "

"I still don't understand what it means."

"Let me tell you about a man named Martin Luther. He was born on this day many, many years ago in Germany. These words were his slogan or motto. Luther read in the Bible that God saves us by grace. We can't be perfect enough to earn heaven. That's the meaning of grace alone."

Grandpa continued, "Many people in Luther's day thought doing good things would get them into heaven. Luther believed we are saved by faith alone. Our good works do not gain us heaven."

"The Bible is God's revealed Word to us. Luther found that the only place you can be sure you have God's Word is the Bible, so he taught the idea of finding God's truth in Scripture alone."

"Luther made it easy to remember, didn't he?" said Chris. "Grace alone, faith alone, and Scripture alone."

"Yes, it is easy to remember and a joy to share," smiled Grandpa.

Read from God's Word

For it is by grace you have been saved, through faith—and this not from yourselves, it is the gift of God—not by works, so that no one can boast. For we are God's workmanship, created in Christ Jesus to do good works, which God prepared in advance for us to do. Ephesians 2:8–10

____Let's do: Draw a picture or make a poster of Luther's slogan. Share that poster with others.

____Let's pray: Dear God, thank You that we receive heaven as a gift. Help us daily read and trust Your Word, the Bible. Amen.

P. L.

Read from God's Word

"Salvation is found in no one else, for there is no other name under heaven given to men by which we must be saved." Acts 4:12

Saved By

What do these things have in common: a "No Homework Coupon," a good catch by a soccer goalie, and an extra day on an assignment?

If you guessed that each has the power to save, you are right. The coupon rescues us from consequences of unfinished homework. The catch by the goalie prevents a score for the opponent. When a teacher gives us more time to complete an assignment, we are saved from turning in poor work.

In these examples people save people from problems, but who will save us from sin? Can we save each other? Can we save ourselves? No.

The only one who can save us is Jesus. His name even means "The Lord saves." Jesus rescues us from the consequences of sin. His perfect life, death, and resurrection gain for us more than any "No Homework Coupon" ever could. Like the goalie, Jesus snatches us from death's grip and the devil's power and makes us winners with Him. Like the bonus time from the teacher, Jesus gives us time forever with Him.

With saving love, Jesus reaches into our lives. With love and thanks in our hearts, the Holy Spirit helps us to share Jesus and His saving message with others.

_____Let's do: Think of times when you were saved from consequences that you deserved. Think of times when you were able to save others from a problem.

_____Let's pray: Dear Jesus, thank You for saving us from the problem of sin. Help us share Your saving message with others. Amen.

P. L.

Little Things Mean a Lot

Read from God's Word

Consequently, just as the result of one trespass was condemnation for all men, so also the result of one act of righteousness was justification that brings life for all men. For just as through the disobedience of the one man the many were made sinners, so also through the obedience of the one man the many will be made righteous. Romans 5:18–19

Suddenly, everything stopped. Signals no longer traveled to earth. The satellite was dead. Scientists searched to learn why.

What they discovered might surprise you. The satellite was a very complex and expensive piece of equipment, yet the problem was with a little screw! One screw was too long and it poked through a piece of metal and caused the electrical system to fail.

A simple 10¢ screw destroyed a 70-million dollar satellite. It is startling to think that something so small can make a difference in something so important.

God created a perfect world. He created people in His own image—perfect. But one "little" sin has caused every person ever born to be full of sin. Adam and Eve's bite of the forbidden fruit caused the entire world, even nature, to be damaged by sin.

Our Bible reading shows us that sin and death came into the world through one man—Adam. We also read that forgiveness and life come through one man—our Lord Jesus Christ! His death on the cross paid for all the sins ever committed.

The damaged satellite couldn't be repaired. You and I can rejoice that our sin-damaged life has been repaired. God's Son, Jesus, through His death and resurrection, repaired the relationship between God and us.

_____Let's do: Why is one little sin so bad? Why is the one sacrifice Jesus made so good?

_____Let's pray: "Chief of sinners though I be, Jesus shed His blood for me, Died that I might live on high, Lives that I might never die." (*Lutheran Worship* 285:1) Thank You, God, for Your gifts of forgiveness and eternal life. Amen.

K. A. S.

Read from God's Word

When they went across the lake, the disciples forgot to take bread. "Be careful," Jesus said to them. "Be on your guard against the yeast of the Pharisees and Sadducees. ... Don't you remember the five loaves for the five thousand, and how many basketfuls you gathered? Or the seven loaves for the four thousand, and how many basketfuls you gathered? How is it you don't understand that I was not talking to you about bread? But be on your guard against the yeast of the Pharisees and Sadducees." Then they understood that He was not telling them to guard against the yeast used in bread, but against the teaching of the Pharisees and Sadducees. Matthew 16:5–12

Adding Flavor to Our World

Paul watched his mother as she carefully measured all the ingredients to make bread. He was surprised at how much flour was needed compared to how little salt and yeast were used.

Paul's mom told him that yeast made the bread light and fluffy. The salt helped the bread taste good. She said Jesus used these very simple things to help His disciples understand the Bible better.

Jesus told His disciples to be careful of the yeast, or bad teaching, of the Pharisees and Sadducees. The Pharisees taught that there were many rules one had to follow to receive salvation. The Sadducees taught that there was no resurrection or heaven. Jesus teaches that He gives us faith to trust in Him for our salvation. By His bitter suffering and glorious resurrection, our Savior prepared a wonderful home for us, where we will live forever with Him.

Jesus also tells us that we are to be salt in the world. Having faith and knowing Jesus as Savior makes our life "flavorful." Our acts of love make the world we live in a more pleasant place.

Bread needs salt and yeast to taste good. We need Jesus and His teaching to have a strong faith. When Jesus fills our life like yeast fills bread, we add good flavor to our world.

_____Let's do: What would bread be like without yeast and salt? Why are Jesus' yeast and the salt of Christians needed in the world today?

_____Let's pray: Dear Jesus, fill us with Your yeast, Your love. Help us to be a good flavor to those around us. Amen.

K. A. S.

The Sea Calmer

The sea was stormy, but the passengers aboard the ferry were unconcerned. The large ship could easily handle the big waves.

While crossing the Baltic Sea that night, the *Estonian* was rocked by 20-foot waves and strong winds. Suddenly, the ship tilted to one side. Within minutes, waves covered the *Estonian*. Of 1,000 passengers, almost 900 lost their lives.

Luke wrote about another boat in a storm. Jesus and His disciples were in a boat on the Sea of Galilee. As Jesus slept, the storm grew stronger. The disciples were sure they would drown.

Frightened, the disciples woke Jesus and begged Him to help. The Son of God stood and simply spoke to the wind and the waves. The storm died down. They continued their journey on a calm sea.

You may experience storms in your own life. Your parents may have disagreements. You may have problems in school. Whatever the storm is, Jesus can and will help you.

Jesus loves you. He doesn't want the storms of life to overcome you. Our Lord may seem to be sleeping at times, but He isn't. He is watching over you. He says to you, "Call upon Me in the day of trouble; I will deliver you, and you will honor Me" (Psalm 50:15).

Read from God's Word

One day Jesus said to His disciples, "Let's go over to the other side of the lake." So they got into a boat and set out. As they sailed, He fell asleep. A squall came down on the lake, so that the boat was being swamped, and they were in great danger. The disciples went and woke Him, saying, "Master, Master, we're going to drown!" He got up and rebuked the wind and the raging waters; the storm subsided, and all was calm. "Where is your faith?" He asked His disciples. In fear and amazement they asked one another, "Who is this? He commands even the winds and the water, and they obey Him." Luke 8:22–25

_____Let's talk: How has Jesus calmed a storm for you? What are some ways to honor Him when He helps you?

_____Let's pray: What a friend I have in You, Jesus! Thank You for caring so much about me. Amen.

K. A. S.

Read from God's Word

Then the king called together all the elders of Judah and Jerusalem. He went up to the temple of the LORD with the men of Judah, the people of Jerusalem, the priests and the prophets—all the people from the least to the greatest. He read in their hearing all the words of the Book of the Covenant, which had been found in the temple of the LORD. The king stood by the pillar and renewed the covenant in the presence of the LORD—to follow the LORD and keep His commands, regulations and decrees with all His heart and all His soul, thus confirming the words of the covenant written in this book. Then all the people pledged themselves to the covenant. 2 Kings 23:1–3

Buried Treasure

Have you ever dreamed about finding buried treasure?

Perhaps the most famous treasures are those buried under the sea. Treasure hunters have discovered tons of gold, silver, pearls, emeralds, and more.

Do you have something special you do not want to lose? For you, this is a treasure.

In the Old Testament we read of another treasure. The people of Israel had begun worshiping idols. King Josiah, who had learned about God from his grandmother, led Israel back to worshiping God. They found the long lost treasure of worship.

One day, when the priest was cleaning idols out of the temple of God, he found the Book of the Covenant (the parts of the Bible written at that time). King Josiah was so excited that he called all the people together to have this book read to them. When they heard the words of God's love for them, they were sorry for their worship of idols. God forgave them. They once again worshiped the Lord.

You can find wonderful treasures in the Bible. God has given us many treasures of hope. They center in the coming of His Son to give us eternal victory. Look up these passages and read the promises found there: Job 19:25; Psalm 147:11; Romans 8:28; Revelation 21:4.

_____Let's talk: Are you upset or discouraged today? What hope and encouragement do you find in God's book of promises?

_____Let's pray: Heavenly Father, thank You for all the treasures You have given us in Your Word. Please help us remember those great and precious promises every day. In Jesus' name. Amen.

K. A. S.

It's Not Easy

Kermit the Frog said "It's not easy being green!" It's also not easy . . .

- being black when everyone else is white;
- or white when everyone else is black;
- having no father at a Father and Son Banquet;
- being the smallest kid at basketball tryouts;
- having to call out your grade when you've gotten a D;
- pretending it doesn't matter when you're called "Fatty";
- defending the most unpopular kid in class;
- going to school when your homework isn't done;
- pretending not to be scared when faced with the neighborhood bully.

Have you ever faced a situation like these? How did you feel?

The little man in our Bible reading also knew such frustration. He wasn't only short but also had the unpopular job of tax collector. He probably had few friends. Yet Jesus chose him out of the whole crowd to visit with. That gesture changed Zacchaeus's whole life.

The next time you find yourself feeling like Kermit the Frog, remember Zacchaeus. Jesus doesn't promise that life will always be easy. He does promise to understand your feelings. Jesus chose you for His own. With Christ as our Savior and Companion we can bear any situation.

Read from God's Word

Jesus entered Jericho and was passing through. A man was there by the name of Zacchaeus; he was a chief tax collector and was wealthy. He wanted to see who Jesus was, but being a short man he could not, because of the crowd. So he ran ahead and climbed a sycamore-fig tree to see Him. ... When Jesus reached the spot, He looked up and said to him, "Zacchaeus, come down immediately. I must stay at your house today." So he came down at once and welcomed Him gladly. All the people saw this and began to mutter, "He has gone to be the guest of a 'sinner.'" But Zacchaeus stood up and said to the Lord, "Look, Lord! Here and now I give half of my possessions to the poor, and if I have cheated anybody out of anything, I will pay back four times the amount." Jesus said to him, "Today salvation has come to this house. ... For the Son of Man came to seek and to save what was lost." Luke 19:1–10

_____Let's talk: Think of a time when you felt singled out. How did you handle it? How does knowing about Jesus' love for you make you feel now?

_____Let's pray: Dear Jesus, although You are so great, You care for the lowly. When I am surrounded by troubles, keep me safe by Your power. Please do everything You have promised, Lord, for Your love is eternal. Amen.

J. L. L.

Read from God's Word

And we know that in all things God works for the good of those who love Him, who have been called according to His purpose. Romans 8:28

God Meant It for Good

The brothers believed their father liked Joseph more than he liked them. They wanted to kill Joseph.

So Joseph's brothers sold him to slave traders who took him to Egypt. In Egypt he was sold to Potiphar, a captain in Pharaoh's army. Things went well until Potiphar's wife falsely accused Joseph of loving her. Joseph ended up in jail and stayed there until God helped him interpret a dream for Pharaoh.

Pharaoh's dream was about seven years of plenty followed by seven years of famine. Pharaoh was so impressed that he put Joseph in charge of storing food so the people would not starve during the famine.

Joseph's brothers were affected by the famine too. They came to Egypt to buy food. Joseph forgave them and gave them plenty of food to eat. God used the bad things that happened to Joseph to bring something good for Joseph, his brothers, and their families.

God continues to use bad things to work for good. God used the suffering and death of His Son, Jesus, to bring you forgiveness of sins. God will be working in your life to bring you good things even when it seems impossible. And God will help you forgive others (brothers, sisters, and parents), just as He did Joseph.

_____Let's do: Read the Bible verse again. Write a prayer that offers thanks to God for providing all you need, including forgiveness and salvation through Jesus.

_____Let's pray: Dear Father in heaven, thank You for all the good things in my life that You give me. Thank you especially for the forgiveness that is mine through Your Son. In Jesus' name. Amen.

J. W.

One in the Lord

Karyn and Kelby raced to watch television. They stopped when they realized the TV was off. Instead, Grandma was waiting for them.

Grandma said, "Let's talk for a while. We're so busy with school and work that we don't have much time for each other. I want us to be close and to show we care about one another."

Grandma, Karyn, and Kelby talked about things they liked and wanted to do together. They realized there were times they didn't show their love and care for one another. They prayed together, asking God to forgive them and help them.

God gives us families. What do you like best about your family? What are some things you don't like about your family? Take time to ask for forgiveness and God's help to show love and care in your words and actions.

We became part of God's family through Baptism. We received the benefits of all that Jesus did when He suffered, died, and rose again. We have forgiveness and the promise of eternal life.

God's family does things together too. We gather to worship, hear His Word, and pray. We are one in the Lord.

Read from God's Word

Just as each of us has one body with many members, and these members do not all have the same function, so in Christ we who are many form one body, and each member belongs to all the others. We have different gifts, according to the grace given us. If a man's gift is prophesying, let him use it in proportion to his faith. If it is serving, let him serve; if it is teaching, let him teach; if it is encouraging, let him encourage; if it is contributing to the needs of others, let him give generously; if it is leadership, let him govern diligently; if it is showing mercy, let him do it cheerfully. Romans 12:4–8

_____Let's do: What do you like best about being a member of God's family? What are things you like to do with other children of God? What are some ways you can show your love and care for one another?

_____Let's pray: Dear heavenly Father, thank You for giving us people who love and care for us. Thank You, too, for making us part of Your family. Forgive us for the times we do not show our love for You and our family. Help us live as Your children in all we do and say. In Your Son's name we pray. Amen.

J. W.

Read from God's Word

Now an angel of the Lord said to Philip, "Go south to the road ... that goes down from Jerusalem to Gaza." So he started out, and on his way he met an Ethiopian eunuch ... reading the book of Isaiah the prophet. The Spirit told Philip, "Go to that chariot and stay near it." ... "Do you understand what you are reading?" Philip asked. "How can I," he said, "unless someone explains it to me?" ... Philip began with that very passage of Scripture and told him the good news about Jesus. As they traveled along the road, they came to some water and the eunuch said, "Look, here is water. Why shouldn't I be baptized?" .... Then both Philip and the eunuch went down into the water and Philip baptized him. When they came up out of the water, the Spirit of the Lord suddenly took Philip away, and the eunuch did not see him again, but went on his way rejoicing. Acts 8:26–39

Help Me Understand

Erica's class was reading *The Long Winter* by Laura Ingalls Wilder. For most of the students, who had always lived in Minnesota, the book spoke of familiar things like snow and blizzards. But to Keiko, who had recently come from Hawaii, the story was strange and hard to understand.

Keiko was worried about the report on the book they were assigned. When Erica asked how the report was going, Keiko admitted that she didn't understand the book at all.

Erica read the book to Keiko and explained what was happening. After that, Keiko wrote her report. Keiko said she could never have done the assignment without Erica's help.

In our Bible reading the man from Ethiopia had the same problem. He didn't understand what he was reading. God sent Philip to explain it to him. Philip used the passages from Isaiah to tell how Jesus was the one who suffered innocently and took away the sins of everyone. The Holy Spirit worked faith in the Ethiopian and he wanted to be baptized.

God can use you also to tell others the Good News about Jesus. Many people hear or read the story of what God has done for us, but they don't understand. The Holy Spirit can use the words you say to help them.

_____Let's do: Is there someone you know who doesn't know Jesus as Savior? Ask God to help you share the Good News in words that he or she can understand. God will be with you just as He was with Philip.

_____Let's pray: Dear Father in heaven, without Your help we know we cannot spread the Good News about Jesus. Send Your Spirit to help us. In Jesus' name we pray. Amen.

J. W.

I Still Love You

Read from God's Word

But God demonstrates His own love for us in this: While we were still sinners, Christ died for us. Romans 5:8

"Mommy, do you still love us?" four-year-old Tab asked from his hospital bed.

"Of course I do," she answered, her eyes filled with tears.

Tab and his brother, Tom, were out of danger now. But for a while the doctors didn't know if the boys would live. They had eaten a whole bottle of vitamins! The boys knew they were supposed to have only one a day, but the vitamins tasted good. And before they knew it, the bottle was empty.

The boys thought their mom would be mad. They threw away the empty bottle so Mom wouldn't see it. Later, Tab and Tom started vomiting. They got scared and told their mother what they had done. She rushed the boys to the hospital.

The boys were given shots to counteract the vitamins. Mother sat in their room, crying and praying that God would spare the lives of her sons. God answered her prayers.

Mother still loved her boys although they had disobeyed her. But more important, God continued to love Tab and Tom. The Bible verse for today reminds us of this.

Not only does God continue to love Tab and Tom even when they do wrong, He also continues to love each of us.

_____Let's do: Read the Bible verse for today for each person in your family. When you come to the second half, change it to say: "While (name) was still a sinner, Christ died for (name)."

_____Let's pray: Dear heavenly Father, thank You for continuing to love us even though we disobey You. Thank You for sending Your Son, Jesus, to die for our disobedience. Help us live a life pleasing to You. In Jesus' name we pray. Amen.

Read from God's Word

For even when we were with you, we gave you this rule: "If a man will not work, he shall not eat." We hear that some among you are idle. They are not busy; they are busybodies. Such people we command and urge in the Lord Jesus Christ to settle down and earn the bread they eat. And as for you, brothers, never tire of doing what is right. 2 Thessalonians 3:10–13

Why Should I?

Meet the Whymee family.

The breakfast things had not been put away. "Why should I put them away?" whined Winnie Whymee. "I wasn't the last to use them."

The garbage hadn't been taken out. "Why should I take it out?" snapped Wendel Whymee. "It isn't mine."

There was dirty laundry everywhere. "Why should I wash it?" yawned Mom Whymee. "It will only get dirty again."

The kitchen floor had three inches of water on it because of a leaking pipe. "Why should I fix it?" asked Pop Whymee. "I'm not a plumber."

Were the Whymees thankful for the blessings of home and family God had given to them? We are just like Whymees when we grumble and complain about the tasks we have every day.

The Bible warns against the dangers of being idle or lazy. If we do not work, we can be led into sinful actions. Jesus worked for our salvation on the cross. God wants to create faith in our hearts and lives.

The same Jesus who loves us and died for us gives our work meaning. He forgives our grumbling and helps us see work as a blessing. We can go about our business with energy from God, sharing the Good News of Jesus through all we do.

_____Let's do: Talk with your family about work. What jobs do you like? What jobs are attitude challenges? Make a chore chart.

_____Let's pray: Father, I appreciate the many blessings You have given me. Help me show my thankfulness to You by gladly doing my share of work. In Jesus' name. Amen.

V. S.

Give Thanks

Give thanks to the Lord, for He is good. He provides us with people who love us and give us hugs, who care if we are sad.

Give thanks to the Lord, for He is good. He gives us healthy food to eat, and sometimes food that isn't healthy but tastes good anyway.

Give thanks to the Lord, for He is good. He gives us the opportunity to go to school and learn, although sometimes it is hard.

Give thanks to the Lord, for He is good. He has created a world full of wonders for us to enjoy.

Give thanks to the Lord, for He is good. He gives us older brothers and annoying little sisters who really are fun to be with.

Give thanks to the Lord, for He is good. He gives us friends to laugh with and share secrets with, to sometimes argue with, but always to make up with.

Give thanks to the Lord, for He is good. He protects us from things that might hurt us. He keeps us strong when temptations threaten us.

Give thanks to the Lord, for He is good. He sent His only Son, Jesus, to die on the cross because of His great love for us.

Give thanks to the Lord.

Read from God's Word

Give thanks to the LORD, for He is good. His love endures forever. Give thanks to the God of gods. His love endures forever. Give thanks to the Lord of lords: His love endures forever. To Him who alone does great wonders, His love endures forever. Who by His understanding made the heavens, His love endures forever. Who spread out the earth upon the waters, His love endures forever. Who made the great lights—His love endures forever. The sun to govern the day, His love endures forever. The moon and stars to govern the night; His love endures forever. Psalm *136:1–9*

_____Let's do: Add your own thanks to the list above. Ask each of your family members to do the same.

_____Let's pray: Thank You, Lord, for all the blessings You have given me. Thank You for the greatest blessing, Jesus. Amen.

V. S.

Read from God's Word

Two are better than one, because they have a good return for their work: If one falls down, his friend can help him up. But pity the man who falls and has no one to help him up! Ecclesiastes 4:9–10

Two for One

"What part of speech is the word *splendidly?"* Cindy asked.

"Adverb," replied Beth.

"This is so confusing," sighed Cindy. "I'm glad you're good at English."

"Talk about confusing!" cried Beth. "I've done this math problem three times and it still isn't right."

"You added when you should have subtracted," Cindy offered.

"I'm glad you're good at math," Beth said.

Cindy and Beth were best friends. You might not think so if you knew them. Cindy loved sports and participated on as many teams as she could. Beth didn't care for sports. She spent her time practicing music.

The girls didn't look alike either. Cindy was taller and wore glasses. She was a little shy and very serious. Beth was shorter and had braces. She talked to everyone she met and laughed a lot.

How could two such different people be good friends? They complemented each other. One girl's weakness was the other girl's strength. They enjoyed their differences.

They shared another friend—Jesus, who died for them and lives for them. Jesus offers His love to everyone, no matter who they are. Jesus makes up for what we need the most—perfection and forgiveness. When Jesus is a part of the group, friendships will be stronger, blessed with His forgiveness and His power.

_____Let's talk: Are you happy for your friend or do you get jealous? Have you tried asking Jesus to be part of your friendship?

_____Let's pray: Dear Jesus, thank You for the gift of friendship. Help me appreciate the differences between my friends and me. Thank You for being my best friend. Amen.

V. S.

Whatever

Read from God's Word

Finally, brothers, whatever is true, whatever is noble, whatever is right, whatever is pure, whatever is lovely, whatever is admirable—if anything is excellent or praiseworthy—think about such things. Philippians 4:8

"There's a sub for Mrs. Armstrong today. I bet she got fired because nobody likes her," hissed Amelia.

"She broke her ankle. We're making cards to send to her."

"Whatever!" Amelia replied. "Did you hear Tony got in trouble for pushing an old lady down?"

"Actually, he was helping Mrs. Thompson. When she started to stumble he caught her."

"Whatever!" Amelia sighed. "Guess what? I have the answers to the science test."

"That's cheating, Amelia. I don't want to cheat."

"Whatever!" Amelia said.

Whatever was Amelia's favorite word. She would begin by saying something that was untrue, unkind, or just wrong. If her friends didn't want to listen, she would answer with her favorite word.

As you read in today's Bible reading, St. Paul also liked the word whatever. Whatever you allow to be in your thoughts, these are the things that will show up in your life. Paul wrote these words as a guideline. We are tempted to do whatever we please. Our sinful nature delights in passing on half-truths and gossip. For our sinful "whatevers" Jesus came. He saves us through His death and resurrection. He forgives our sins and sends us out as His servants. With God's help we read His Word and share His Good News.

_____Let's do: What things do you want God to help you do? Ask Him today. He is willing.

_____Let's pray: Dear Lord, guide me through Your Holy Spirit to fill my thoughts with things that are pleasing to You. In Your name. Amen.

V. S.

Read from God's Word

"This is what the LORD Almighty says: 'In a little while I will once more shake the heavens and the earth, the sea and the dry land. I will shake all nations, and the desired of all nations will come, and I will fill this house with glory,' says the LORD Almighty." Haggai 2:6–7

Earthshaking

Have you ever heard the term *earthshaking*? What could be so powerful that it could make the earth shake?

When your teacher surprises you with a science test, it might not be earthshaking, even if your knees wobble.

Stampeding horses can cause the ground to shake.

The powerful force of hurricane winds can shake trees and damage homes.

People who live in parts of the world hit by earthquakes have seen the destructive power that shakes the earth as its layers shift.

History has shown that an atomic bomb can not only shake but also destroy everything for miles. Could there be anything more powerful than that?

Yes. The power of God. God is powerful enough to shake the heavens and the earth. He is powerful enough to create our world and each of us in it. His love for us is powerful enough to send His only Son, Jesus, to die and rise in triumph so our sins are forgiven.

The God of all power has chosen you to be His child. How powerful does that make you? He gives you His power to confess what has gone wrong each day. He gives you the power of His forgiveness. He gives you the power to love others.

Our powerful God loves you—now that's earthshaking news!

_____Let's talk: What other things do you feel empowered to do because of God's love for you? How can you share this power with others?

_____Let's pray: God of power, God of love, thank You for loving me and making me Your child. Thank You for forgiving my sins for Jesus' sake. Amen.

V. S.

Pass It Along

Read from God's Word

May the God of hope fill you with all joy and peace as you trust in Him, so that you may overflow with hope by the power of the Holy Spirit. Romans 15:13

"Jesus loves me this I know ..." Carrie sang softly as she climbed the steps on the school bus.

"... for the Bible tells me so," the bus driver sang softly. He wasn't sure how the song had come to mind, but he kept humming as the children got off the bus at school.

"Little ones to Him belong ..." Rex sang as he walked into school. "Good morning, Mr. Winston," Rex said as he passed his teacher in the hall.

"Good morning, Rex," Mr. Winston replied. "They are weak, but He is strong ..." he sang as he passed the principal's door.

As the principal finished her paperwork and left her office, she was singing in a quiet voice, "Yes, Jesus loves me ..."

Mrs. Ross, the librarian, was preparing a new book display when the principal walked past her. As the students came into the library they could barely hear Mrs. Ross singing, "Yes, Jesus loves me ..."

There are many ways to spread the Good News. Carrie's hope and joy in the Lord spilled out in song. God used Carrie and she didn't even know it. Sometimes God uses us in ways we are unaware of. God will also use you to tell others about Jesus!

_____Let's do: What are some ways you can think of to share the Gospel? Draw a cartoon showing the actions in this devotion.

_____Let's pray: Thank You, Jesus, for loving me. Help me be a bold disciple and tell others about You. Amen.

V. S.

Read from God's Word

Though the fig tree does not bud and there are no grapes on the vines, though the olive crop fails and the fields produce no food, though there are no sheep in the pen and no cattle in the stalls, yet I will rejoice in the Lord, *I will be joyful in God my Savior. Habakkuk 3:17–18*

Bad for Good

A young man was driving home from school. Suddenly, there was a terrible accident. The young man was taken to the hospital, but he died.

His parents were very upset. They were joyful that their son was in heaven, but they were also very sad that he would no longer be with them.

In another part of the hospital a girl was very sick. Unless the doctors could find a new heart for her, she would die. As the girl's parents sat next to her bed praying, the door opened and a doctor came in.

"There was a terrible accident today," he began. "A young man died. His parents want to donate his heart so your daughter can be healthy."

Bad things happen because we are sinful and live in a sinful world. But God is in control. He loves us and cares about us. He can take the worst thing and bring some good from it.

That is what He did for us on the cross. He took our worst problem, sin, and solved it with His best solution. Jesus. We can trust this same God, who solved our worst problem, to work out all the problems in our lives for good. That's quite a trade—bad for good.

_____Let's do: Think of something bad that happened to you that has turned out to be good.

_____Let's pray: Father God, thank You for loving me. Thank You for caring about me even when things are going bad. Amen.

V. S.

Oh, Baby

Read from God's Word

For You created my inmost being; You knit me together in my mother's womb. I praise You because I am fearfully and wonderfully made; Your works are wonderful, I know that full well. My frame was not hidden from You when I was made in the secret place. When I was woven together in the depths of the earth, Your eyes saw my unformed body. All the days ordained for me were written in Your book before one of them came to be. Psalm 139:13–16

"Mom," Angela whispered, "I thought Aunt Laura was going to have a baby. She doesn't look like it."

"That's because the baby is still too small to see. It will keep growing until Aunt Laura looks bigger. But right now, it's still so small Aunt Laura can't even feel that the baby is there," Mom replied.

"If it's too small to see and too small to feel, when does it become a real baby?" Angela asked.

"The very moment a child begins to grow inside the mother, before the mother or father even know it's there, it's a real baby. God loves that tiny baby from the very moment it begins to be," Mom continued. "God can see that tiny little one. He knows who that child will be, what he or she will look like. That child is as precious to God as you are."

"You mean God has known and loved me longer than you and Dad have?"

"Yes, Angela. When God showed His great love for us by sending Jesus into the world, it was for all people—grown-ups, children, tiny babies, and even those not yet formed."

Angela looked at Aunt Laura again. "I'm going to start praying for this baby today—my newest and tiniest cousin."

_____Let's talk: How does it feel to think God has known you longer than anyone else?

_____Let's pray: Dear Jesus, thank You for becoming a tiny baby and coming into the world to show Your love to me and all others, no matter how big or how small. Thank You for giving me life and for caring about my life. Amen.

V. S.

Read from God's Word

The tongue of the wise commends knowledge, but the mouth of the fool gushes folly. ... The tongue that brings healing is a tree of life, but a deceitful tongue crushes the spirit. Proverbs 15:2, 4

Be a Firefighter

Lightning flashed. One tree began to burn at the top of a mountain. It burned slowly before it began to spread to other trees.

Firefighters came to this mountain to put out the fire. As they worked, sudden strong winds fueled the fire. Soon the entire mountain was burning, and the firefighters were forced to run for their lives.

How could something so small turn so quickly into something dangerous?

Our tongue and the words we speak with it can be compared to the spark of lightning that set the single tree on fire. Have you ever heard a story about someone that was unkind or untrue? Did the story stop with you or did you pass it along to someone else? Each time the story gets told to someone else, it may change. It may get bigger and bigger until it is completely out of control.

We have all sinned with our tongue. We have hurt others—even our friends. Who can love us when we talk like that? God does! He leads us to feel sorrow for what we have said. He offers us forgiveness. As we reflect on this amazing love, we are led to respond with new words of thanks and praise.

_____Let's do: Write your own proverb about the "tongue of the wise" and the "mouth of the fool."

_____Let's pray: Dear Lord, please help me use my tongue for prayer and praise. Amen.

V. S.

Consequences

Jeffrey caught the football and was immediately tackled by two of his friends on the opposing team.

"First down!" Jeffrey called. Out of the corner of his eye he saw one of the flower bushes.

"Hi, Jeff," his mother said later that afternoon. "I noticed one of my flower bushes outside is in pretty bad shape. Know anything about that?"

"What's wrong with it?"

"Looks like a first-down tackle."

Jeffrey paused for a moment. "Sorry," he finally said. "It was an accident."

"Thank you for being honest and for apologizing. I forgive you. We can get another bush. I'll take the cost for it out of your allowance."

"I said I was sorry," Jeffrey protested. "Why do I have to pay for it?"

"All our actions have consequences," Mom explained. "It's important to confess when you've done wrong. But you are not made righteous because you confess. God forgives you because Jesus paid the consequences for all sin when He died on the cross."

Read from God's Word

Have mercy on me, O God, according to Your unfailing love; according to Your great compassion blot out my transgressions. Wash away all my iniquity and cleanse me from my sin. Psalm 51:1–2

Slowly, Jeffrey's thoughts turned from resentment to thanks. He considered the consequences Jesus had suffered, the price Jesus paid.

Jeffrey walked back to his mom. She could see a big difference in his face. She said, "Let's go dig a hole for the new bush." Jeffrey went to the garage for the shovel.

_____Let's talk: Why is it important to think about consequences before doing something? How can consequences be blessings?

_____Let's pray: Thank You, Lord, for forgiving me when I mess up. Give me the strength and courage to accept the consequences of my actions without complaint. Amen.

V. S.

december

Contributors for this month:

Peter J. Meyer

Pat List

Greta Heinemeier

Jonathan Maier

Mary Lou Krause

Annette Schumacher

Dot Nuechterlien

Eager to Do Good

Read from God's Word

"Come now, let us reason together," says the LORD. "Though your sins are like scarlet, they shall be as white as snow; though they are red as crimson, they shall be like wool." Isaiah 1:18

John was anxious to go sledding with his friends. Running home from school, he accidentally plowed into Mrs. Albers. She was carrying her groceries. Cans and boxes went everywhere.

"I'm sorry," stammered John as he dashed off.

When John came home from sledding, his father was on the phone. Dad was not smiling. After he hung up, his dad asked John if he remembered running into Mrs. Albers.

"Yes, but ..." John stopped when he noticed his dad still frowning. After a moment John said, "I owe Mrs. Albers an apology, don't I?"

"Yes, you do. It's a good thing you only knocked the groceries out of her hands and didn't knock her down."

The next morning after John had helped Mrs. Albers clear her walk of snow, they sat down for a cup of hot cocoa.

"I am sorry for running into you yesterday," said John.

"Oh, I forgive you, John," Mrs. Albers said. "God forgives me. He makes my sins whiter than snow that covers the ground. There's enough forgiveness—and snow—for everyone."

"If there are other jobs you could use help with around the house this month, please let me know. I'd like to help."

Mrs. Albers smiled and said, "John, you can come over anytime."

_____Let's talk: Who has forgiven you? Who can you forgive?

_____Let's pray: Gracious God, thank You for making my sins whiter than snow through your forgiveness. Amen.

P. J. M.

Read from God's Word

The people walking in darkness have seen a great light; on those living in the land of the shadow of death a light has dawned. Isaiah 9:2

More Than a Decoration

"Who noticed something different this Sunday?" Pastor Klein asked during the children's message. Of course, everyone had noticed the Advent wreath.

"An Advent wreath is made of evergreen branches," said Pastor Klein. "Green is the color of hope and new life. An evergreen tree always stays green, and Christ is always our hope for eternity.

"An Advent wreath is round. Just as a circle has no beginning or end, neither does Jesus' love for us.

"There are five candles on our Advent wreath. This week we lit one. Next week we'll light two. The third week, we'll light the pink candle, the joy candle. Then on the fourth week, we'll light all four of the outside candles.

"The white candle in the middle, the Christ candle, is lit on Christmas Eve. When we see the bright light from all the candles together, we think of the night Christ was born to be a great light to the world that was still in darkness. And we'll think of Jesus' words: 'I am the light of the world.'

"So you see," said Pastor Klein, "our wreath is more than just a decoration. It helps us prepare for the Savior's coming."

_____Let's do: Ask your parents to help you set up an Advent wreath in your home. Then during family devotion time, light the appropriate candle and say together, "Jesus is the light of the world."

_____Let's pray: Hark the glad sound! The Savior comes, The Savior promised long; Let ev'ry heart prepare a throne And ev'ry voice a song. (*Lutheran Worship* 29:1)

P. L.

To Serve Others

Read from God's Word

If anyone speaks, he should do it as one speaking the very words of God. If anyone serves, he should do it with the strength God provides, so that in all things God may be praised through Jesus Christ. To Him be the glory and the power for ever and ever. Amen. 1 Peter 4:11

A man was sorting through the shoes at the church rummage sale. He tossed one pair after another into a pile. Maria asked if she could help. "No thanks," the man said and walked off.

A little later Maria noticed the same man rummaging through the old radios and other electronic gadgets. Her father went over to see if he could help. Maria's father came back a moment later. He had been rudely told to leave the man alone.

Then Mrs. Hoffmann, the sweetest lady Maria knew in the church, asked the man if there were any baked goods he might like. Although he didn't speak nicely at first, Mrs. Hoffmann kept right on being nice. When he left, the grumpy man had a smile on his face and a cheery good-bye for Maria!

Maria asked Mrs. Hoffmann, "What did you do that made that man change?"

"He is a widower who lives down the street," replied Mrs. Hoffmann. "I simply showed him kindness as a fellow Christian."

God loved us while we were ugly and crabby with sin. His love changes us so completely that we are able to love others who are difficult to love.

"Maria," said Mrs. Hoffmann with a smile, "God will grant you His power to love the unlovable too."

_____Let's do: Think of someone with whom you can share this special love.

_____Let's pray: Heavenly Father, grant me Your love to share with my family and friends today. Help my words to be kind and my actions gentle. Amen.

P. J. M.

Read from God's Word

The day of the Lord will come like a thief in the night. … You, brothers, are not in darkness so that this day should surprise you like a thief. You are all sons of the light and sons of the day. We do not belong to the night or to the darkness. So then, let us not be like others, who are asleep, but let us be alert and self-controlled. For those who sleep, sleep at night, and those who get drunk, get drunk at night. But since we belong to the day, let us be self-controlled, putting on faith and love as a breastplate, and the hope of salvation as a helmet. For God did not appoint us to suffer wrath but to receive salvation through our Lord Jesus Christ. He died for us so that, whether we are awake or asleep, we may live together with him. Therefore encourage one another and build each other up, just as in fact you are doing. 1 Thessalonians 5:1–11

Countdown

People were very concerned about what might happen at 12:00 a.m. on January 1, 2000. When the computers turned to 00 for the year code, it could create problems for banks, airlines, and other businesses.

For the years leading up to the year 2000, there were all sorts of forecasts. What would happen when the computer clocks changed? Some said planes would fall out of the sky. Cars would stop running. Some feared they would have no water or electricity.

Did all the predictions come true when the clock changed from December 31, 1999 to January 1, 2000?

They did not. Computers were safe. Power stayed on.

Our Bible reading tells about another significant event in our future—the second coming of Jesus. As we look forward to Jesus' return, we need not worry. Our future is secure in God's hands. The God who planned our salvation through Jesus is guiding and leading us through our life.

While we wait, we are prepared for Jesus' return. God holds us firm, strong, and steadfast until the day of Christ. The Bible tells us to put on faith, love, and hope. We receive these blessings and the gift of salvation through our Lord Jesus Christ. God Himself prepares us for His second coming.

_____Let's talk: What upcoming events worry you? What makes these events seem scary? How does God help you prepare for these events?

_____Let's pray: Dear God, You are the Lord of all time. Help me to trust You as I look at the significant events in my life. Amen.

P. J. M.

No Mystery

Derek found a note in his desk at school. He could not figure out where it came from or what it said. The note was written in code. No one in Derek's class knew where the note had come from.

That night Derek showed the note to his father. They tried to decode the message—no success. Derek's dad said, "We need the key. No key, no message."

The next morning at school Derek was surprised to find another note in his desk. This one was not in code. He read it and found what he had been waiting for—the key. Derek deciphered the first note. It said:

"Derek, This is a special note to tell you that Jesus Christ is your Savior. I want you to remember how much He loves you. He is with you every day. Mr. Meyer."

During religion class Mr. Meyer was smiling. "Yesterday I watched many of you try to help Derek figure out the message. Since it was in a secret code, you couldn't figure it out."

Derek read the deciphered note aloud. Mr. Meyer explained how the Bible had been written. God inspired the writers to put down His message. God's message is about His love and forgiveness for us in Jesus Christ. Isn't it nice that God's message isn't a secret?

Read from God's Word

For prophecy never had its origin in the will of man, but men spoke from God as they were carried along by the Holy Spirit. 2 Peter 1:21

_____Let's do: Write a secret coded Christmas message to a friend. Don't forget the key.

_____Let's pray: Dear God, help us to read and to share Your good news with everyone. Amen.

P. J. M.

Read from God's Word

I love you, O LORD, my strength. The LORD is my rock, my fortress and my deliverer; my God is my rock, in whom I take refuge. He is my shield and the horn of my salvation, my stronghold. ... In my distress I called to the LORD; I cried to my God for help. From His temple He heard my voice; my cry came before Him, into His ears. ... He reached down from on high and took hold of me; He drew me out of deep waters. He rescued me from my powerful enemy, from my foes, who were too strong for me. They confronted me in the day of my disaster, but the LORD was my support. He brought me out into a spacious place; He rescued me because He delighted in me. The LORD has dealt with me according to my righteousness; ... He has rewarded me. Psalm 18:1–20

Rescued

The movie "The Perfect Storm" was based on the real-life experience of a group of commercial fishermen who were caught in a fierce North Atlantic storm. As the weather got worse, other boats headed to shore for safety. The men on this boat never returned home.

There were a lot of special effects in the movie. Although the audience knew it was only a movie, the sense of dread and fear was very strong.

At times our own lives feel the same way. Problems and difficulties come and whip around us just as the nasty storm tossed the ship and her crew. We panic and become scared. We begin to feel as though there is nothing we can do.

Our Bible reading reminds us that the Lord is our rock. Rocks and mountains are not easily moved, so a rock is a good place to be during a storm. The wind can blow hard, the waves can splash, but the rock is secure. God promises that He will be our rock—our refuge to protect us.

God the Father sent His Son, Jesus, to conquer our biggest problem. Jesus has defeated the storms of sin, death, and the devil. We can be sure He will see us safely through any trouble in our lives.

_____Let's do: Find a rock and place it by your bed where you will see it every night as you fall asleep and every morning as you wake up. When you look at it, say to yourself: "Jesus is my rock. He is my strength and salvation."

_____Let's pray: Dear God, You are our rock, refuge, and fortress. Keep us safe no matter what problems or difficulties we encounter here on earth. In the name of Jesus. Amen.

P. J. M.

An Invitation

Imagine that you were planning a special party. You have the best entertainment, beautiful decorations, delicious food, and gifts for each of your guests. But instead of being excited about the party, your friends have refused to have anything to do with you. What would you think? What would you do?

You would be upset. You would wonder what was wrong with your friends or why they rejected your invitation.

Our heavenly Father is throwing that kind of party. You are invited to God's grand feast! At the baptismal font, with the splashing of the waters and with God's Word, you were invited. When you hear the Word of God, the Holy Spirit works in your heart. Through the power of the Word, you are invited to the greatest party of all time.

Not everyone who is invited will attend the feast of heaven. Some who hear God's Word will reject it. Some will not believe. But for those who have been given faith it will be more wonderful than we can imagine. All of the people of faith will be there.

Jesus will be there too. He not only paid the price for the victory party but is also waiting there for us to come.

Read from God's Word

"The kingdom of heaven is like a king who prepared a wedding banquet for his son. He sent his servants to those who had been invited to the banquet to tell them to come, but they refused to come. … Then he said to his servants, 'Go to the street corners and invite to the banquet anyone you find.' So the servants went out into the streets and gathered all the people they could find, both good and bad, and the wedding hall was filled with guests. But when the king came in to see the guests, he noticed a man there who was not wearing wedding clothes. 'Friend,' he asked, 'how did you get in here without wedding clothes?' The man was speechless. Then the king told the attendants, 'Tie him hand and foot, and throw him outside, into the darkness, where there will be weeping and gnashing of teeth.' For many are invited, but few are chosen." Matthew 22:1–14

____Let's talk: How would you make a party special if you were in charge? Talk with your friends about what you think heaven will be like.

____Let's pray: Dear God, thank You for giving us the gift of eternal life in heaven. Help us to share Your love and message. In Jesus' name. Amen.

P. J. M.

Read from God's Word

But godliness with contentment is great gain. For we brought nothing into the world, and we can take nothing out of it. But if we have food and clothing, we will be content with that. People who want to get rich fall into temptation and a trap and into many foolish and harmful desires that plunge men into ruin and destruction. For the love of money is a root of all kinds of evil. Some people, eager for money, have wandered from the faith and pierced themselves with many griefs. 1 Timothy 6:6–10

All I Need

Jody and her friends were talking about what they would do if they had all the money in the world.

"I'd buy a beautiful mansion and three sports cars," said Paul.

"I'd buy every kind of toy ever made," Marta claimed.

"Well, I'd buy a huge ice cream sundae for everybody in the class," laughed Jody.

Anne didn't say anything at first. "I don't know what I'd buy," she finally said. "I've got everything I need. I have a mom and dad who love me, a warm house to live in, and a sister who keeps me company. I've got good things to eat and toys to play with. And Jesus as my best friend. What more could I need?"

Anne knew something very important. Many people want things they don't have. But Anne realized that God had given her everything she needed.

God doesn't give us just food and clothing. Are there some things you have that you don't really need? Why did God give them to you? He gives us all we need and more because He loves us. He loves us so much that He gave us the most important thing ever—His Son, Jesus. Jesus is our Savior and His love and forgiveness is our greatest treasure.

What a wonderful, loving, generous God we have!

_____Let's do: With your family or friends, list things that God has given you that begin with each letter of the alphabet.

_____Let's pray: Heavenly Father, help us remember to thank You daily. In Jesus' name we pray. Amen.

P. L.

Broken Promises

Read from God's Word

See that what you have heard from the beginning remains in you. If it does, you also will remain in the Son and in the Father. And this is what He promised us—even eternal life. *1 John 2:24–25*

Janine's dad had promised to take her to the circus. She thought about the lions and tigers, the dancing bears and trapeze artists. The more she thought about it the more excited she got.

But when Mom came in the room, Janine could tell from the look on her face there was a problem.

"Dad just called," her mom said. "He's really sorry, but one of the machines at work broke and he has to wait for it to be repaired. By the time he gets home, it'll be too late to go to the circus."

Has someone ever broken a promise to you? Can you think of someone who never breaks a promise? God promises to take care of you, be with you, answer your prayers, and help you in time of trouble.

The most important promise God made took many years to come true. In the Garden of Eden, the Lord promised a Savior to Adam and Eve. After many years Jesus fulfilled God's promise. He lived a perfect life yet died on the cross to take the punishment for our sins.

Because of God's great love for us, we know that heaven will be ours. That's a promise that will come true. God said so! "This is what He promised us—even eternal life."

_____Let's talk: Think about a time when someone broke a promise to you. Was it something they couldn't do anything about? Have you forgiven them for that broken promise?

_____Let's pray: Dear God, we know You would never break a promise to us, and we thank You for that. Help us truly appreciate the gift of Your Son, which You gave us so we can live with You in heaven someday. In His name we pray. Amen.

P. L.

Read from God's Word

Lift up your heads, O you gates; be lifted up, you ancient doors, that the King of glory may come in. Who is this King of glory? The LORD strong and mighty, the LORD mighty in battle. Lift up your heads, O you gates; lift them up, you ancient doors, that the King of glory may come in. Who is He, this King of glory? The LORD Almighty—He is the King of glory. Psalm 24:7–10

An Advent Story

This story takes place in the time of knights, castles, kings, and peasants.

Imagine that you live in the Kingdom of Glory. The king cares for the village and protects it. Your job in the village is to take care of the cows. Every morning you go to the pasture outside the village to do the milking.

One morning you see a horse and rider on top of a hill. When you recognize him as one of the knights of evil, you run back to the village and climb the church tower to look around.

Sure enough, the forces of evil have surrounded the village and will soon charge down from the hills to capture the villagers. You ring the church bell, wake everyone up, and tell what you have seen. Everyone is frightened. Does the King of Glory know the danger? Will He come to save the village? Everyone is talking or crying.

You look into the distance again. "There's a cloud of dust in the distance!" you shout. You see the leading horseman carrying the banner of the King of Glory!

He is coming! The King of Glory is coming to defeat evil and keep us safely in His kingdom. Get ready for the King! That's the exciting news of Advent.

_____Let's talk: How are we like the peasants in the story? Whose coming do we look for during Advent?

_____Let's pray: Jesus, our King of Glory, we wait for Your coming to rescue us from sin and the forces of evil. Make us happy people who love to serve You in Your kingdom. Amen.

G. H.

Fitting In

There was a puzzle piece named Pablo. He didn't like his shape. *I'm funny looking,* he thought. So Pablo changed his shape.

When it came time to put the puzzle together, something was wrong. All the pieces fit but one. The puzzle couldn't be finished. Pablo's neighbor asked if he wouldn't mind changing back to his old shape so the puzzle could be completed.

Pablo didn't want to be left out of the puzzle so he returned to his own shape.

Then Pablo noticed that his coloring was plain and white. *That won't do,* he thought. *White is not exciting.* So Pablo changed his color to bright orange.

The puzzle was completed with Pablo in his proper place. The pieces together formed a picture of Jesus. It was a beautiful portrait except for a bright orange spot on Jesus' white gown.

Once again Pablo's neighbor spoke to him. What Pablo was told made him feel good about who he was. Quickly he returned to his former color. This made the portrait of Jesus perfect.

We are each a valuable part of the body of Christ. He has redeemed us and given us an important position. We don't have to be like someone else or change who we are. God made us just as He wanted us to be.

Read from God's Word

As it is, there are many parts, but one body. The eye cannot say to the hand, "I don't need you!" And the head cannot say to the feet, "I don't need you!" On the contrary, those parts of the body that seem to be weaker are indispensable, and the parts that we think are less honorable we treat with special honor. And the parts that are unpresentable are treated with special modesty, while our presentable parts need no special treatment. But God has combined the members of the body and has given greater honor to the parts that lacked it, so that there should be no division in the body, but that its parts should have equal concern for each other. If one part suffers, every part suffers with it; if one part is honored, every part rejoices with it.
1 Corinthians 12:20–26

_____Let's talk: Pretend you are Pablo's neighbor. What did you say to Pablo to make him change back to his original color? What might you say to a friend who doesn't think he or she fits in?

_____Let's pray: Lord Jesus, thank You that I have a special place in Your body. Help me be all that I was made to be. Amen.

J. M.

Read from God's Word

But Mary treasured up all these things and pondered them in her heart. Luke 2:19

Take Time to Treasure Up!

Things were a bit hectic at the first Christmas.

Remember the bustling streets of Bethlehem, the crowded inns, the surprise appearance of the excited angel choir, and the rush of visitors shortly after the Savior's birth? In the midst of all this activity, Mary took time to treasure up and ponder (think about) what the Lord was doing.

The devil would like to use the flurry of activity during this season to distract us from treasuring up the Savior's birth. Here's an idea for an Advent calendar. It has daily reminders of God's great plan to save us by sending Jesus. Make cutouts of felt or paper and decorate your own calendar or a triangle-shaped Christmas tree background. Each day from now until Christmas, add a shape and take time to read and think about the Bible message.

_____Let's do: Tell someone else about your treasuring time. Make this calendar with a friend or give it as a gift.

_____Let's pray: Lord, bless me in this Advent and Christmas season as I think about Your wondrous birth and treasure it in my heart. Amen.

M. L. K.

Wisdom, Not War

Read from God's Word

I do not trust in my bow, my sword does not bring me victory; but You give us victory over our enemies, You put our adversaries to shame. In God we make our boast all day long, and we will praise Your name forever. Psalm 44:6–8

A young man in South Africa saw the oppression and poverty of his people. The suffering and injustice made him angry.

One night the young man and several of his friends demonstrated their anger. They started some fires. When the police came, the demonstrators scattered.

The man hid in a church. While he was hiding, he heard the Scriptures being read from Ecclesiastes 9:13–18. In the story, a poor but wise man saved a city from a powerful, oppressive king. The Holy Spirit was at work. "Wisdom is better than weapons of war, but one sinner destroys much good," the reader was saying.

The Word of the Lord was stronger than a sword. The young man's heart was changed. He went to the police and confessed his crime.

The police were surprised. "Why do you surrender?" they asked.

"Because the Lord has shown me that godly wisdom is better than war," he answered.

The police saw the change in the young man. They did not prosecute him. He entered a seminary to train for the ministry. Today he is a leader of God's people. He proclaims, "Guns and weapons will not heal our country. Only the Good News of salvation in Jesus Christ can change the hearts of people."

_____Let's do: How would you express the Good News of salvation in Jesus? Why is this Gospel so powerful?

_____Let's pray: Lord, You give us certain victory over our enemy Satan. By the power of Your Holy Spirit, melt hearts that are hard with hatred and fill them with Your love. In Jesus' name. Amen.

M. L. K.

Read from God's Word

But just as you excel in everything—in faith, in speech, in knowledge, in complete earnestness and in your love for us—see that you also excel in this grace of giving. I am not commanding you, but I want to test the sincerity of your love by comparing it with the earnestness of others. For you know the grace of our Lord Jesus Christ, that though He was rich, yet for your sakes He became poor, so that you through His poverty might become rich. 2 Corinthians 8:7–9

Playing Ball in a Wheelchair

Recess was a lonely time for Liz. On most days the third graders would play ball or tag. Liz had to sit still in one place—her wheelchair.

One day Liz heard William say to the teacher, "Mrs. Cooper, I just got stitches. Do you think I should play tag?"

Mrs. Cooper looked at William. "Perhaps it would be better if you let them heal. If I get you a Nerf ball, would you play with Liz? She has to sit by herself every day."

William agreed to play with Liz. He put some stones on the ground to mark the bases. Liz tossed the ball to him. William pretended to hit the ball. He ran around the bases. Liz shouted with joy.

Again and again they played. William was the batter, catcher, and runner all in one. At first William felt sorry for Liz, but then he truly had fun with her. They became better friends after that, and he talked often to her.

God's Holy Spirit helped William give of himself without expecting a return for his efforts. Jesus showed such total caring for us when we were helpless sinners. He went all the way to the cross to save us.

_____Let's talk: Why did Jesus, who was rich, become poor? What are some ways we can show Jesus' love by giving of ourselves to others?

_____Let's pray: Lord, forgive us for giving to others in the hope that we get something in return. Help us reflect Your unselfish love in the way we care for others. In Jesus' name. Amen.

M. L. K.

Countdown to Christmas

Read from God's Word

But when the time had fully come, God sent His Son, born of a woman, born under law, to redeem those under law, that we might receive the full rights of sons. Galatians 4:4–5

The countdown is on. Everywhere we are reminded, "Only 10 shopping days until Christmas!"

Actually the countdown to Christmas started long ago. It started when we messed up the world with our sin. It started with Adam and Eve in the Garden of Eden. God promised that He would send a Savior to crush the devil's power.

The countdown continued for many, many years. It was easy for God's people to forget the big day they were anticipating. When they thought His countdown wasn't going fast enough, they were tempted to trust themselves more than God. Sometimes they forgot God's Word. They blamed God's leaders for what was going wrong.

Still, the countdown continued day after day, century after century. God didn't stop loving His people.

Then one night the angels burst out of the sky singing, for God's Christmas countdown was complete. The baby Jesus, who would save the world from sin, was born. The glory of that day radiates to us. We are Christians living in the time of fulfillment. We know that God keeps His promises. We can trust Him to forgive our sins and take us to heaven.

_____Let's talk: What do you think is the best part about God's plan? How can we be sure that God will keep us safe in the countdown to eternity in heaven?

_____Let's pray: Dear Jesus, thank You for coming to save us, as Your Father said You would. Forgive us for being impatient with Your plan. Fill our days with praise and bring us safely to heaven with You. Amen.

M. L. K.

Read from God's Word

But whatever was to my profit I now consider loss for the sake of Christ. What is more, I consider everything a loss compared to the surpassing greatness of knowing Christ Jesus my Lord, for whose sake I have lost all things. I consider them rubbish, that I may gain Christ and be found in Him, not having a righteousness of my own that comes from the law, but that which is through faith in Christ—the righteousness that comes from God and is by faith. I want to know Christ and the power of His resurrection and the fellowship of sharing in His sufferings, becoming like Him in His death, and so, somehow, to attain to the resurrection from the dead. … Brothers, I do not consider myself yet to have taken hold of it. But one thing I do: Forgetting what is behind and straining toward what is ahead, I press on toward the goal to win the prize for which God has called me heavenward in Christ Jesus. Philippians 3:7–14

The Right Gift

Is it hard to find the right gift for someone you know? You're not the only one with this problem. Entire catalogs have been designed to offer gifts "for the person who has everything."

It's easy to envy people who seem to have everything. You may think, *How perfect their life must be!* But in Philippians 3 the apostle Paul reminds us that no life is perfect, no one has everything.

Paul could brag about his family heritage and how well he kept the Law. But he knew that something was missing. Because of sin, we all need Jesus and His righteousness. In fact, Paul says that he considers "things" mere rubbish compared to the righteousness that comes from faith in Jesus.

If you believe that Jesus died to take away your sins, you have been made holy. You are clothed in the righteousness of Christ. Because of Jesus you can enter heaven.

Take another look at someone who seems to have everything. How could you be sure he has what is most important—faith in Jesus Christ?

_____Let's do: Send a Christmas card with a Gospel message. Explain how you have everything in Jesus. Sing carols that praise your Savior. Read today's Bible selection together.

_____Let's pray: Heavenly Father, thank You for giving me a Savior, Jesus Christ. Amen.

M. L. K.

The Real Christmas

Our first Christmas in Nigeria had none of the outward signs of a North American celebration. In our tropical village home there were no electric lights or evergreen trees. The village market sold plenty of pineapples, bananas, and squash, but no Christmas cards or manger scenes.

Villagers cut long palm branches and stuck them in the ground along the pathways. On Christmas Day, colorful flowers were tied to these branches. Sometimes they formed an archway at the house or church entrance, greeting every visitor with celebration.

The language in the mud block church was new to us, but the singing was powerful and jubilant. We recognized the great rejoicing. Smiles were all around. Joy overflowed from grateful hearts. "Abasi [God] has sent a Savior. Now we can sit with Him forever in heaven," the people sang.

The real Christmas was here. Rejoicing in God's gift of a Savior was all that mattered. Later that afternoon, as I shaped a manger scene from the clay outside my door, I thanked God for His simple, clear message of love for all people.

Jesus came to us in a humble way to display the greatness of God's love. Even the palms outside our door seemed to stand taller, proclaiming the praise of our triumphant Lord.

Read from God's Word

This is how the birth of Jesus Christ came about: His mother Mary was pledged to be married to Joseph, but before they came together, she was found to be with child through the Holy Spirit. Because Joseph her husband was a righteous man and did not want to expose her to public disgrace, he had in mind to divorce her quietly. But after he had considered this, an angel of the Lord appeared to him in a dream and said, "Joseph son of David, do not be afraid to take Mary home as your wife, because what is conceived in her is from the Holy Spirit. She will give birth to a son, and you are to give Him the name Jesus, because He will save His people from their sins." ... When Joseph woke up, he did what the angel of the Lord had commanded him and took Mary home as his wife. But he had no union with her until she gave birth to a son. And he gave Him the name Jesus. Matthew 1:18–25

_____Let's talk: What are some things that distract you from the real meaning of Christmas? How can you focus more on what God has done?

_____Let's pray: Pray for missionaries who celebrate Christmas in other cultures. Ask God to bless their witness.

M. L. K.

Read from God's Word

Sing to the LORD a new song, for He has done marvelous things; His right hand and His holy arm have worked salvation for Him. The LORD has made His salvation known and revealed His righteousness to the nations. He has remembered His love and His faithfulness to the house of Israel; all the ends of the earth have seen the salvation of our God. Shout for joy to the LORD, all the earth, burst into jubilant song with music. Psalm 98:1–4

Singing Our Greetings

The angels started it. Those heavenly beings sing praises before God's throne day and night, every day. But Christmas night was different. God's holy Son was sent to earth to rescue sinners.

So the angel choirs exploded with joy, lighting the night sky with God's glory. In jubilant, majestic chords they sang, "Glory to God in the highest, and on earth peace."

The shepherds never forgot this heavenly concert. Joy filled their hearts as they ran to see the Savior lying in the manger.

We are not so different from the shepherds. In God's Word we have heard the birth announcement of our Savior. By faith we know He came to rescue us from the devil's power. This is wonderful news! We express our joy by telling others and praising God.

Perhaps you know someone who would enjoy a singing Christmas greeting. If you like, team up with a friend or two or three. Decide on a Christmas song or hymn you can sing with joy. Knock on the door of a friend or neighbor and begin singing. Let your songs echo the joy of the angels on that first Christmas Day!

_____Let's do: Why is singing one of the best ways of praising God? Which Christmas songs or hymns do you like best? Sing them!

_____Let's pray: O Lord, my God and Savior, I sing to You with all my heart. You have done wonderful things. Glory to You in the highest! Amen.

M. L. K.

Draw a Missionary

Let's draw a missionary. Isaiah 52:7 starts with beautiful feet—"How beautiful on the mountains are the feet of those who bring good news, who proclaim peace, who bring good tidings, who proclaim salvation."

Think of people waiting for news. Suddenly the sound of the messenger's feet is heard. Whatever it takes to deliver the message of victory, these feet are ready to go. Think of other lands where such feet have traveled. Think of city streets where such feet have dared to go with the Good News. Draw running feet.

Next come the lips. When God asked, "Whom shall I send?" Isaiah answered immediately, "Here am I. Send me!" (Isaiah 6:8). Missionary lips are full of praise. They are full of words about Jesus, who came to save us. Draw lips open and filled with messages of salvation.

Missionary hearts are big. "We love because He first loved us!" they say. Make a heart bursting with love.

God calls all His saved ones to be His telling ones. Listen prayerfully to Jesus' words: "I am sending you … to open their eyes and turn them from darkness to light, and from the power of Satan to God, so that they may receive forgiveness of sins and a place among those who are sanctified by faith in Me."

Read from God's Word

"On one of these journeys … I saw a light from heaven, brighter than the sun, blazing around me and my companions. We all fell to the ground, and I heard a voice saying to me in Aramaic, 'Saul, Saul, why do you persecute Me? It is hard for you to kick against the goads.' Then I asked, 'Who are You, Lord?' 'I am Jesus, whom you are persecuting,' the Lord replied. 'Now get up and stand on your feet. I have appeared to you to appoint you as a servant and as a witness of what you have seen of Me and what I will show you. I will rescue you from your own people and from the Gentiles. I am sending you to them to open their eyes and turn them from darkness to light, and from the power of Satan to God, so that they may receive forgiveness of sins and a place among those who are sanctified by faith in Me.'" Acts 26:12–18

_____Let's talk: Talk about your picture of a missionary. How does the picture look like you? Like your parents? Like your pastor and teachers?

_____Let's pray: Dear Savior, here am I. Send me to share Your love and mercy with many other people, by the power of Your Spirit. Amen.

M. L. K.

20 december

Read from God's Word

Rejoice greatly, O Daughter of Zion! Shout, Daughter of Jerusalem! See, your King comes to you, righteous and having salvation, gentle and riding on a donkey, on a colt, the foal of a donkey. I will take away the chariots from Ephraim and the war-horses from Jerusalem, and the battle bow will be broken. He will proclaim peace to the nations. His rule will extend from sea to sea and from the River to the ends of the earth. Zechariah 9:9–10

A Not-So-Very-Small Gift

Everyone wondered what could be in the big box. It had to be something wonderful since it needed so much space. The ribbons were undone, the wrapping torn away, and the box opened. Inside was—another box.

That box was opened. Inside was still another box. The third box was opened—another box. Box after box was opened until only one was left. When the small box was opened, it contained a marvelous gift.

Long ago, people knew that a Savior was coming. Many thought God would send a glorious king. They envisioned a powerful man who would rule over mighty armies and kingdoms.

What they got was a baby born in a stable. He grew up as a carpenter's son. He wore common clothes and acted like a servant. He was crucified as a criminal. That is not what people expected in a savior. God was like a huge package. Could His Son be such a small, humble person?

Jesus is a king more glorious than a thousand Solomons. He is a resurrected, eternal ruler. Through Him we have been given the greatest gift of all—salvation.

Let Christmas delightfully surprise you. Be amazed at the mighty love a tiny baby brought.

_____Let's talk: When have you received more than you expected? How did that feel? How does God continue to give you more than you ever expected?

_____Let's pray: Thank You, Father, that through a very small gift, the baby Jesus, I have received the greatest gift of all—eternal life. Amen.

J. M.

Christmas Is ...

Christmas is ... How would you finish that sentence? Your friends might say, "Presents!" Your mom might say, "Shopping, decorating!" Your brother or sister might say, "Baking cookies with Grandma!"

People celebrate differently. People also give differently, at Christmas and all through the year. Your parents and teachers give you many things to help you. Although your brothers and sisters may bother you sometimes, think of the fun and joy they bring into your life. Your friends and grandparents share good times with you.

Christmas is ... giving. It is a good time to give to those who give so much to us. We don't have to buy presents (although that's fun too); we can give our thanks and our time.

Of course, here's the most important thing about Christmas: Christmas is God giving to us. Because He brings us peace without end, Jesus is the best gift and God the Father is the best giver.

We give our love and praise to the Savior, who gave His life for us. We also give love and praise to the Father, who gives us wonderful gifts all through our lives.

What gifts of time and help can you give to the people in your life? What special gifts can you give to God? Why might you want to?

Read from God's Word

For to us a child is born, to us a son is given, and the government will be on His shoulders. And He will be called Wonderful Counselor, Mighty God, Everlasting Father, Prince of Peace. Of the increase of His government and peace there will be no end. He will reign on David's throne and over His kingdom, establishing and upholding it with justice and righteousness from that time on and forever. The zeal of the LORD Almighty will accomplish this. Isaiah 9:6–7

_____Let's do: Make gift coupons for family members. Example: "Coupon good for breakfast in bed on December 26." You could distribute the coupons during your gift exchange.

_____Let's pray: Dear Father, thank You for giving us Your Son. Help us to give Your love to others. Amen.

A. S.

Read from God's Word

"Be still, and know that I am God; I will be exalted among the nations, I will be exalted in the earth." Psalm 46:10

Hustle, Bustle

This is an exciting time of the year—the last few days before Christmas. We have enjoyed parties, sung carols, and feasted on holiday cookies and candy.

School is out until after New Year's, but there is plenty to do. Your family may shop for presents, clean the house, or cook special food for the celebrations ahead.

Churches and Sunday schools might have special programs and worship services. Maybe you will be caroling for the elderly and shut-in people in your community.

With all of the hustle and bustle, it is no wonder people sometimes feel exhausted before Christmas even arrives! It is important to let God's Bible verse remind us that while holiday preparations and activities are enjoyable, in the long run that's not what Christmas is all about.

The baby Jesus was God's gift to the whole world. He came to free us from our sinful lives so we could trust in God's promise of salvation. That is the true meaning of Christmas and a great reason to celebrate!

_____Let's talk: Are you truly prepared for Christmas? What are your plans for celebrating the birth of our Savior?

_____Let's pray: Thank You, dear Father, for loving us so much. Thank You for sending Jesus to be our King! Amen.

D. N.

Four Candles

The church service was about to begin. The organ was playing softly when Greg, the acolyte, walked up to the altar holding a long candlelighter.

Beside the altar was a huge Advent wreath. Since this was the Fourth Sunday in Advent, Greg lit all four candles.

Mindy, Greg's little sister, was sitting with their mom and dad in the second pew. When she saw Greg light the final candle, Mindy said loud enough that everyone could hear, "Look! It's a big green birthday cake with four candles!"

People smiled at Mindy. Some people were surprised a bit later when Pastor Henry, who had also heard Mindy's comment, mentioned it in his sermon.

"Our Advent wreath is like a birthday cake," he said, "with one big difference. While lighting the wreath every week, we have been looking forward to the birth of the Savior. A birthday cake means looking backward to the time when someone was born.

"A birthday usually brings family and friends together to celebrate God's gift of a loved one. But the birth of Jesus unites the entire world in celebrating God's gift to the whole human race. God gave us His Son, as a baby, to be our Savior."

When the service ended, Greg and his parents gave Mindy special hugs. And so did Pastor Henry!

Read from God's Word

A voice of one calling: "In the desert prepare the way for the Lord*; make straight in the wilderness a highway for our God. Isaiah 40:3*

_____Let's talk: Can you think of something you now understand better than when you were a young child?

_____Let's pray: As the Advent wreath helps us prepare for Your coming, dear Jesus, prepare my heart each day for Your life within me. Amen.

D. N.

Read from God's Word

And there were shepherds living out in the fields nearby, keeping watch over their flocks at night. Luke 2:8–18

A Time of Angels

Angels appear in movies and on television shows. Many people wear angel jewelry or have angel calendars on the wall. Children living in places where snow falls sometimes lie on the ground and swing their arms up and down to make snow angels.

The Bible tells us that God uses angels as messengers. At times they speak to individuals, and at other times they appear to groups of people. Have you ever thought about what it would be like to have a visit from an angel?

Today, on Christmas Eve, we especially remember the angels who came to the shepherds on the night Jesus was born. They had a wonderful message to deliver: "Glory in the highest," they sang, "a Savior is born in Bethlehem."

If angels came to deliver a message to us, God would help us do exactly what the shepherds did. He would help us drop everything and run to see for ourselves!

Today the message that our Savior was born comes to us in the words of the Bible. It is such Good News that we tell it to one another and we sing about it in many Christmas hymns and songs.

_____Let's do: As you read the words of this favorite Christmas carol, imagine angels singing to you as they did to the shepherds.

_____Let's pray: Hark! The herald angels sing, "Glory to the newborn king; Peace on earth and mercy mild, God and sinners reconciled." Joyful, all you nations, rise; Join the triumph of the skies; With angelic hosts proclaim, "Christ is born in Bethlehem!" Hark! The herald angels sing, "Glory to the newborn king!" (*Lutheran Worship* 49:1)

D. N.

Gloria—Carol—Noel

Read from God's Word

The shepherds returned, glorifying and praising God for all the things they had heard and seen, which were just as they had been told. Luke 2:20

Do you know someone named Gloria? What about Carol? Or Noel?

Some parents give children names like these because of the influence of Christmas music. As the angels sang, "*Glory* to God in the highest," we also sing *carols*—known in French as *noels*—to praise God for sending Christ.

Singing and making music with instruments are ways God lets humans express their feelings. Singing makes the message very clear and powerful.

Let's do an experiment. First, look at the difference between speaking and shouting. Try this: in a quiet voice, say the words "Go, team." Now shout, "Go, team!" See what a change that makes? Shouting adds feeling and energy to the words.

Singing is similar: your whole body is more involved. Say the words "Glory to God." Now sing them quietly. See how more of your "self" gets into the expression? Next sing loudly. Your whole body gives energy to those words of praise.

God's plan of salvation is so marvelous, so wondrous, that we can hardly imagine it. Like the shepherds, we glorify and praise God because a baby was born. This was not just any baby: He was the Son of God Himself.

Let's sing praises to God for all the things we have seen and heard this Christmas!

_____Let's do: Choose a favorite carol to sing or speak. Let your lips glorify and praise God.

_____Let's pray: Great God, we can hardly keep quiet when we think of what You have done for us. Accept our songs and praises for Jesus. Amen.

D. N.

Read from God's Word

This mystery is that through the gospel the Gentiles are heirs together with Israel, members together of one body, and sharers together in the promise in Christ Jesus. Ephesians 3:6

Boxing Day

In Canada and Great Britain, the day after Christmas is called Boxing Day.

Many years ago, people gave presents in little boxes to those who worked for them or gave them special service. Waitresses, mail carriers, and teachers were often remembered on Boxing Day.

Today Boxing Day is just another holiday—a second Christmas Day. Most people in Canada and Britain do the same things Americans do on December 26. They play with new games and toys, go shopping, or visit relatives.

For some people December 26 means Christmas is over. They might take down their tree and get ready for New Year's.

For Christians, though, Christmas never ends. Many churches celebrate the First and Second Sundays after Christmas, followed by the Epiphany season. (Epiphany means an appearance or a shining forth.)

On these Sundays, we hear Bible stories about Jesus' early life and the fact that He came for the whole world. Jesus came for everyone in every time and every place. During Epiphany, the Gospel lessons show Jesus' great power and His saving love.

Our celebrations are not over the day after Christmas. The birth of the Christ Child is a gift God gives us every day: Christmas, Boxing Day, and forever.

____Let's talk: To whom would you give a gift if you celebrated Boxing Day this year? Can you share the joyful message of Christmas with them in some other way?

____Let's pray: Thank You, Lord Jesus, for coming to earth as God's forever gift to us. Amen.

D. N.

St. John the Divine

On December 27 Christians give thanks to God for St. John the Divine, the man God inspired to write the Book of Revelation.

There were many men named John during and after Jesus' life. Many scholars think this John was a close disciple of Jesus. Others are not sure because no records exist to make it clear.

Whether he was the same person or another man, we are sure of one thing. John was inspired by God to write about the vision of what he called "a new heaven and a new earth."

In those days, people were required to worship the Roman emperor. Whoever refused was punished. John had been banished to the island of Patmos because he would not give up believing in Jesus Christ. God had him write the book to encourage other Christians and to declare that no power on earth will ever conquer the kingship of the true Messiah. The message of Revelation is that we should not be fooled. It may look like the evil ones of the world are winning the struggle, but they will fail in the end.

Instead, everyone who is baptized and believes in Jesus is "more than [a] conqueror," and has the assurance of God's promises to love, forgive, save, and deliver us. We will live forever with God.

Read from God's Word

Then I saw a new heaven and a new earth, for the first heaven and the first earth had passed away, and there was no longer any sea. I saw the Holy City, the New Jerusalem, coming down out of heaven from God, prepared as a bride beautifully dressed for her husband. And I heard a loud voice from the throne saying, "Now the dwelling of God is with men, and He will live with them. They will be His people, and God Himself will be with them and be their God. He will wipe every tear from their eyes. There will be no more death or mourning or crying or pain, for the old order of things has passed away." He who was seated on the throne said, "I am making everything new!" Then He said, "Write this down, for these words are trustworthy and true." Revelation 21:1–5

_____Let's talk: What Bible verses do you remember that remind you Jesus has already won the victory?

_____Let's pray: Praise to You, dear God, for inspiring John with Your vision in the Book of Revelation. Help us to trust Your promise of salvation, through Jesus. Amen.

D. N.

Read from God's Word

The people walking in darkness have seen a great light; on those living in the land of the shadow of death a light has dawned. Isaiah 9:2

Winter Solstice

Throughout the fall, the days become "shorter" as the amount of sunlight decreases each day. This is noticeable until we reach the winter solstice on December 21.

Near the Arctic Circle and in parts of the Northern Hemisphere, the sun does not clearly appear at all. Stars shine and streetlights stay on 24 hours a day!

People who live in the far north miss the sun during the long winter. Some feel tired, sad, or gloomy. Some people fly south to find relief in the daylight and warmer temperatures.

In a way, the prophet Isaiah described life like a constant winter solstice. People walking and living in spiritual darkness were unhappy and afraid. They had no hope. But God had mercy on His people and sent His Son, Jesus Christ, to be the Savior.

With the birth of Jesus, a great light came into the world. The deep darkness of sin and separation from God is gone. Now, "The Lord will be your everlasting light, and your days of sorrow will end" (Isaiah 60:20). Jesus is our light and our salvation—even on the darkest days of winter.

_____Let's talk: Have you ever been in a very dark place? Even a tiny light can make a big difference. Jesus was not a tiny light. He brought "great" light into the world. Nobody has to live in spiritual darkness any longer.

_____Let's pray: Fill me with Your light, dear Lord, so I will not be afraid of darkness. Help me to share the message of Jesus with others so they will trust You too. Amen.

D. N.

The Big White Bear

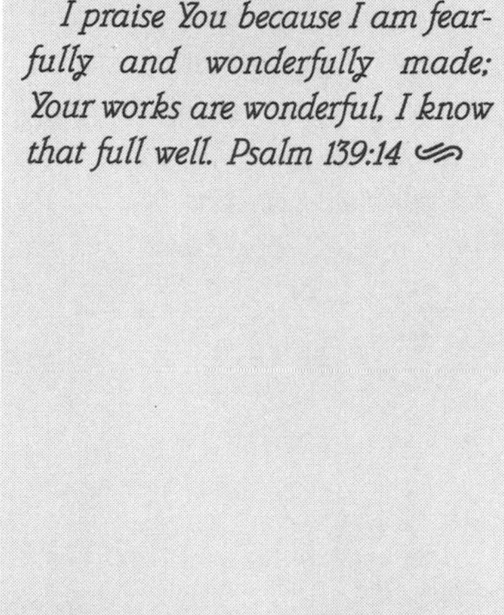

Read from God's Word

I praise You because I am fearfully and wonderfully made; Your works are wonderful, I know that full well. Psalm 139:14

The first thing travelers see in the airport in Anchorage, Alaska, is an enormous polar bear. It stands about 10 feet tall on its rear legs. Fortunately, it is stuffed and locked in a glass case.

A real live bear can be pretty scary. You would not want to meet one in the woods or on a forest path.

An interesting thing about polar bears is their color. Since they live only in the far north (except in zoos, of course), they appear white so they can blend into the snow. Actually their fur is clear and reflects the snow. No one can see them from very far away.

In the past, bear fur was considered a great prize for making clothes, rugs, and blankets. People ate bear meat to stay alive during long cold winters. The fur and meat of the polar bear helped people to live. Every creature God made has a purpose and can be useful to the rest of the world.

People have special purpose too. We were made to praise God and proclaim His glory, telling others the Good News about Jesus. This helps others hear about forgiveness of sins, peace and joy with Christ, and eternal life.

Bears and other creatures are wonderfully made. So are we. Thanks be to God!

_____Let's talk: What is your favorite way to praise God? What are your favorite things in the world that God made?

_____Let's pray: Thank You, dear God, for making all creatures and for creating me special. Help me to serve and praise You. For the sake of Jesus. Amen.

D. N.

Read from God's Word

"Therefore, my brothers, I want you to know that through Jesus the forgiveness of sins is proclaimed to you. Through Him everyone who believes is justified from everything you could not be justified from by the law of Moses." Acts 13:38–39

New Year's Resolutions

Nathan and Natalie sat at the kitchen table, each with a piece of paper and pencil.

The twins had challenged each other to write 10 New Year's resolutions. When they read their resolutions aloud, they laughed. Some were exactly the same! Both said they would do their homework as soon as they got home from school. Both would be more cheerful when Mom or Dad asked them to do a chore. And both wanted to try harder to get along with each other.

Making resolutions can be a good way to improve our habits and behavior. The New Year is a good time to think about our actions. The end of one year and start of another is an opportunity to do things differently.

That's the way it is with forgiveness too. In God's promises at Baptism, we are led to repent of wrongdoing and are given the promise of God's help. We have forgiveness and are adopted as God's sons and daughters. We are changed and live as God leads us.

Jesus has already overcome all sin and evil in our place. With God's help, we make resolutions to start over. This New Year, make a resolution to remember God's help and forgiveness every day.

_____Let's talk: Do you make New Year's resolutions? How successful are you at keeping them?

_____Let's pray: Be with me, Lord Jesus, and help me live in a way that points others to You. Help me forgive others for Your sake. Amen.

D. N.

My Favorite Night

When I was a child, New Year's Eve was my favorite night. It was the only time my parents let my sisters, brothers, and me stay up after midnight.

Read from God's Word

Cast all your anxiety on Him because He cares for you. 1 Peter 5:7

After supper we went to church for a service thanking God for the year that was ending and asking His blessing for the new year ahead.

When we went home, we made popcorn, sat at the dining room table, and began to work. Our job for the night was to put together a jigsaw puzzle. We would work until nearly midnight. Then we went back to church.

The church where my dad was the pastor had a tall bell tower. We climbed up the tower and at exactly midnight we all pulled on the rope to ring the bell, announcing that the new year had arrived.

Today we all have happy memories of December 31 and we still like puzzles. The best part of what I learned during those times is that God is in charge of each year—the old ones and the new ones.

The future is uncertain. Facing a new year reminds us that although we don't know what lies ahead, we need not worry. For Jesus' sake, God promises to be with us every step of the way.

_____Let's talk: How does your family celebrate the new year? What are your hopes and dreams for the new year that begins tomorrow?

_____Let's pray: Thank You, dear God, for Your tender care for me and all Your children. Thank You for our Brother, Jesus, who showed us what Your love means. Amen.

D. N.